# LEARNING TO TEACH, TEACHING TO LEARN

Stories of Collaboration in Teacher Education

# LEARNING TO TEACH, TEACHING TO LEARN

Stories of Collaboration in Teacher Education

Edited by
*D. Jean Clandinin*
*Annie Davies*
*Pat Hogan*
*Barbara Kennard*

**Teachers College, Columbia University**
**New York and London**

Published by Teachers College Press, 1234 Amsterdam Avenue
New York, New York

The authors acknowledge the support of the Social Sciences and Humanities
Research Council of Canada for this research.

*Library of Congress Cataloging-in-Publication Data*

Learning to teach, teaching to learn : stories of collaboration in
    teacher education / edited by D. Jean Clandinin . . . [et al.].
        p.    cm.
    Includes bibliographical references and index.
    ISBN 0-8077-3223-0 (pbk.).  —  ISBN 0-8077-3224-9
    1. Teachers — Training of — United States.   2. Student teaching —
United States.      I. Clandinin, D. Jean.
    LB1715.L428      1993
    370.71′0973 — dc20                                    92-35077

ISBN 0-8077-3223-0 (pbk.)
ISBN 0-8077-3224-9

Printed on acid-free paper
Manufactured in the United States of America

99  98  97  96  95  94  93     7  6  5  4  3  2  1

# Contents

# Foreword

This lovely book *shows* what it means to teach, to learn, and to grow. It does not simply tell. As each participant's story unfolds, the general themes appear again and again, each time enriching the reader's understanding and demonstrating in convincing terms how the participants have grown. The narrative inquiry is developed around five themes: growth, rejection of the theory/practice dichotomy, collaboration, language and communication, and improvisation. Student teachers, cooperating teachers, and university supervisors join together to tell us a sophisticated and complex story of people growing as learners, teachers, and wiser human beings.

The stories told here are not sentimental accounts of "shooting the breeze." Children learn, and that learning is well documented, but they learn something about life and learning itself as well as the standard material of the regular curriculum. Teachers, looking at the children and remembering the pain and joy of their own childhood, reflect on the centrality of relationships in teaching, and they share these reflections with one another and with us.

Although the stories highlight love and connection — not science and technique — some wonderful techniques emerge. Teachers use their own stories to learn "chaptering" — how to plan lessons with a narrative thread, how to reflect on their teaching as one might on a chapter: Does it have continuity? Is there some drama and excitement? Is there a theme? Do the reader-participants care what happens to the characters? Is there a beginning, middle, and end? Do reader-participants want more? Readers may find themselves reflecting on their own professional practice and, even, on the composition of their lives in ways these teachers illustrate.

One of the wonderful things about this book is that we hear women talking about professional practice. A couple of men join the conversation. They *join* it; they do not dominate it, nor are they silenced by it. All through the book we hear stories of being silenced, recovering voice, and learning to speak both as individuals and in concert. The resulting stories represent a powerful rejection of much we have learned to accept passively in teacher education. I hope they also reflect a true picture of teacher education's future.

Nel Noddings
Stanford University

# Acknowledgments

Our acknowledgments are to places, conversations, and most especially to the people that form the experiential text of our lives. We owe much to long walks in Centennial Park, to days and nights in the "Clubhouse," and to our week of conversation at Beach Acres.

Conversations took many forms and occurred in many places. Some were spontaneous, others planned, but all of them were "real." They occurred in small groups and large groups, at the university, in schools, in our homes, and on the phone. They all helped us to figure out the stories told in this book.

We owe all the participants in the Alternative Program a great deal. It took courage and imagination for all of us, particularly the student teachers, to be part of exploring new possibilities.

Thank you to our families and friends for waiting patiently and giving us space as we wrote these stories in the evenings, on the weekends, and in the summers. As we worked together, the four of us developed an intensely close and caring relationship with each other and with chocolate.

We greatly appreciate the patient work of Sherilyn Grywul, who has typed endless drafts of the manuscript. Thank you. Sarah Biondello has supported us and believed in the value of our work. We acknowledge our debt to Sarah for believing that student teachers' and cooperating teachers' stories need to be heard in the conversation of teacher education. Thank you also to Melissa Mashburn who made us rethink and revise as we worked our way through her editing.

D.J.C.
A.D.
P.H.
B.K.

# LEARNING TO TEACH, TEACHING TO LEARN

Stories of Collaboration in Teacher Education

# CHAPTER 1

# Teacher Education as Narrative Inquiry

## D. Jean Clandinin

In elementary school classrooms, in seminar rooms of graduate school, in walks and talks with good friends, in writing projects, and in our journals, my colleagues and I began to be aware of the ways in which we, as teachers, were writing our lives (Heilbrun, 1988) as we worked in our classrooms. As we listened to each other's stories and told our own, we learned to make sense of our teaching practices as expressions of our personal practical knowledge (Clandinin, 1986; Connelly & Clandinin, 1988), the experiential knowledge that was embodied in us as persons and was enacted in our classroom practices and in our lives. It was knowing that came out of our pasts and found expression in the present situations in which we found ourselves. For many of us it was an acknowledgment that had been missing as we lived out our lives in the prescriptive environments of schools where our stories as teachers had not been valued and the kind of knowledge we possessed had not been given voice.

With the realization that we were writing our own lives as knowing people came a sense of the need to give voice to our experiences and to find places where we could begin to figure out what it was that each of us knew as teachers. We began to tell stories of our experiences as children, as teachers, as students, as women, as men, and as people in our Western society. We came to see, as we reconstructed our lives, the ways in which they were storied ones. We came to make sense of what we were doing both as living our stories in an ongoing experiential text and as telling our stories in words as we reflected on life and explained ourselves to others.

As we acknowledged these new ways of talking about our knowledge and our lives, we looked back over our stories and journals to find the narrative threads of our individual lives. We saw the ways in which we had been shaped by our culture, our gender, our institutions, and our profession, but we also saw that each of us had learned to write her life in unique ways that came from her personal experience of the world.

We began to know our own stories better by hearing others' stories. As we listened to others' stories, we not only heard echoes of our own stories, but saw new shades of meaning in them. We learned to value each time we wrote in our journals, responded to another's journal, told one of our stories, and listened to another's story. Through these experiences we gained new possibilities for writing our lives differently.

As we read the work of researchers and practitioners and talked about their ideas and how they helped us make sense of our lives, we also saw new possibilities for changed practices. Each was an educative experience. We knew as we listened and as we spoke and wrote our stories, to value the knowing that we had come to see in our work and in ourselves.

This new sense of ourselves as knowing people emerged over time as we developed a language and ways of working with each other. We learned to make spaces for each other in which to hear our voices, to know that in our voices were our ways of making sense of ourselves and of our work. Words such as Britzman's (1990) helped us to find ways of talking about what we were figuring out.

> Voice is meaning that resides in the individual and enables that individual to participate in a community. . . . The struggle for voice begins when a person attempts to communicate meaning to someone else. Finding the words, speaking for oneself, and feeling heard by others are all a part of this process. . . . Voice suggests relationships: the individual's relationship to the meaning of her/his experience and hence, to language, and the individual's relationship to the other, since understanding is a social process. (p. 14)

Britzman's words about what it means to have a voice gave us a sense that we could find ways of talking about our knowing that were part of how we lived our lives. We began to tell stories of other experiences to which we had not given voice, stories of many experiences that formed the texts of our lives. The distinctions placed between who we were as professionals and who we were as persons blurred as we talked about our lives and the ways in which we worked with children and each other in schools and classrooms, in our homes, and among our families.

As we wrote about our work and the knowing found in our work and in our lives, we began to wonder about the ways in which teacher education was constructed and lived out. We began with wondering about graduate programs in education, staff and professional development, and the ways in which such programs were constructed. The language and the strategies of these programs emerged from talk of one vision, one way of knowing, of skills that could be coached. This language seemed disconnected from the meaningful experiences of our lives. We began to write and talk about other ways of continuing to have educative experiences, other ways of making connections to our lives and our work and to the people with whom we worked each day. As we wondered about the experiences our institutions constructed for us, we began to talk of preservice teacher education. We found the language of teacher education an uncomfortable one with its talk of standards, percentages, skills, strategies, exit and entrance criteria. We had come to feel uncomfortable with this language because we had learned to talk about our own teaching in terms of personal and practical knowing, emotionality, moral dilemmas, and ethics of caring. Noddings (1986) helped us to express some of what we felt about the language of teacher education when she wrote that "we approach our goal by living with those whom we teach in a caring community, through modeling, dialogue, practice and confirmation. Again, we see how unfamiliar this language has become" (p. 502).

Noddings's words helped us begin to question the feelings we had when we found ourselves trying to live out our lives bounded by the structures of teacher education. We felt constrained by unfamiliar boundaries, boundaries that we had begun to break out of when we thought about our lives as teachers of children. The ideas of expert–novice, prescriptions for "right" practice, and generic rules that could be applied in any situation felt as uncomfortable in teacher education as they had in how we were beginning to speak of our teaching. And yet our talk of friendship, ethics of caring, and what Elbow (1986) calls the believing game seemed to have no place in discussions of teacher education. We found no place for making sense of teacher education as part of our ongoing narratives of experience (Connelly & Clandinin, 1990) or for seeing teachers as holders of personal practical knowledge. When we wanted to talk about student teachers as learning to live and tell their stories in practice, of personal knowledge being made practical, we became lost in the gaps and silences of the institutional stories of teacher education.

Quietly and cautiously, we had begun to question the lived story of teacher education, a story rooted in long institutional narratives of university–professional relationships. In the pages that follow we tell of our wondering about teacher education. We describe the ways in which we tried to construct and live out a new story of teacher education, through a collaborative experimental program.

## PLANNING THE PROJECT: BEGINNING THE INQUIRY

The story of this inquiry into restructuring or restorying the lived and told stories of teacher education has, as all narratives of experience do, multiple possible beginnings. I could begin to tell this story, or more appropriately these stories, in many ways depending on the temporal, personal, or institutional frame I placed around the story. I could begin, for example, with each of the participants' narratives of experience situated within particular institutional, cultural, and social stories. If I took that as my starting point, I would trace the narrative threads that led each participant to the program. I might, for example, begin with a telling of my story that highlighted an image of community rooted in my experiences as a child in a rural community in Alberta. I was raised to be in tune with the rhythmic changes of the seasons, nurtured by parents, family, and community members whose very survival depended on being responsive to nature and other community members. But that is only one of the possible narrative threads that led me to this new program in teacher education. There are many such threads, some more telling than others.

The story could begin with such a telling for any participant in the program. I might, for example, begin with Pat Hogan's story with its narrative roots in a search for place within a community, with establishing a community both in which to feel she belonged and that sought to move forward some mission that gave place to others. There are many such possible narrative beginnings. The characters in this story were 28 student teachers, 28 cooperating teachers, five university teachers, other team partners, school administrators, and countless children and parents. I could begin this story with any of their stories, with each participant's story told in many ways.

There are other possible narrative beginnings. Another beginning could be, for example, the discussions of my research on teaching seminars on different conceptions of teaching fostered by the work of John Dewey, Philip Jackson, Elliot Eisner, Joseph Schwab, Madeleine Grumet, Bob Yinger, Eleanor Duckworth, Donald Schön, David Hawkins, Michael Connelly, Deborah Britzman, and Vivian Paley. This telling of the story would begin with the questions raised by seminar participants about why our institutions "did" teacher education as they did if scholars held different conceptions of teaching, of curriculum, of teacher education.

I could also begin with each cooperating teacher's story of student teaching, of teacher education, of methods classes, of working with student teachers in other years. Those, too, would be possible beginnings to the story of the inquiry.

I could also begin by telling of the connections among the participants. Many joined the program because they had friends in the program. They wanted to share a further adventure, to participate with colleagues and to engage in a collaborative inquiry into teacher education. They wanted to learn to live and tell their stories of teaching, of curriculum, and, perhaps, of their lives differently through working in more connected ways with valued colleagues. In this telling, I would begin with stories of collaboration, of caring, of participants playing the believing game, trying to see things from another person's perspective. I would raise questions about how the story of teacher education would look different if university teachers and cooperating teachers took seriously and tried to live out the ideas talked about in courses on teaching and curriculum.

The story could also begin with the students who participated and how they sought out the program, hearing that their friends were coming. They, too, had heard stories of "the dreaded practicum year" that was both the best year of the program and the worst. They wanted to be part of living a different story of teacher education. Becoming participants in the program with us allowed them that possibility.

All are possible beginning points and, depending on which one I select, I would give a different telling of the story. In any telling, however, I would want to note some common marks. I would emphasize that the inquiry was marked by a search for voice, a search for place. In the inquiry all participants tried to take each other seriously. They tried to listen closely to their own voices, the voices of other participants, and the voices of theory as they struggled with a new story. All participants tried to come to new understandings of the ways in which their stories had been lived out within social, cultural, and institutional stories that had both shaped their knowing and continued to shape the new stories they were trying to live and tell. The inquiry was marked with deep emotions. Colleagues in different small groups and large groups laughed and cried together as they came to understand what it means to teach and to be a teacher. It was an inquiry marked by the moral issues of what it means to engage in educative experiences with children, with teachers, and with other people. The story told of the inquiry is one in which the participants cared deeply about what was happening and have, as a consequence, learned a great deal about other possible stories to live and tell in teacher education.

But I have here sketched out the barest of possible beginning points for these stories. As the stories are told in the pages that follow, I hope the richness of each particular story will allow others to imagine different ways I might have told the story.

## A TEMPORAL TELLING OF THE STORY

When called on to explain the Alternative Program to others, I have found myself constrained by the customary narrative form of beginning, middle, and end. I first outline the inquiry's purposes and name the participants. I describe the activities in which participants engaged and the outcomes of the program. I will do some of that here so readers get some sense of the development of the program and of our inquiry.

The story I most often tell begins with a meeting called by Dr. Kathy

Skau, department head of Teacher Education and Supervision at the University of Calgary. She called a small group of faculty together to discuss possibilities for an experimental program in teacher education. Teacher education is often a topic at the autumn department retreat, but rarely do department members come together after the retreat to make changes in the program. This is partly because teacher education is a faculty-wide responsibility but also because when they return from the retreat faculty members are immediately caught up in the demands of teaching. The formation of a group to discuss a possible alternative program was something new. The group eventually consisted of Garry deLeeuw, Garth Benson, Suzanne Kurtz, Pat Hogan, and Jean Clandinin. Marilyn Stratton, an instructor in the required educational administration course, also joined the group albeit somewhat later. Bill Hunter worked with the students in a computer course although he stayed at the periphery of the inquiry.

During the fall of 1988 and winter of 1989, the group met to discuss program issues in teacher education and what would constitute an alternative to the present program. We discussed the kinds of experiences we would want student teachers to have, what kinds of parts we would want to play in relation to students, and how we would work with schools and teachers. In our proposal for a small amount of University Special Projects funding we wrote:

> We seek to promote a different relationship between theory and practice. Rather than beginning with the theory and methods of instruction, the proposed alternative program begins its sequence of instruction in practice and, as student teachers begin to develop understanding of practice, various theoretical readings are introduced. Here the starting point of teacher education is in practice because it is from this perspective that individuals construct their own personal knowledge of teaching. This practical starting point gives students a grounded way to make sense of the theories, models and research they encounter in university classes. Furthermore, the proposed program acknowledges students begin teacher education with personal knowledge acquired from their prior experience. Both the experiential knowledge and the practical starting point provide a context in which students can plan, experiment, reflect and read in order to develop their teaching knowledge. Through this process, students construct and reconstruct their own personal practical knowledge. (Clandinin & Hogan, 1989, p. 2)

In the proposal, we attempted to explain the shape of the plot outlines of the imagined new story of teacher education. It was, however, with little understanding of the ways in which each of our stories would be lived out within the new program constraints.

As the small group discussed possibilities, we situated the program in ongoing work in narrative inquiry and personal practical knowledge. Personal practical knowledge is

> A term designed to capture the idea of experience in a way that allows us to talk about teachers as knowledgeable and knowing persons. Personal practical knowledge is in the teacher's past experience, in the teacher's present mind and body, and in the future plans and actions. Personal practical knowledge is found in the teacher's practice. It is, for any one teacher, a particular way of reconstructing the past and the intentions of the future to deal with the exigencies of a present situation. (Connelly & Clandinin, 1988, p. 25)

This perspective viewed the knowledge of experienced teachers as legitimate, as something different from theoretical knowledge, although we saw theoretical knowledge as part of teachers' knowledge (Elbaz, 1983; Lampert, 1985). Teacher knowledge was seen as constructed and reconstructed in practice and through reflection upon practice (Britzman, 1990; Clandinin, 1986; Hogan, 1988). Teacher knowledge was described as biographical (Grumet, 1988), embodied in who we are as people, and enacted in our practice.

Our group used this theoretical foundation to help us think about what we might do differently as we structured an alternative program in teacher education. We drew on earlier work where I had imagined that

> by adopting a personal knowledge perspective, reflection gains importance as a critical element in teacher education. By making reflection an integral part of three kinds of teacher education experiences (observation, student teaching and other courses), an intellectual experience is set up. Student teachers have not yet worked out a dynamic relationship between their imagery and other dimensions of their personal knowledge and practices. The significance of personal knowledge in curriculum is that we must go beyond theoretical principles and rules of teaching and beyond practical description of action found in statements of strategies and routines. We would focus on ways of thinking and on plans and programs by which teachers and student teachers may reflect on themselves as knowing, teaching beings. Examining research knowledge, participating in applied research, observing other teachers teaching, trying out ideas developed elsewhere can all be valuable if they are part of a process of professional interaction, action and reflection. (Clandinin, 1986, p. 175)

However, in the program, we wanted to emphasize teacher education as a collaborative inquiry in which collaboration was essential between student teachers, university teachers, and cooperating teachers. We wanted to look at teaching not as the transmission of knowledge but as collaborative inquiry involving students and teachers at all levels. This would involve shared work in a practical setting among student teachers, cooperating teachers, university teachers, and children. We saw this collaborative process as similar to collaborative research in which there is a joint living out of all participants' narratives so that participants are continuing to tell their own stories but the stories are now being lived out in a collaborative setting (Connelly & Clandinin, 1990). The inquiry, however, was not to begin with prespecified problems to which theory or sets of rules were applied, but was to begin with the phenomena of a teacher's classroom practice and a student teacher's intention to develop his or her practical knowledge.

The collaborative inquiry would occur in the practice of teaching through the process of reflection-in- and -on-practice (Schön, 1983, 1987). This would allow our program to recognize that people say and do different things in different circumstances and, conversely, that different circumstances bring forward different aspects of their experience to bear on the situation. According to this view, a person's personal practical knowledge depends in important measure on the situation (Clandinin & Connelly, 1988). Through this reflective process of constructing and reconstructing personal practical knowledge, the temporal and social/cultural horizons of each participant would, we hoped, be expanded and changed.

We imagined this process would be ongoing throughout the practicum year with constant opportunity for reflection-in- and -on-action. The participants would continually construct and reconstruct personal practical knowledge as they engaged in practice. Their ongoing practice would be the framework for understanding theories and for constructing and reconstructing practical knowledge.

## ADDING OTHER PARTICIPANTS TO THE STORY

When the group of university teachers had worked out the ideas sufficiently well for Pat and I to write the proposal, it was time to begin work with teachers who might be interested in participating with us. Our group wanted to be able to include their knowing in the ways we structured the program. While we recognized the constraints of the temporal cycles of the university week and year and the constraints of the number and names of necessary courses, we sensed we had flexibility to try out new variations on the themes set by the proposal, the people working in the program, and the temporal cycles of schools and university.

At this point we had set up a weekly cycle for the student teachers that named their courses and gave a temporal sequence to their weeks. They would be in the schools on Monday, Wednesday morning, and Friday. Tuesday and Thursday mornings would be spent in four methods of instruction courses (mathematics, science, social studies, language arts). The methods courses would be integrated with each other as much as possible. Tuesday afternoon would be spent in an advanced computer applications class, and Thursday afternoon would be spent in a required educational administration class. Wednesday afternoon would be spent in small group seminars in the schools. This schedule met the requirements for coursework and practicum in the elementary route professional program.

The yearly cycle had been set in order to have the student teachers begin work with the teachers as early in the school year as possible (late August or early September). They would stay on the school cycle until the end of April. However, we scheduled some full weeks in the schools with no university classes, and we also allowed a one-week break in each term with no university or school expectations. These nonscheduled times were for work on assignments. We hoped student teachers and cooperating teachers could negotiate flexibility around these cycles. We also agreed that students would keep dialogue journals, but we had only tentative discussions on this topic. Other than this framework, we hoped to negotiate the rest of the shape of the story with student teachers and cooperating teachers.

Our university group sent out invitations to teachers and principals with whom we had worked in other settings. We talked with each of them individually to find out their interest and to tell them briefly about what we envisioned. They gave us names of other teachers who might be interested. Friends of friends were invited. The first meeting of interested school people was April 6, 1989. We shared our ideas and, in small discussion groups, we heard theirs. A steering committee of 14 teachers plus five university teachers was set up. Over the spring months the steering committee met. The program began to take shape in these discussions.

The plot of the story began to unfold quickly in April when we spoke to prospective students. We visited classes to distribute brochures and invited students to an information meeting. There we shared the sketchy ideas for an alternative program in teacher education. We provided as much information as we could about the program and talked about what we hoped would be its collaborative nature. We asked them to consider what we had in mind and, on the basis of their intentions, to choose whether or not to work with us. Decisions were out of our hands at that point as registrations for the 28 spaces in our program were to be filled by the admissions office on a first-come, first-served basis. Many of the students who eventually came to work with us in the program stood in line from early in the morning on registration day to ensure a spot. Clearly they too saw a need for an alternative program in teacher education.

In discussions with the university teachers and cooperating teachers, both in the steering committee and in the large group meetings, many issues in the inquiry began to surface. These issues added to the ones our university group had imagined. The issues emerged from the different institutional stories that shaped and constrained each participant's knowing as well as from each participant's narrative of experience.

In these discussions, points of tension were noted. As we analyzed field notes of these meetings, we found issues about the journals. For example, questions were raised about how to have the journals be "true reflections" rather than reflected journals and places to fulfill course requirements or explain classroom activities. Other questions were raised about how to work with cooperating teachers, a university teacher, and student teachers in small journal group settings. These questions were linked to the notion that we needed to be writing and talking together in order for collaboration to lead to changed practice. We talked frequently about trusting relationships as the key to the program. Issues of evaluation occupied a great deal of the discussion early in the deliberations. Questions were raised about how to view evaluation differently given the collaborative nature of the relationships and the reflective nature of the processes with which we were involved. In the field notes we wrote:

> Given that we and the students are trying to make sense of classrooms and our work as practitioners, and that the students are trying to make sense of theory in light of their own experience in our classrooms, much of the evaluation will be a kind of self-evaluation occurring in a collaborative relationship that gives students a great deal of voice. (Notes to file, May 18, 1989)

Those notes drew our attention again to the importance we were placing on this as a collaborative inquiry.

> It is important to keep in mind that in fundamental respects, evaluation is an ongoing process in which all persons involved need to have equal voice. It is important also to remember that we will not be alone, but that we will have many others with whom these questions can and will be explored. (Notes to file, May 18, 1989)

As the stories in our program emerged, these notes took on importance. We began to be aware of the possible tensions in learning to live a

new story of teacher education. Other issues that foreshadowed our awareness of the institutional boundaries of our knowing were issues about working with in-school administrators and negotiating new relationships for
student teachers with school administrators. In early meetings we discussed
the need for continuity and consistency between the schools and the university. In part, this was a concern about the student teachers' weekly and
yearly cycle being different from the school's cycle. We all sensed the possible tension that would result from this, but we could not imagine other
possibilities that would fit within the university constraints. A frequently
expressed concern was how difficult it would be to learn to live out the new
story we were creating in the inquiry rather than falling back into the stories
we had experienced in teacher education.

## BRINGING THE PARTICIPANTS TOGETHER

By June's end, the yearly school cycle necessitated the calling together
of the 28 students, 28 cooperating teachers, and five university teachers for
an evening planning session. This was the first meeting of the whole group.
After that meeting, it was left to the university teachers to match students
with teachers and to inform everyone of the paired relationships. At the
meeting some of the cooperating teachers and student teachers made their
own matches and let the university teachers know their choices. The
matches left to the university teachers were made on some of the standard
criteria about geographical location, time and family constraints, and subject matter specialties. The university teachers informed the student teachers and cooperating teachers of their partners in early July. The stage was
set for the program to begin with the late August–early September meetings
in the schools.

## NARRATIVE THEMES IN THE INQUIRY

Narrative themes, in many ways interrelated, emerged from the inquiry. We discuss five important ones here.

An important narrative theme in the inquiry was a view of teacher
education as part of the ongoing writing of student teachers' lives, not a
separate preparation for something disconnected from what came before
and a readying for what is to come after. Teacher education was seen
as part of the ongoing storying and restorying of students' lives. Teacher
education experiences were part of ongoing narratives of experience, narratives that were being continually revised and rewritten as individuals found

new ways of making sense of their work as teachers and as people, and as they found themselves in new situations.

Another narrative theme in the inquiry was a questioning of the separation of theory and practice, a questioning of the view that we learn theory in order to apply it to practice. In our inquiry we tried to make new sense of how theory and practice might be connected; we tried to engage in a dialogue between our practices and theory, a dialogue mutually informing to both theory and practice, to researcher and practitioner. In this view, theory was not seen as superior to practice but as in a kind of dialectical relationship to practice. The dialogue or conversation between theory and practice resulted in new understandings for both.

A third narrative theme was collaboration. In our inquiry we wanted to learn to listen to each other so that together we might all learn to make new sense of practice and learn to live more moral lives in our teaching (Coles, 1989). We engaged in making sense of teacher education with each other, that is, with our student teachers, with cooperating teachers, and with university teachers. When we worked with others, we were able to see more clearly new possible stories. We did not see our work as teachers as changing or transforming children or each other. That was not our project with student teachers. We did not see ourselves as the ones who held the power to transform others. As we worked with each other, our attention was drawn to other plot lines and other ways of living and telling our own stories. This happened because we engaged with each other with intensity, paying careful attention to how others were telling and living their stories. When we became participants in their stories, their stories changed. When they became participants in our stories, our stories changed. The experience was educative for each of us.

A fourth narrative theme was a search for language to talk about the ways each of us made sense of ourselves as people and as teachers. We wanted to develop a language of teacher education that allowed description of ways of finding a place in order to feel part of a personal and professional community. We wanted a language of teacher education to talk about who we were and about what lives we were writing for ourselves.

A fifth narrative theme was improvisation or what Bateson (1989) calls desperate improvisation. We engaged in an inquiry in which there were many ways of knowing, many ways of making sense, and many institutional stories. Yinger (1987) has written about practice as improvisation in which teachers improvise around a theme. Improvisation became a theme for the ways we learned to live new stories of practice. There were many improvisations as student teachers, cooperating teachers, and university teachers tried to figure out what it meant to learn to live a new story.

## PURPOSES FOR WRITING THE STORIES

We have several purposes for undertaking to write our stories in this book. We undertook this inquiry into teacher education in part to serve our own purposes as cooperating teachers and university teachers. We wanted to work with student teachers in new ways, ways that would allow them to see a range of possibilities for themselves as teachers. Cooperating teachers also participated, in part, in order to engage in an educative experience for themselves. They wanted to learn to live new stories of practice with the children in their classrooms. As cooperating teachers and university teachers, we also wanted to learn to live new ways of storying our own practices in teacher education. In part, then, when we write down the stories we have lived in this inquiry, it is to record for ourselves the new stories we have learned to live and tell.

But in writing this book we hope to reach a wider audience of practitioners, including cooperating teachers, student teachers, and university teachers. I have written elsewhere about the purposes of writing narratives for a larger audience.

> Narrative inquiries are shared in ways that help readers question their own stories, raise their own questions about practice and see in the narrative accounts stories of their own stories. The intent is to foster reflection, storying and restorying for readers. (Clandinin & Connelly, 1990, p. 20)

These are our purposes. We want to engage readers in considering what our stories of teacher education allow them to see in their stories and practices of teacher education.

In earlier writing (Clandinin & Connelly, 1990) I used Crites's (1975) words to suggest how people should tell their stories in ways that encourage readers to be reflective about their practices and to invite them to engage in a restorying of their stories. Crites (1975) noted that the completeness of a story consists

> in the immediacy with which narrative is able to render the concrete particularities of experience. Its characteristic language is not conceptual but consists typically in the sort of verbal imagery we employ in referring to things as they appear to our senses or figure in our practical activities. Still more important the narrative form reproduces the temporal tensions of experience, a moving present tensed between and every moment embracing a memory of what has gone before and an activity projected, underway. (p. 26)

As I thought about our purposes in writing this book and in telling our stories for others, Crites reminded me that these stories are not models or solutions to the problems of teacher education but are stories that highlight the tensions each of us experienced as we lived out our personal stories embedded within the cultural and institutional stories of teacher education, schools, and universities. I want to foster reflection on the ways individuals and institutions live and tell stories of teacher education. Perhaps our stories begin to do that.

In subsequent chapters, several participants tell their stories. Through these chapters we highlight the ways many of us came to make sense of our experiences in the program and of teacher education more generally. This book has been put together by a small group of practitioners, university teachers, student teachers, and cooperating teachers, who were interested in writing about their experiences in this inquiry into teacher education. What we have done as editors is to offer a range of possible stories of experience. In Part One of this book three student teachers have authored chapters in order to give their accounts of their experiences of learning to teach. Part Two of the book is collaboratively written by student teachers and cooperating teachers in order to tell stories of their experience of working together in teacher education. In Part Three, chapters are written by cooperating teachers who wanted to tell their own stories of new possibility in their practices and in teacher education. Finally as editors and authors of the book, we have written about new insights into teacher education that we hope highlight some possible ways to restory teacher education.

> What matters is that lives do not serve as models; only stories do that. And it is a hard thing to make up stories to live by. We can only retell and live by the stories we have read or heard. (Heilbrun, 1988, p. 37)

## REFERENCES

Bateson, M. C. (1989). *Composing a life*. New York: Atlantic Monthly Press.

Britzman, D. (1990). *Practice makes practice: A critical study of learning to teach*. New York: SUNY Press.

Clandinin, D. J. (1986). *Classroom practice: Teacher images in action*. London: Falmer Press.

Clandinin, D. J., & Connelly, F. M. (1988). Studying teachers' knowledge of classrooms: Collaborative research, ethics and the negotiation of narrative. *The Journal of Educational Thought, 22*(2A), 269–282.

Clandinin, D. J., & Connelly, F. M. (1990). Narrative and story in practice and research. In D. Schön (Ed.), *The reflective turn: Case studies of reflective practice* (pp. 258–282). New York: Teachers College Press.

Clandinin, D. J., & Hogan, P. (1989). Special projects proposal. University of Calgary.

Coles, R. (1989). *The call of stories: Teaching and the moral imagination*. Boston: Houghton Mifflin.

Connelly, F. M., & Clandinin, D. J. (1988). *Teachers as curriculum planners: Narratives of experience*. New York: Teachers College Press.

Connelly, F. M., & Clandinin, D. J. (1990). Stories of experience and narrative inquiry. *Educational Researcher, 19*(5), 2–14.

Crites, S. (1975). Angels we have heard. In J. B. Wiggins (Ed.), *Religion as story* (pp. 23–63). Lanham: University Press of America.

Elbaz, F. (1983). *Teacher thinking: A study of practical knowledge*. London: Croom Helm.

Elbow, P. (1986). *Embracing contraries: Explorations in teaching and learning*. Oxford: Oxford University Press.

Grumet, M. (1988). *Bitter milk: Women and teaching*. Amherst: University of Massachusetts Press.

Heilbrun, C. (1988). *Writing a woman's life*. New York: W. W. Norton.

Hogan, P. (1988). *A community of teacher researchers: A story of empowerment and voice*. Unpublished manuscript, University of Calgary.

Lampert, M. (1985). How do teachers manage to teach? Perspectives on problems in practice. *Harvard Educational Review, 55*(2), 179–194.

Noddings, N. (1986). Fidelity in teaching, teacher education and research for teaching. *Harvard Educational Review, 56*(4), 496–510.

Schön, D. (1983). *The reflective practitioner: How professionals think in action*. New York: Basic Books.

Schön, D. (1987). *Educating the reflective practitioner: Toward a new design for teaching and learning in the professions*. San Francisco: Jossey-Bass.

Yinger, R. (1987). By the seat of your pants: An inquiry into improvisation and teaching. Paper presented at the annual meeting of the American Educational Research Association, Washington, DC.

# PART ONE

# TELLING OUR STORIES: THE STUDENT TEACHERS' STORIES

Three student teachers have written accounts of their experiences in the program. Their stories are important ones to hear as we explore teacher education. As the participants in the Alternative Program worked together, we learned to make spaces for their voices.

Chapters 2 to 5 give partial accounts of how three student teachers learned to make sense. We selected these stories because they provide examples of different ways of learning how to reflect on learning in order to live a story of teaching. Helen Mahabir has written an autobiographical account that connects her early experiences of schooling with her experiences in the program. Kathryn Cope has written of her work with a child in her classroom and of the ways she learned to make sense of her work as a teacher while she worked with him. Jean Fix has offered an account of the ways in which she saw her story reflected in the stories of children in her classroom.

CHAPTER 2

# Autobiography as a Way of Knowing

## *Helen Mahabir*

You are about to enter the world of Helen Mahabir. This chapter journeys through my life as a student in London, Ontario, and as a student teacher at the University of Calgary, and my imagined life as a future teacher.

What is the purpose of reflection? Why would I want to discuss my childhood feelings and attitudes toward the four subject areas I'm studying and teaching? Should my fears and apprehensions be set aside as I begin my new career as a teacher? How important are our pasts? What do they tell us? We can gain an understanding of the world and its incidents through the discipline of history; however, we rarely emphasize the importance of studying our own past to gain a better understanding of who we are as individual members of society. Reflection allows me to analyze my past feelings and then relate them to my present attitudes and situation. Reflection helps me to weave the connections between my past experiences of education and my present understanding of negotiating curriculum. As I write about and share these stories I become aware of where I come from, where I am, and where I would like to be in the future.

I would like to set the stage. I went to school in London, Ontario. I attended Emily Carr Public School from grade 4 to grade 8, and Sir Frederick Banting Secondary School from grade 9 through grade 13. Emily Carr was considered one of the tougher schools in London. Kids who couldn't be controlled in other schools came to ours and remained in the "White Portable" on our school grounds. Though this special class was a prime target for ridicule, I befriended some of the kids from the "Portable." They seemed normal to me and I didn't understand why they were considered uncontrollable. Generally speaking, I was an easygoing child who was always willing to help even substitute teachers. I enjoyed being the classroom representative and helping at school events. In grades 7 and 8 I spent a fair amount of time helping to organize different school activities. I have fond memories of my time at Emily Carr.

Emily Carr school was an open area school. In the younger grades the dividers were scarcely drawn, which created a fairly noisy learning atmosphere. Our desks were arranged row by row, supporting strict seating assignments that were organized by the teacher. We all faced the front of the class where the teacher stood to teach us. The philosophy of education at Emily Carr was traditional with a rigidly structured curriculum. The subjects were taught at specific times of the day and week, and connections between subjects were not acknowledged or encouraged. Flexibility and integration were not a part of my education. Talking while working was prohibited and discussions were always teacher-controlled. Small groups or paired situations were rarely employed. Most of my learning occurred in isolation.

Sir Frederick Banting connected the "well-off-doctor" neighborhood with the "other-side-of-the-tracks" kids. Emily Carr students were considered the "other-side" kids. This, however, did not inhibit me. I seemed to get along with most teachers and students. I made friends with people from all the various cliques in school. I continued my involvement with organizing events through participating in the Student Council. Academically, I did not have any problems either. I was an Honor's student throughout high school. Overall, my secondary education was extremely positive.

I don't remember feeling constrained by the teacher's authoritarian role in the classroom. I accepted the quiet, teacher-pleasing role of the student and never questioned my actions. Because I played the game so well, as the pleasant child who did not rock the boat, I slipped through the system without any problems. I learned to accept authority in elementary school. I learned that the teachers were the ones who had all the answers, and if I ever wanted to get anywhere in life, I had better listen and do what I was told to do. The teacher shaped how we, the children, would think, feel, learn, and act toward others because she was the ruler in our classroom.

## SUBJECT BOUNDARIES AND FEELINGS
## OF DISCONNECTION

While I enjoyed school for the most part, I recall subject difficulties. My science story has been a long and ongoing battle. Grade 7 was the first year I distinctly remember disliking science. Throughout that year I did not understand the concepts covered and did not relate well to the experiments that we had to do in class. On my report card it was the lowest grade. I "needed improvement." I know that I was very upset because I didn't "need improvement" in any other subject. Science consisted of seemingly disconnected laboratory experiments. One of our biggest chores was writing up the experiment in our "Lab Books." Each experiment was numbered and written in a specific form: purpose, materials, method, observations, results, and conclusions. My observations and results were usually different from those of other students. I never reached the expected "right" answer. Science became a struggle for me, and something to which I did not relate. I could not figure out at the age of 12 how any lab experiment would affect me in the future. Science was taught out of context and did not relate to my life, and I adopted the idea that it never would. This negative attitude has affected my motivation and ability to learn about science ever since.

Grade 9 reinforced my view of science as disconnected from my life. I remember studying about an air conditioning system and how it worked. It seemed ridiculous. In grade 13 chemistry I memorized most of the Periodic Table. I vaguely remember my teacher describing the attraction of atoms like partners dancing together. I liked that image. Other than that I always categorized science as one of my worst subjects and definitely the one I disliked the most. I played the game. I memorized what I needed to know for the tests. I filled in the information for the experiments and tried to find the teacher's answers in order to pass the course. I never gained an understanding of or an interest in what science was really all about. Now as a university student I become easily frustrated and anxious when I work with science concepts in my methods classes, but my anxiety level has been reduced. I have finally come to know science in a different way by working with children. I have experienced learning in meaningful contexts with units of study being shaped by their curiosity. I have become more relaxed by living a process of collaborative inquiry guided by real questions generated in the classroom community.

Social studies did not create the same negative experience that science did for me. It was simply ambiguous. I don't remember any particular topic of interest. I do remember keeping a social studies notebook; coloring in maps with pencil crayons; receiving "dittos" that we always smelled; folding these sheets of paper into one-quarter of their size and pasting them into our social studies notebook. These irrelevant memories form a stronger image for me than the topics we studied. I remember doing projects and gathering most of the information from the encyclopedia. This was not learning. It was keeping us busy, creating products that satisfied the curriculum mandates. We were not given the opportunity to explore or discover our feelings and ideas about the topics.

My secondary school curriculum supported the division of social studies into separate areas. It was compulsory to have one history, and one geography course in grade 9. By grade 13 I took courses in Canadian/British history, geography (human and urban), man in society, and sociology. I have always been fascinated by different cultures and the interrelationships that exist among people and their environments. Our main sources of information for most of these courses were textbooks. Even though they were dry and left nothing to the imagination, I learned as much as I could. Urban geography, taught by Mr. Oliver, became my favorite subject. In his course, we did not analyze people in urban communities, but focused on the geographical significance of urban concepts. Mr. Oliver's approach to teaching intrigued me. He was determined to make our learning experiences as real as he could. He brought in hundreds of slides that provided visual examples of the concepts we were discussing. He took pictures of Highway 401 (while he was driving); he rode in planes and helicopters to get landscape scenes; he climbed up fences to get pictures of urban blight; he even disobeyed warning signs that trespassing would cause more erosion to get us pictures of the Scarborough Bluffs. He warned us not to attempt any of his stunts. We had some interesting discussions in class, and always had time to laugh. Mr. Oliver, affectionately known as Uncle Ollie, gained respect from his students because he respected our ideas and opinions. His caring manner and enthusiasm for geography made our classes exciting. I am glad that I spent some time reminiscing about his classes because it helped me to realize how important it is to be excited about learning and to share one's enthusiasm.

If I had been asked 7 months ago about my elementary math experience, I would have said it was wonderful for I was a successful student. I have always learned about math strictly from a textbook. I remember I had to memorize the multiplication tables and then chant them in class. In grade 4, we proceeded up and down our rows of desks rhyming off each answer. I don't think I ever recited the answers to $7 \times 8$ and $9 \times 6$ because they still confuse me. I had, however, sufficiently memorized what I needed to know in order to achieve the correct answers. I completed the math work sheets or tests with little difficulty and I found speed tests challenging. This streak of success followed me until the first few years of high school. I was encouraged by my math teacher in grade 10 to join the Math Club, which I did for a short time before I lost interest. By grade 11 I had noticed a trend. My final grades in math had declined a few percentages in each year since grade 9. I knew I did not fully understand trigonometry, especially when it was applied in word problems. I realized the extent of my difficulty only when I failed my grade-12 math midterm. It felt like my world had fallen apart because I had never failed an exam before. I worked twice as hard and brought up my mark. The math concepts became increasingly more difficult in university. I failed calculus in my first year at the University of Western Ontario and struggled through permutations with the aid of a tutor the next year.

What happened throughout the years that allowed me to become so weak in math? Why couldn't I make the connections necessary to understand the university courses? There may be many reasons. However, analyzing my past experiences allows me to see that I did not fully understand the connections that existed in math. I had memorized the basic facts for elementary school but I did not comprehend the combinations and patterns that were evident in mathematical computations. My foundation of understanding in math was weak. I had an unstable base that could not withstand the more complex concepts of math. As my foundation in math collapsed, I became frustrated trying to figure out meeting points for trains, the angle of cliffs, and the volume of pig troughs. This conclusion was highlighted as I evaluated my understanding of the various concepts discussed in our math methods course and as I worked with my grade 3 students.

In my schooling, I failed to see connections in the language arts. They were broken down into individual areas and taught separately. We learned about the rules of grammar, and completed written exercises using the defined rules in various sentences. Our weekly spelling lists came from the spelling textbooks and not from our writing or the topics we were studying in class. We read silently at our desks from readers provided in our classroom. I never developed an interest in reading because I read irrelevant stories in elementary school; I was forced to read boring books in high school; and then I read dry, factual information in textbooks for my university courses.

Writing was taught in fragments. We analyzed punctuation, sentence structure, and order of paragraphs. I did not fully understand what the whole picture looked like. I did not have the opportunity to explore reading/writing connections, and I realize that my writing reflected my disinterest in reading. Most of my essays for university were criticized for awkward sentence structure. I lacked confidence in my writing skills and therefore spent a great deal of time trying to perfect my work. Writing does not come easily to me.


## REFLECTION AS PART OF COMING TO KNOW

Having shared some of my past stories about the four subject areas, I move into the present. It is through my relationship with Pam Rinehart, my cooperating teacher, that I come to see teaching from a different perspective. As I connect my past to my present situation, I realize that my relationship with Pam is the bridge between the two experiences.

Each of us brought our past experiences and expectations into our new relationship. Pam had already experienced intern teaching in a collaborative situation. I had the knowledge I'd gained through university. I entered the relationship quite hesitantly, waiting to see what role she wanted me to play. I was conditioned to see her as the expert. I would play the quiet accepting role of student. As the student teacher, I believed I knew nothing and would have to learn everything. The only way for me to learn would be to do as I was told, to listen to the advice of my cooperating teacher, and to internalize the proper methods of teaching proposed by my university professors. My personal story would not matter. Any papers would reflect opinions of "well-educated" theorists or professors and all I would need to figure out was how to splice together quotes and connecting words to fulfill the requirements for the course. What a surprise I had when I discovered the reality of the situation. The reality for me lies within the story I share with Pam, the story of our collaborative relationship.

One of my early entries in my journal describes my searching for the boundaries of this new relationship. Everything was tentative. As the student teacher, what was my role? Where was my place in the classroom? How should I act? I wanted to somehow figure out what Pam was thinking and feeling.

> There's just one last thing I would like to mention. It's in regards to discipline. I have automatically assumed the role and have asked some kids to lower their voices, keep on working, listen, etc. I hope I have not overstepped my place. I am sorry if I have. I have been told that my personality can easily be dominating and I don't want to come off like that. Please, feel free at any time now, or later to clarify any situations that are uncomfortable for you. I do not mean to be that way and a reminder always helps. I want this year to be a good one for both of us and I feel an open and honest relationship will complement our working together. (Journal entry, September 7, 1989)

I soon realized Pam's expectations for our relationship when she responded in my journal. My former conception of the role of a student teacher started to change. Pam was not playing the role of the cooperating teacher that I had imagined. Her manner and easygoing attitude allowed me to relax and figure out things at my own pace, a pace at which I was comfortable to explore, discover, and learn.

> I'm glad you have! You are a teacher in this class too and so you should take on that role. The kids need us to be consistent so it would be difficult if you didn't respond according to your feelings. We can be very honest with each other and you need to find your rhythm in

the class. Respond in ways that feel right to you. (Journal entry, September 7, 1989)

In my journal I shared the uncertainties and questions that I had with respect to teaching. Having Pam and Pat Hogan, my university teacher, respond in my journal provided a place for me to figure things out with their support. Writing about my struggles allowed me to develop a feeling for self-evaluation. As Pam and Pat validated and acknowledged my feelings and understanding of my situation, I found I gained peace of mind and acceptance as a teacher. As I struggled with aspects of teaching that were new to me, Pam and Pat storied similar experiences from their teaching careers. I could relate my experiences to their situations and examine their strategies or answers to see if they were relevant to mine. With their help I gained confidence in my ability to work things out. In my journal I discussed classroom management, something that has haunted me for a long time. Pam acknowledged my fears. She did not, however, provide answers. She supported my feelings of concern as she storied her experience.

> I was just thinking, I forgot how management and disciplining once kept me up at night. I remembered that in my intern year I had several weeks of recurring nightmares. In the nightmare I would ask the kids to do something and they would laugh and walk out. I would be left in this empty room crying. I think I realized some time after that, discipline was mostly a result of my state of mind. When I'm relaxed and feeling like myself, I have the confidence to respond naturally and I do not get into power struggles. Fear can take away self-confidence and then discipline becomes an issue. (Journal entry, November 11, 1989)

I have expressed only a very small part of the relationship I developed with Pam. It may have started out as a student teacher/cooperating teacher relationship but now I value it as a friendship. Through this friendship, Pam has encouraged me to discover who I am as a teacher. I formed my own answers because I was allowed to make mistakes and learn from them. Pam's understanding and support in our collaborative relationship have enabled me to develop a confidence in myself as a teacher. This confidence grew through Pam's openness and willingness to learn with me. I was no longer a student teacher but a team-teacher sharing a unique experience with a very special partner.

Our journal dialogue helps me to make new connections, but most of all, Pam's words made me feel important, a real teacher.

Helen, I like your thinking back over the events in a more general
way. Sometimes it's hard to feel where things are going when one is in
the midst, but looking back a thread emerges and then the continuing
direction becomes more clear. This kind of looking back, seeking connections, is how a rhythm for the year develops. I like reading your reflections because I see things more clearly when we reflect together.
(Journal entry, October 23, 1989)

Looking back at Pam's and my grade 3 class this year, I am amazed at
the "realness" of our situation. There were no false fronts as Pam and I
presented ourselves to the class. We shared storied experiences from our
lives. I believe this made us more real as the children connected with our
stories and shared their own. We experienced a community atmosphere in
which we all participated. Our shared conversations created a supportive,
caring environment; a safe place for all of us to learn and take risks.

## EXPLORING POSSIBILITIES FOR INTEGRATION

In this environment my shared conversations with Pam allowed me to
think about new possibilities for the integration of various curriculum areas. It was exciting for me to see that I could remove subject boundaries. I
discovered this through sharing carefully chosen literature that was connected with social studies themes. I knew that I was creating a context for
the children to make more meaningful connections. Our study of native
people was enhanced by reading and responding to two novels: *Trouble
River* (Byars, 1969) and *Stone Fox* (Gardiner, 1980).

In science the children kept moon journals. They made observations,
sketches, questions, and predictions, and even wrote poetry that connected
with the significance of the moon for the native people. In computers, we
attempted drawing the moon, planets, and stars with Logo. The children
created their own curriculum in art as they represented the native people's
artifacts and way of life in their paintings and plasticine play. An integrated
curriculum manifests a natural environment for learning. The children are
interested in learning more about the topic from different perspectives,
which allows them to discover the connections and thereby integrate the
curriculum.

In working collaboratively I discovered that I could express and explore my felt sense of how integrated learning might be constructed within
a classroom community. By reflecting on past storied experiences and my
experiences with children, I see the possibility for becoming closer to all

children, for becoming more sensitive to their needs and to my own. I am more comfortable with the uncertainty that lies ahead.

> The more I think about it the more I realize how emotional my life is going to be in this profession. But, I would not want it any other way. Dealing with children and their lives opens a door of caring and understanding and loving. It's a passionate profession and one that deserves to be full of life, love, and excitement. One I feel closer and closer to as this year ends and the hope of my own classroom becomes closer to reality. I look forward to the purple glow that lies ahead. (Journal entry, March 15, 1990)

## REFERENCES

Byars, B. (1969). *Trouble river.* Toronto: Viking Press, Penguin Books Canada.
Gardiner, J. R. (1980). *Stone Fox.* New York: Crowell.

CHAPTER 3

# Pictures, Letters, Words:
# One Child's Stories

## *Kathryn Cope*

There is no way that you can miss Wally when you walk into our classroom. Tiny, with enormous black eyes and a bum that never stops moving, he jumps (literally) with incredible enthusiasm and interest into everything that we do. Never afraid to try and always full of ideas and suggestions, Wally brings with him into grade 1 spirit, originality, and a wonderful sense of humor. All of these things are reflected in his story writings, from picture stories with a few letters added, to stories about ants raiding picnics and stealing hot dogs. This chapter is about his stories and the growth and development of Wally's story writing during his first 8 months in grade 1.

I particularly noticed Wally because of his energetic, fun-loving sense of himself as an individual. I like kids like this. I remember myself as a quiet child. While I was not at all like Wally on the outside, there was much going on inside of me, in my imagination.

As I was planning the style and layout of this chapter, I really thought about how I could present Wally's work in a way that would make it decipherable without making it sterile, removing the charm and individuality of his work in an attempt to make it "readable." Wally's stories are wonderfully rich and inventive, but they are also very difficult to read unless you know his way of sounding things out and writing them down. Often it is more fun to sit down and try to figure out what a child has written than it is to pick up a translation and read that instead. However, reading the original text can take a lot of time and sometimes it's impossible to figure out what the child has written. I have decided to compromise and include both Wally's stories and my translations.

## STORIES IN PICTURES

At the beginning of the year, our story writing consists of journal writing, where the children write stories using a combination of pictures, letters, or words, depending on what they want to do. Like most of the other children in the classroom, Wally tells his first stories with pictures and a few letters. As shown in Figure 3.1, the picture holds the meaning and the words are just there for accompaniment. While this doesn't really seem like a big deal, it indicates to me several things about his abilities at the beginning of the year. That he tells his stories by pictures is not important — pictures are stories too. What is noticeable here is that he knows that letters can tell stories along with pictures. He may not know many letters and he does not seem to understand the connection between sound and letters, or

**Figure 3.1**

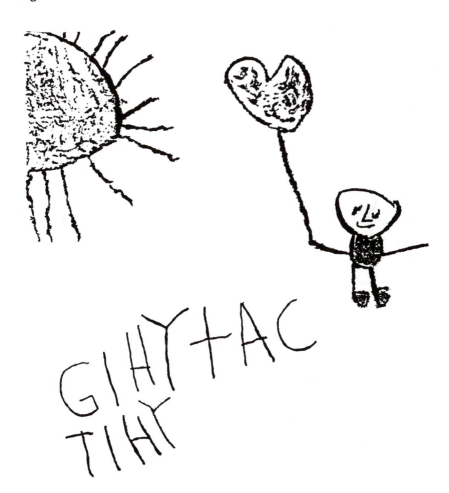

that letters can be grouped in different ways to mean different things, but that will come.

## ADDING LETTERS

After several weeks we begin to introduce sentence frames for the children to use in their story writing. We focus on three for a while: "I can see . . . ," "Once upon a time . . . ," and "One day in the fall . . . ." Wally incorporates these frames into his writing easily and can repeat them back when reading a story, but he has not yet come to recognize them as separate words. He shows here the new letters that he has learned, including *m, s,* and *f*—the first letters we covered.

The story in Figure 3.2 is about a secret game that he played with his friends, and it shows several things.

**Figure 3.2**

**Figure 3.3**

(One day in the fall) I played a secret game with my friends. (Journal entry, Oct. 6, 1989)

Here I have an advantage in that I know he is writing about a secret game because he told me. If he had not done so, I would be pretty clueless about what this story is all about. Wally shows here that he is starting to make connections between sounds and symbols, and his experiences with phonics are getting him used to listening for the first sound and letter. He seems to be putting that knowledge to use—Does the "m" stand for "my," the "f" for "friends," "src" for "secret"? As Wally continues writing, these connections become clearer and clearer to see. By the way, the secret game is Ring-Around-the-Rosy; he told me that too!

I know the sample in Figure 3.3 does not look very exciting, but I chose it anyway because it shows a few big steps for him. We have a language arts center on bears. The children complete the frames to describe what bears can do.

(Bears can) bears can stand up.
(A bear can) bears can bite. (Journal entry, November 6, 1989)

Wally has developed a tendency here to repeat the frames at the beginning of his sentences, which can make it pretty hard to figure out what he has written. Wally has difficulty reading his work back if he does not remember what he has written, and sometimes it takes a good deal of sleuthing and some guesswork to figure out what is on the paper. These two are among the first examples of his work that can be understood without his assistance. Once you remove "Bears can" or "A bear can" from the beginning of the sentences, it's easy to see the answers "bite" and "stand up." The pictures help. Wally is starting to hear more than one dominant sound in words and he is starting to write more of these sounds down. Not only is he noting the first and last letters in these words, but he's having a go at the stuff in between as well.

Say what you like about Wally's stories, they are always very individual and very different. Wally never has to come up and ask for a topic to write on like other children in our room. He is very confident of his own ideas; he seems to have little difficulty coming up with new ideas for each story, and few stories are alike. November's journal entry in Figure 3.4 illustrates how Wally writes like he speaks.

There's some red and there's black and some green and some yellow and some blue and there's brown. (Journal entry, November 22, 1989)

Wally rarely sits when working at his desk. Instead he puts one knee on his chair and leans over his desk for support, whispering loudly and listening carefully to every sound he makes. The sounds that he hears are recorded on the paper. When he says "and there's some," he hears the familiar sounds of *n*, *d*, and *sm*, and so he writes these down.

He writes this story at a time when he seems to be listing the things that he knows. After he describes the colors, he goes on to write the alphabet song and then list various things in and around the classroom. We explored the colors at the beginning of the year and so Wally knows where to find all the color words posted on the walls in the classroom. I am impressed by his apparent confidence in his own abilities. He is willing to try words on his own even though he knows where to look for the "right" spelling. This confidence is characteristic of Wally. He is always willing to try.

Wally's confidence in using his new letters is improving but his ability to remember finger spaces is not. Many of his stories are difficult, if not

**Figure 3.4**

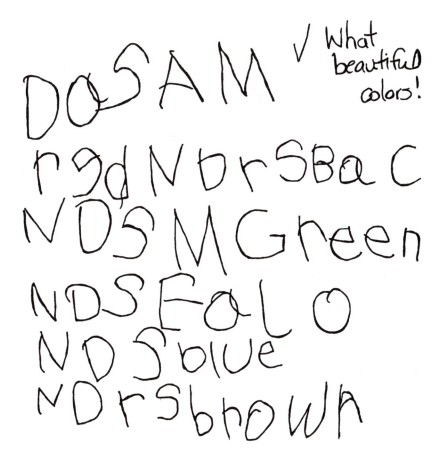

impossible, to decipher, and in Figure 3.5 much has to be figured out using the context in which he writes.

(Last line of verse.)
run run fast as you can can't catch me I'm the gingerbread man. (Journal entry, December 15, 1989)

Knowing that this is the story of the gingerbread man and knowing the song that the gingerbread man sings as he runs away helps immeasurably. Without this background information we would probably never know what

**Figure 3.5**

SoDo hU _K9TeeT

íoDurAnA oD moɑ

NICɣ VI∩ʰ WTOUT₀

rɑ∩ʰɑ1ʃc ∩U+cc∩í∩Øʰ8ɑoɑɑ∩

this means. As it is, I can only figure out "old man" at the end of the second line and the last line, but the others are a mystery. Not only is it difficult for me to read, but Wally finds it very frustrating as well. He writes so much and then goes back to it only to find letters and words that have lost their meaning, and I am powerless to help him. While he loves to read books to the children, he is hesitant to read his own stories to them and needs a lot of encouragement and help.

## USING WORDS

After Christmas Wally's stories begin to blossom in length, creativity, and style. The story "Sledding with the Smurfs" in Figure 3.6 comes out of a center activity. Wally's originality shows through again in this story. While everyone else lets their Smurfs go tobogganing and then go home for hot chocolate, Wally's Smurfs get to do a little bit more.

> One day the Smurfs was going in the deep woods and they found a gorilla talked to them and they went to their home and they went to the shortcut and found their home. The end. (Journal entry, January 15, 1990)

This story illustrates how Wally uses "da" for so many words as in day, the, they, them, there. We've been stressing "th" sounds since the beginning of the year, but Wally has either taken no notice or decides to write the way it sounds to him. The finger spaces are helping Wally to see how the clusters of letters mean different things and he is learning that there is more to words than the first letter or sound that you hear. Since the finger spaces are now a regular feature of his stories, it is a lot easier to help him with the deciphering of what he has written and Wally is enthusiastic about reading his work again.

The majority of the class starts using descriptive words in April, but Wally has been using them since February. Maybe he picked them up from books, maybe from other children around him. It really doesn't matter. He chooses to use these words for his story in Figure 3.7. Wally has control over his stories and what he will do with them. He doesn't need to follow us around checking spelling and making sure that what he's doing is right. He knows what he wants to do and he is comfortable going ahead and doing it.

> One day a big monster was flying in the long grass. He fell down. The end. (Journal entry, February 6, 1990)

Whether it is gorillas, giant earth worms, monsters, or anything else that Wally includes in his stories, his ideas are usually all his own. He still experiences difficulty reading his stories back and he tries to keep them down to under a page. Other children get more paper for two words because

**Figure 3.6**

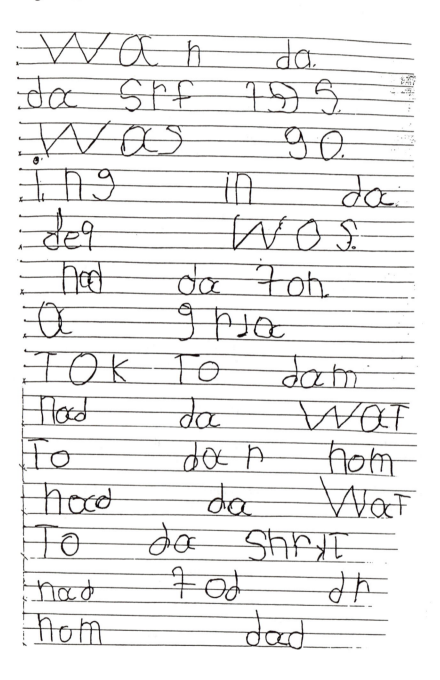

**Figure 3.7**

Wah da a dig
mosr was
7-Jing in da
Jo gras hofou
doh dahd

they like the feeling of writing two-page-long stories. Wally, however, is content to cram it all on one page and get it over with. This story, written in his spare time, is a typical example of his stories at this stage, lots of big scary things and "violence." Wally has written some wonderful dinosaur stories, but unfortunately neither one of us can read them. Often when he writes, he gets very excited and writes quickly, and these are the stories that stump him when he tries to read them. When he thinks his words through, he is able to hear the sounds that he needs to get the words down in a way that he will recognize later on.

The story in Figure 3.8 starts out as one of my idea cards on special people in families but finishes up being a story about Wally's best friend. It is not hard to figure this one out but a little background might help. Wally had been away in the morning and when he arrived in the afternoon, a boy

**Figure 3.8**

wan da, michael
was mi Besf fen.
and he was mi
Port nr and heks moing
and We Wakt up
and we mok Pancks
Wen it was hloWen.
u hoy I em
mic hael. fen Bes
He miS me and
mic hael Was a
Bat and i Was
a varpiih and We
fikrtret The end.

named Michael lavished him with hugs and kept telling him about how he had been missed.

> One day Michael was my best friend and he was my partner and next morning we waked up and we make pancakes when it was Halloween. You know I am Michael's best friend. He miss me and Michael was a bat and I was a vampire and we trick-or-treated. The end. (Journal entry, March 26, 1990)

I am not sure why Wally goes back to Halloween time here but the Halloween words that he uses are interesting. We had not looked at this vocabulary since the big day, and to me his spelling of these *hard* words, like trick-or-treating, vampire, and Halloween, indicates how confident he is becoming in his abilities to sound out words and write on his own. This is the first time too that he uses "the end" instead of "d and," which can look like "dead" if you are not reading carefully.

The last story, in Figure 3.9, shows how much Wally has grown. This story really does not need translation.

> Happy Bunnies
> One day Happy Bunny was going to a picnic with his friends. They found a perfect spot for the picnic. They ate hot dogs and ants were coming by and then they ate the hot dogs. When the rabbits woke up they didn't have the hot dogs. The end. (Journal entry, April 2, 1990)

His stories now show a definite beginning, middle, and ending. He understands the connection between sounds, symbols, and meanings. He has a collection of sight words and when he encounters something unfamiliar or doesn't remember the spelling, he sounds things out slowly and carefully to make sure that he has all the sounds and letters.

The odd "da" pops in, but for the most part this has been replaced with "th," something that he changed on his own. I notice how Wally spells "they"—thea. Does he recognize "th" as being spelled "the," and if you add an "n" to make "then," then adding an "a" must make "they"? I forget sometimes what a difficult language English can be to learn, and Wally's rules for spelling sometimes make more sense to him than conventions do. Sometimes he is willing to listen to my explanations, sometimes not. I see that children in this grade 1 class are free to develop their own rules, which are changed or discarded as they learn more and figure more things out. As a student teacher in this classroom, my story of Wally's work stops here, but his stories will continue to grow and develop.

Wally's stories taught me that "good" stories are not necessarily good

**Figure 3.9**

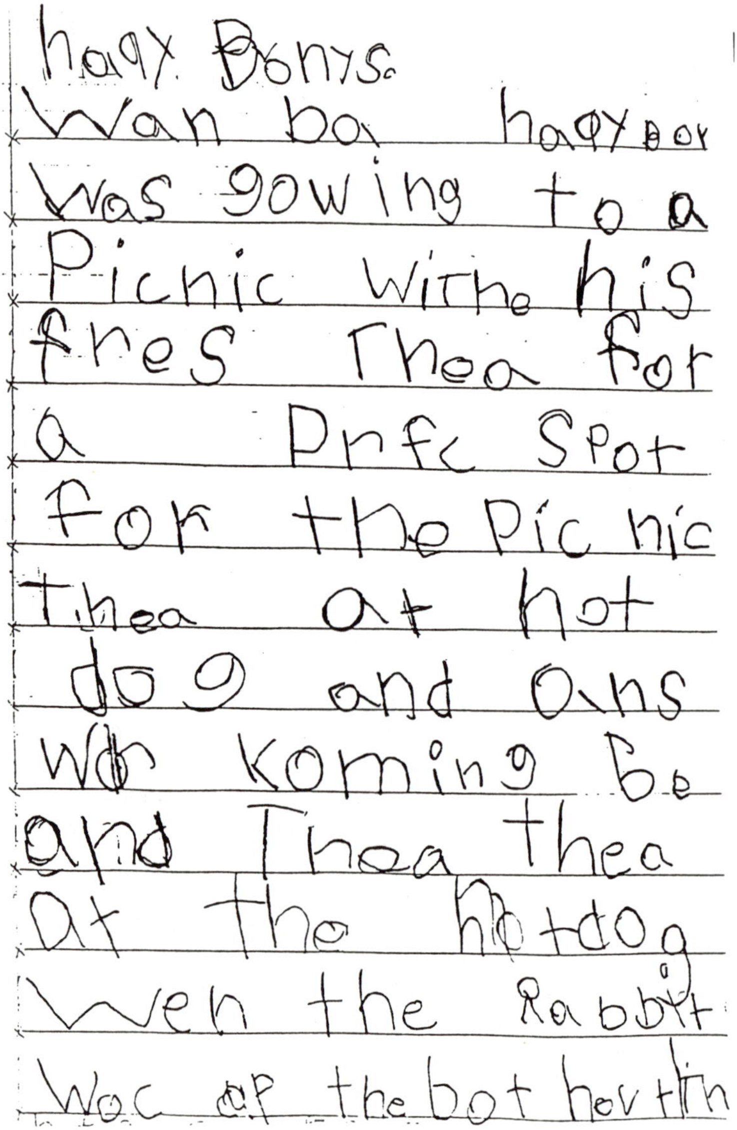

haqy Bonys.
Wan boy        haqy boy
Was gowing   to a
Picnic witho his
fres Thea for
a       Drfc Spot
for  the Pic nic
Thea   at  hot
doo  and Ons
Wa Koming  Be
and Thea thea
At  the  hotdoo
Wen  the  Rabbit
Woc af the bot hovtth

just because all the words are spelled correctly, all the letters touch the lines, and every sentence ends with the proper punctuation. Wally taught me that any story written by a child is a good story because it is an expression of who that child is and what that child is all about. As I work with my grade 3 children now, Wally's stories remind me to look beyond the words on the page to celebrate the story that is being told.

# CHAPTER 4

# Connecting Reflections

## *Jean Fix*

I remember seeing her when she was about six. Oh, I had known her long before then but as I recall, this was the first time I really *saw* her. She was struggling through some reading. A book on dance. Ballet. Right then, I think "to struggle" could have become her motto. Perhaps it was a good thing she was never aware of the notion until much later — until "struggle" could be translated into "challenge."

The classroom is busy today. I'm trying hard to pay attention to many children and their individual needs. It seems an unending task as I try to focus on the lesson I am struggling to complete. Children are buzzing, and I'm conscious of the noise level. As long as they are on task things are well, I hear myself think. Amir's* sheet doesn't appear to be done. Why? I wonder. I hear myself correcting his efforts. He was doing well last day. Oh darn, it's almost time for music. Why is he not responding? I correct more. I am aware he is looking down — but not at his work.

She was reading orally that day trying to combine her memory of words with the sounds she understood each letter must have. "Ballet" stumped her. Time after time she pronounced the "et" and each time she was corrected. She wanted to read well and I think on the whole she was, except for this seemingly small infraction. But each time she was corrected, she felt as though she had failed somehow. Her repeated error and the continuous editing began to negate all that she had accomplished. She finished only remembering her errors.

I make sounds to get the children ready for their next class. Amir has gladly packed up. Escape from my tenacious manner. Hmmm. Her face clouds over Amir's and an understanding washes over me. I take a few

---

*The children's names have been changed to pseudonyms in this chapter.

moments to speak to Amir, to reassure him, to give him accolades for what he knew, to leave on a positive note. He smiles. The class is leaving and the buzz starts to dissipate.

She was in grade 3 when I "saw" her again. Sitting in the third row from the window, fourth desk down. Questions were being asked. She knew the answer and reached her hand up.

But another little person was called upon. I saw the look of surprise on her face when her peer was not responding. If she knew the answer, everyone must know it. I could see she was trying to make sense of this thought. She shifted in her seat and bit on the end of her pencil. It appeared to her that she was never called upon for an answer when she was sure of something, only when she was not.

There is something about today in my classroom I don't feel all that comfortable with. The lesson itself is fine. Well, more than fine. It is one of those lessons that seems to have wings. I start the plane and the children pilot it. But my questioning techniques in order to gather information leave me feeling grounded. There must be a way to field responses without always picking specific children out to do so. I call on Negin, whose hand is up. Sean blurts out the answer. I look at Sean. He shrugs. Negin repeats what Sean has said.

She bit down hard, shifted again and said what she knew out loud. Immediately she was told to sit on the bench and face the blackboard at the front of the room. Tears welled up. She was going home. But the teacher only spoke her directions louder—with more authority. So, she sat at the front, on the bench, facing the blackboard, deciding never to put her hand up again.

Suddenly, it strikes me. I get everybody to work in pairs—easily enough done as they sit mostly in twos. They can help each other, talk to each other, and get a chance to say everything they know. I look around, things appear at first to be a little chaotic. Sean is busy, happily explaining his knowing to Azin. From the back of the room Scott has his hand up. He is asking me a question. So, that's what hands are for—to get my attention, to ask me questions. A two-way street! That feels better. This way, hopefully, I won't miss anyone.

She was in grade 4 when I saw her reading out loud again. She was standing at the front of the class taking her turn. I was so pleased for her. Her reading flowed. She was tracking—running her finger along the printed page. Unfortunately, that tool was not acceptable in her classroom, and when she became conscious of her finger she immediately pulled it away. Too late. She knew she would be penalized. And as she continued to read she stumbled and tripped over every word. When she finished and took her seat, she could only picture herself as a poor reader.

Whenever I see her reflection in my grade 2 class I work hard at allowing children to use as many tools as they need in order to help them see themselves as viable learners. I want them to see themselves as successful.

I have a class period free for preparation today. As I finish up some marking I can see Michael out of the corner of my eye. I recognize the body language. I have come to understand—there is a story in there and I can help if I take the time to listen. I can help with connections only if I am aware of what parts need connecting! I move toward him, grab a vacant chair, and pull it up next to him. He starts to talk immediately. "I can't . . . I don't know how." I nod and suggest that we can figure it out together. I start by drawing pictures of money, asking how many pennies are in each coin, helping him differentiate between them. "Money has just the same numbers in them as when we add and subtract," I hear myself saying. "A nickel is five cents, which is like five pennies or five ones. If you have five cents and you give me two, how many do you have left? We could use the same numbers with beans or pencils." "Three," he said simply. "Three cents or three beans." "Right, depending on what we are working with. Math is based on patterns." "Oh," Michael looked up at me. "Nobody told me. I can do this." His body language reads a different story. As I sit and watch Michael, she blends into mind.

Years later someone told her that math was primarily built on patterns. Seeing her struggle through all those years of schooling and not making connections between even the simplest pattern, leaves me wondering why no one pointed this out to her long before then. Her world of education was a far cry from discovery-teaching, discovery-learning, so I knew that was not the motive behind not explaining and sharing connections. She was up against rote memory, rote math. Automatically clicking into math patterns based on previous work obviously was not the way she easily interpreted math. She saw everything as independent units—not interrelated at all. Consequently, the more complicated the symbols, the more she felt intimidated by the whole process. Not getting it became her pattern.

I smile to myself, aware of the classroom once again. It was good to explain patterns to Michael. Maybe my connections are not his, but if I do not share mine, perhaps he will not recognize his own.

I saw her again in grade 8. She was thirteen. I suspect she was resigned to not battling through school at a high academic level any longer, but still I remember hearing the anxiety she felt when she continued to be placed in a lower-level reading group. I think she was struggling for an identity of some sort. Something that would set her aside — in a positive light. One happened. Not entirely without a struggle, but at least the struggle had a new angle to it. It was challenging.

I am not sure of science with all of its implications. Relax, I think to myself. You can learn with the kids. Tom's answering questions — taking an interest in everything we are doing. That's neat, although perhaps a bit unusual. He is making wonderfully clear connections. I call him a scientist. His eyes light up and he replies, "Ya!" And for the first time this year I see Tom become entirely engulfed.

I remember her anxiety as she sat and waited her turn on the raised platform. She was so afraid. It was the same kind of fear that can be heard ringing in your ears when something important is about to happen. She only understood her nervousness. But she got up on the stage and did her stuff. She was intense, totally swept up in the moment. Every pore believed in what she was doing. It was not until she sat back down in her chair that the nervousness took over again.

Her teacher was talking — she turned. "In all my years of teaching nobody has done a finer job at this type of exercise than what I have just seen. And I do not mind saying, I have just given out the highest mark I have ever given." She smiled, the fear eased, an inner voice gave her a hug. She had found a place.

Tom is speaking clear, knowing thoughts, and in this instant I see him on a raised platform. I ask the class to quiet down so they can hear Tom's voice. I sense how important his voice is — not to me necessarily, but to him. I cannot help but wonder if Tom is not somewhat aware of the importance of science to him; the comfort of this place.

She was on the stage when I walked into the back of the auditorium to see her again. She was just a year older but something was different about her. I could feel her nervousness as she began her audition piece. I felt even her nervousness was displayed in a somewhat different fashion. I had to think for a moment before I realized what it was. She had poise — a more confident manner. Her nervousness was built from the adrenaline running through her system — not from pure unknown fear. Her piece was good. I could see the transformation from her to the character she took on. The picture she visioned was clear — believable. She was lost in her picture and so was her audience. When she finished and took her seat among her peers, the drama teacher offered her the poppy he had just picked up off the floor. It was like being handed an ovation. I could sense she was beginning to "believe" off the stage as well. Even if — just for this moment.

"Ms. Fix, he called me dumb." "Do you think you are dumb?" I ask William gently. He shakes his head. "Well, believe in what you know." He nods. A few minutes later I suggest to William that he talk about his plant. What he sees, what he knows. He looks hard in his plastic cup and says he sees nothing but thinks something is trying to grow. I ask him what he thinks it is that is trying to grow. "A big, strong root" is his reply. I wink at him. William believes — even if just for this moment.

From here on, drama became timeless for her. Never did it become too much work or too much energy. Here was where the struggling ceased to exist, as if by some mystical power. There was acquiescence between her inner voice and her pictures. Drama had empowered her.

It was not until college, after years of self-reflecting, that I noticed she really began to trust her inner voice outside of drama. I suspect it had something to do with her English professor at the time. This person was keen on her writing. She loved her pictures. Ideas were not overlooked in favor of finding grammatical errors.

This evening I am trying to read the children's science logbooks. The words are often difficult to make out. I use my red marker to correct spelling so I can read what they have written.

She enjoyed the way the professor listened. In class the professor would paraphrase what the students were expressing. She made a point of acknowledging their voices, both orally as well as in their written work. The professor would make overhead copies of students' essays and use them to discuss the merits of their work. It was the first time her writing was ever celebrated in this manner. She noticed on her papers that the professor would quietly make corrections. Never did she try to rewrite the students' words. She listened to their writing with as much intensity as when she listened to them speak.

As the picture of her sitting in this English class fades, I get a sharp sense of the ambience I am creating with my red marker. I put it down and start to read their impressions out loud. It is not as difficult as I first anticipated. On the contrary, it is easier. I listen to what is written. And as I listen, I realize my original purpose for the logbooks. They were to be a tool for observations. The kids' observations, not mine.

I see her often these days. We actually have become quite good friends. Oh, she still struggles through with some things but understanding is apparent — even to her. She sees struggling as part of her journey.

The realization that pictures play such an important role in her life allows these pictures to become her thoughts rather than constantly trying to sever one from the other. These pictures collectively have become her stories.

Now, when I see her in my classroom — her stories become mine. The mirror she holds up in front of me gives me the opportunity to observe and understand what I might have chosen to negate.

Her reflection becomes mine.

**REFLECTION**

Every time she looked in a mirror
She saw precisely what she expected
Until she went beyond the boundaries
To explore the crevices and peaks.

The layers of her reflection
Were not easily seen at first
They hid behind her perceptions
Laying dormant until she searched.

And long after her inviting —
Editing and coloring went on
Shading in an understanding
Of who she thought she was.

But many parts of equal importance
Got lost without her knowing
So now when she looks at her reflection
She tries to go beyond
                                   to see what she cannot.

# PART TWO

# LEARNING TO TEACH BY LIVING TEACHING

In this part, we share stories of collaboration. These stories illustrate the shared meaning that was constructed as student, cooperating, and university teachers worked together. In Chapter 5 Annie Davies, Pat Hogan, and Benita Dalton describe how journals provided a way for all participants to reflect on practices. Annie and Pat tell their story lived out with Benita, a student teacher, and the ways journal writing and response became a conversation of practice.

The next three chapters were authored by pairs of cooperating teachers and student teachers. Deb Nettesheim and Sherri Pearce use gift giving and receiving as a way to describe their relationship. Angela Barritt and Kerry Black use parallel stories to construct a way of giving an account of their work together. Barbara Kennard and Lynn Johnston-Kosik tell of their struggle to learn to work together in a series of poems that form a conversation. For them, poetry became a means of connection, a way of beginning the conversation.

In Chapter 9, Annie Davies reflects on her work with Benita Dalton as she tells stories of planning, stories that tell how she and Benita learned about what it means to plan in the context of their shared practice. In Chapter 10, Pat Hogan and Carol Flather tell a story of their work together as Carol tried to find her own voice and a place in her classroom as she worked with children. In Chapter 11, Pat Hogan tells a story of Joanne, a story of a dilemma we experience as teachers when students are silent. Pat tells her story of the dangers of constructing a story for a silent student to live out.

# CHAPTER 5

# Journals: The Conversations of Practice

*Annie Davies, Pat Hogan, and Benita Dalton*

The use of journals in the Alternative Program has a long narrative history. Many of the teachers who worked in the program had used journals in the context of graduate courses and in their personal lives. Some had begun to experiment in their work with student teachers in the regular practicum using the traditional logbook as more of a dialogue journal. One of the narratives that shaped the use of journals in the program was our story of working together with a group of practitioners who used reflective journals to research their own practice. Our work with four other teachers over 2 years prior to the fall of 1988 led all of us into the Alternative Program, but it also helped shape how we envisioned journals being used by student teachers.

## THE JOURNAL IN THE TEACHER-AS-RESEARCHER STORY

In the context of our teacher-researcher group, we learned how teachers' belief in the unique nature of their evolving practice could be a starting place for inquiry. We found that journal entries could be seen as written conversations of practice that evolve over time. The recorded data could be reviewed as historical text to which teachers return in order to gain new understanding of practice through reflection.

As our story unfolded it became a story of personal and professional growth and the journals became central to each person's development. They provided an occasion for learning and a place for thinking to be recorded. Annie reflected on how personal and professional growth became intertwined.

> The journals then aid the broader goal of development of the self in the professional realm but perhaps more importantly at the personal level and that feeds back into the professional level. The journal group provides a

function that is latent and perhaps unanticipated by us (by me at least). I knew I'd find out about my teaching but didn't expect some of my other "personal findings." (Hogan, 1988, pp. 5–6)

The members of our group each discovered their own purposes for keeping a journal and their own directions for inquiry. As each individual purpose for writing unfolded, the style and structure of each book evolved. Each teacher wrote a different journal. The journals changed over time as focus and direction emerged and as individuals learned and grew. Questions emerged and changed shape. Annie addressed this as she described how her journal allowed a reconstruction of experience.

Journals give time to build an awareness of options—time to find threads—to go back and reflect again—to go back knowing more and to read again with "fresh eyes." We see things we weren't able to see then. (Hogan, 1988, p. 9)

As we sorted out our purposes for keeping journals and for inquiring into our practice, we came to recognize how belonging to a community helped us to grow. Written response in the journals became an important dimension of that growth. It was important to both those who gave and those who received the responses. In composing responses, we engaged in reflecting on the entries in light of our own experience. Our responses represented an extension and a reconstruction of our personal practical knowledge and served to increase personal awareness of and confidence in our knowing. As a result of engaging in this form of critical thinking, new questions arose. In responding to others, we also attempted to answer these new questions. Our confidence in ourselves and our voices strengthened. Whenever we engaged in responding to anyone else's journal, we entered into a dialogue or conversation that enhanced our connection with the other person. We came to know other people's thoughts as well as their feelings. We read about their uncertainties, their problems, and their aspirations. We shared our ideas and our emotions, offering encouragement and support. Our responses come from the head and from the heart. We came to appreciate, trust, and care about each other.

The sharing of journals became an important experience for everyone in the group. Responses were validating, confirming, and motivating. Feedback and questions generated further levels of reflection for each individual. Annie wrote, "I need an audience. The other collaborators are very important. They see things I cannot because I am too close to it" (Hogan, 1988, p. 7). The questions of others caused new insights and new learning.

Reading and reacting to responses from other group members was complicated but powerful. With each set of responses we experienced different reactions to our thoughts, and we had the opportunity to reconsider our original ideas when we reread our entries in light of the responses.

Our participation in the group gave us a chance to examine our beliefs and the assumptions underlying them. We developed a growing sense of what was "right" for us as teachers. We gained the courage to ask questions about important educational issues and to explore and challenge what we were being asked to do in our classrooms. Our dialogue was genuine. We neither glossed over our differences nor ignored our sameness. The integrity of each individual was preserved. We communicated and shared in an environment that welcomed differences and celebrated similarities.

## THE JOURNAL IN THE ALTERNATIVE PROGRAM

When we began to think about a new story of teacher education, we knew we would have to incorporate journals into the program. We hoped that some of our experiences with journals in the teacher-researcher group could be recreated for student teachers. We knew how important response would be to the student teachers' sense-making of what was going on in the context of their coursework and their classrooms. We also had begun to understand how dialogue in the journal could be a mutual construction of knowledge, so it seemed important to create ongoing conversations in both contexts. We decided to have each student teacher keep a journal in two parts. One part would be kept in dialogue with the university teachers who were currently teaching the methods courses. This would afford university teachers the opportunity to see what was of interest and concern to the students in their practice. It would help clarify when particular theoretical issues might be appropriate for the on-campus components of the program. It would help university teachers to be a part of the students' conversations with theory.

The other part would be a classroom journal kept in dialogue with the cooperating teacher and the university teacher responsible for that student's small group seminar. This would create a three-way conversation of practice where all participants engaged in the inquiry. As the student teacher recorded observations and reflections, questions and wondering thoughts, the cooperating teacher and university teacher would respond, offering support, encouragement, and another perspective on thinking about life in the classroom. In our responses we could make connections with the student teacher and with each other both personally and professionally. We knew we could further the student teacher's thinking but we also knew that in making responses we too would figure out more about ourselves and our teaching.

When we made the journals a central part of the program, we wanted to recognize each student teacher's unique way of coming to know practice. We knew we could not prescribe a format for how the journals should be kept but instead tried to allow each student teacher the opportunity to find purpose and direction in his or her writing. This wasn't as easy for some students to grasp as it was for others. Some students struggled initially with the institutional story of what it was "the university wanted." Gradually many of them came to believe we were giving them ownership of their journals.

We could tell many stories of how student teachers used their journals and of how cooperating teachers and university teachers became a part of the process. We could tell many stories about what we learned. Each story would be as unique in voice and style as the individual teachers who participated in the program. Instead we attempt here to tell just a few stories that represent something of the range of experiences with journals.

## ANNIE'S STORY OF THE JOURNAL IN
## THE PRACTICUM EXPERIENCE

The topic of journals was high on the agenda on the first day that Pam Rinehart, my teaching partner, and I met Helen Mahabir and Benita Dalton, our student teachers. Pam and I talked about our previous journaling experiences and explained what we had come to know over the previous 3 years as teacher-researchers. We told Helen and Benita that we would continue to write our own reflective journals and that they were welcome to read and respond to them. Our previous journals served as models of what a journal might look like. The colorful pages of Pam's coiled notebook and the clown on the front of mine contrasted sharply with the usual practicum logbook used by the university. To us they symbolized "choice." Our special journals were places where we chose to write. We wrote about things that mattered to us in our practice, things we were trying to figure out. We valued our writing and the written responses of trusted colleagues. We talked of the relationships that had developed over time. Our enthusiasm served to allay Helen's and Benita's fears. They chose their special journals and all four of us began to write.

Pam and I responded to each other as well as to our student teachers. Benita was able to read Pam's response to me and was also drawn to respond to my journal. She quickly got a feel for the human quality that is the essence of thoughtful response and adopted an easy conversational tone as she wrote in her own journal. She began to see an unexpected versatility in my use of a journal. She witnessed my process of reflecting in order to plan future experiences for the children. Her observations led her to ask questions so that she might better understand how to use a journal.

> I see that you are using your journal for your planning as well. Is this meant to be or does it just happen? I guess with experience you learn how to integrate the subjects together. It's neat to watch you do this. I hope to be able to achieve this as well. (Journal response, September 13, 1989)

Benita quickly learned that the journal was not just a place for simply "telling" what was going on in the classroom. She continued to question what she saw, and I found myself using my journal to explain things to her. I wanted her to understand why I did things in a certain way. I recognized that my classroom looked very different from anything that Benita might have experienced in her own schooling. I felt a moral responsibility to help her to find her place as my team partner working in a classroom environment structured by me.

Through daily writing as a member of the classroom "community of writers," Benita began to find her place, her voice, and a "self" she hadn't known. The following journal comments reflect her growth and confidence as a writer as she received responses from me and from Pat, the university teacher responsible for her small group seminar.

> I was amazed at myself in that I was actually able to write. As a child I could never think of anything to write about so I would sit for the majority of the time. (Journal response, September 15, 1989)

> The students had a lot to write. I was the same. I could have kept writing for hours. I find that I have learned more in these first couple of hours of writing than I did in two years of English classes. (Journal response, September 18, 1989)

> I am enjoying writing and thinking through my writing, something that is very new to me. (Journal response, October 2, 1989)

In less than a month, Benita had a sense of just how powerful writing to learn can be. It was good to read the following response:

I don't feel like I am being evaluated. I feel like I am working with Annie rather than under. This is a good feeling. (Journal response, October 6, 1989)

Pat's response in Benita's journal also made me feel that I had found a way to build a collaborative relationship through the sharing of our journals and ourselves.

You have really figured out what it means to collaborate. Am I surprised? (Journal response, October 6, 1989)

Benita felt secure in a community of journal writers where all of us asked questions and gained support and encouragement through response. She wrote at length and her journal shaped itself. She knew there was no "right way" to do this. She trusted the process and those who provided response.

After 4 months Benita had a sense of making her journal work for her. Her reflective entries were extensive, involving a complexity of integrated thoughts summoned by situated classroom events. The following response describes her experience as she worked with our grade 3 students in math:

I am very comfortable with the math unit maybe because it is money and I have worked with a lot of money over the years. The math is going much faster than I had anticipated. I have designated partners to work together when working with the "real" money bags. I tried to partner strong with weak so that the stronger partner can be a teacher to the other person. Also I tried to pair them so they could work together or one person would influence the other to work rather than fool around. I have noticed some problems already with certain groups but I will wait a couple more days. Maybe things will straighten up before I have to make changes. The class was so excited when I handed out the real money. It seemed like the best thing since sliced bread. The class is fairly comfortable with assembling money. I haven't said anything about how to arrange the money, but I have noticed that some of the class made an order from the largest coin to the smallest. Tomorrow I will work on the arrangement of the coins. I had seen a couple of groups go back to the idea of piling their money. So it is difficult to count the money at a glance. They did the same thing when they worked with the base 10 blocks at first. Interesting! One very important discovery I made today when I was helping Lorraine* with money after school was that if you can't count by 5s or 10s starting at a given number, then you have a hard time trying to count up money. I would like to work with counting with 5s and 10s a little longer. (Journal response, January 9, 1990)

I am now able to see this response as a story, Benita's story of making sense of practice. The comfort she describes as she works with the math unit comes from her many years of experience as a cashier for Co-op Food Stores. She was able to tell the children real stories about cash and customers, and the shared stories gave her a way into the unit as well as an aura of credibility. Her careful structuring of paired working relationships among the children reveals her understanding of the classroom story that she has been living. She uses a structure that is well established, but takes time to designate specific paired relationships, drawing on her knowledge of individual children to form these pairs. This too is part of her story because she struggled with individual behavior problems and felt that structuring situations was what she needed to do in order to feel comfortable. Her planning reveals an attention to details that will allow her to be successful from a classroom management point of view. It also shows an equal concern for maximizing the learning opportunity for the children. I see her story as inextricably linked to the classroom story that she is part of, and to the individual stories of each child.

When Benita comments about the math "going faster" than anticipated, I see her ability to pick up the rhythm of her students, to gauge their knowing and be prepared to adjust her plans according to the needs and leads of her students. Equally, she shows a patient reflective stance in relation to problems. She feels comfortable "waiting" yet is prepared to change. I feel her willingness to be guided by the situation and her own knowing. As she watches the children handling the money, she gets a lead for her next lesson. I see her ability to find the next logical step, the link to connected, meaningful experience. She thinks about the children's instinctive desire to pile things up, linking it with a previous observation. She knows this is not helpful as they count. Her comment "interesting" lets me know that she is thinking about this phenomenon. I see a connected presence with the children, a willingness to wonder and gradually understand better each child's world. Benita's ability to connect with individual children such as Lorraine allows her to move from the particular to the generalizable. She is able to pinpoint an important step or skill, that of counting by 5s or 10s, and resolves to spend sufficient time so that the children will not

---

*The children's names have been changed to pseudonyms in this chapter.

have difficulties. Lorraine's story helps Benita to pace and time her lesson with care in a unique negotiation of curriculum.

I could talk about this journal response as a means to evaluate Benita. In that voice I could say that the response shows her ability to deal with aspects of planning, organization, the negotiation of curriculum, and effective classroom management techniques. But the journal experience generates a different voice. Benita does not anticipate evaluation. She expects response, a personal connected response at the moment that she lives the experience. The written responses that Pat and I give her are based on particular connections triggered by our lived experiences. As I read her journal, I circled the word "real" when she described her use of real money. Beside the word, I wrote:

> Keep this word in your head as a guiding principle for teaching. You are a real teacher when you make things real for children. (Journal response, January 9, 1990)

To the casual reader this response may seem inadequate, even disconnected, but embedded within it are two very particular shared stories, which we mutually understood. In Benita's case the word "real" took on huge significance after our classroom work with *The Velveteen Rabbit* (Williams, 1975). The velveteen rabbit's story of becoming real was synonymous with Benita's concept of becoming a real teacher. Benita also understood my beliefs about real experiences for children, and my comment was an attempt to validate her decision to use real money in the math unit. Pat was drawn to continue the dialogue and to pick up on another point.

> This notion of real makes it relevant for kids. It connects with their world and makes sense for that reason. I wonder what kinds of problems you're noticing with the groups. (Journal response, January 9, 1990)

Pat's wonder made space for Benita to discuss the problems she had noticed in certain groups. Benita's comment had particularly caught Pat's attention because of her own interest in groups and the ways they worked. Working with groups formed a big part of Pat's story. She was interested in what was going on. I, on the other hand, did not feel compelled to respond to the problems, feeling that Benita had this under control and would sort it out for herself. I read my own story of "somehow I will figure this out" in her actions. I realize now just how much our own stories influence what is given or received within the journaling process. I understand the importance of different perspectives, different connections, different voices that are real voices enabling each of us to make sense of experience and engage in a spirit of inquiry that guides our future knowing.

Benita's journal was also a place where I could write to explain my thinking and share ideas that were important to me. In January, I took the lead with the novel *Trouble River* (Byars, 1969) because I wanted Benita to see how I worked with chapters in the novel. I also wanted her to see how I conceptualized the school year as a series of chapters. In her journal I wrote:

> I wanted to do this book because I want you to experience the chaptering idea. If we understand chapters, then we understand continuity and if we can provide continuity of experience for children then our "classroom texts" will be a pretty stunning story that kids won't forget. Does this make sense or is the image too far off? I'm convinced this chapter stuff is really important but I am at an intuitive point with it. I think it really stretches the thinking of the kids. I'm interested in your thoughts and perceptions. I think I'm getting at structure, Benita, and then the rhythm of chapters as they come together. It is demanding for any of us. (Journal response, January 9, 1990)

Because this was important to me Benita also took it on. It became important to her. Her journal response shows her willingness to think hard, to collaborate, and to be part of a shared inquiry.

> Annie started *Trouble River* today by Betsy Byars. She had prompted the class to start thinking about chapters . . . why we have chapters . . . what are they like? It made me think of chapters in a very careful way. I had addressed this idea of a chapter and misunderstood what Annie was asking. I thought that she meant the structure and not the story. But this is good for me to think about the structure of a chapter. A chapter is like a mini-picture of a whole screen text. The chapter does have a distinct beginning by telling the reader something new or introducing new characters. But a chapter can also be a continuation of something from a previous chapter. The chapters within a book connect ideas, each chapter having an idea, but it is related to the whole book. When I am reading and I want to quit I look to see how many more pages until the end of a chapter. In a sense the end of a chapter is a natural pause or time for a commercial. Chapters also break the text into sections, clumping the same ideas together. (Journal response, January 9, 1990)

Pat's response also served to validate our inquiry. In addition, we could both see Pat making sense of her own story.

> I'm convinced that Annie is the only person who does this kind of work with chapters . . . it is really important stuff. It's neat you get to do this with her . . . I'd like to be there too. I tend to think of my life, my story, in terms of chapters. There seem to be periods or chapters in that story that have a beginning and ending yet somehow link to the next chapter, creating some kind of narrative unity. (Journal response, January 9, 1990)

The narrative unity that Pat suggested allowed me to circle back to the idea of understanding the school year in terms of a story with chapters.

> I wonder if we should think of a day as a chapter, a unit of study as a chapter that will link to something and not just be a meaningless chapter, disconnected and floating in children's minds. (Journal response, January 9, 1990)

Our wondering voices, each prompted by the other, acted as catalysts that primed our thinking within this collaborative relationship. Benita finds a focus, makes it her own, and extends the dialogue still further.

> I want to pay close attention to Annie's work on *Trouble River* because then I can learn about chapters and continuity. One of my biggest problems in children's literature was that I became frustrated with the in-depth analyses made by other students in my class because they read too far into the book. I never learned about the chapter and how to look at it from a child's view. I am looking forward to this learning experience. (Journal response, January 10, 1990)

As conversations are continued, intensity builds and true feelings are voiced. I respond again:

> Literature isn't for *right* interpretation. It's for *thinking* and coming to know "self." The "wondering voice" is so important . . . more important than I really understand or can find words to explain. It allows us to be "open" to future possibility, to be lead by the situation, to become part of that situation in a connected way. (Journal response, January 11, 1990)

In ongoing conversations of this kind we come to see a bigger picture. We recognize beginnings and endings, we define chapters and begin to have a sense of the continuity of experience as the text of our lives. As teachers, we must pay attention to the ways we construct the texts for the children in our care.

## JOURNALS: FINDING VOICE IN COLLABORATIVE RELATIONSHIPS

Collaborative relationships are very much like friendships. They are the coming together of two individual stories and the making of room for another's story in one's own so that a shared story might be constructed as work is undertaken together. Initial encounters in new friendships are often tentative. A conscious effort is made to figure out who we are in relation to others and who they are in relation to us. We attempt to show something of ourselves and to make space for the others to do likewise. Offers and invitations are extended; hospitality and acceptance are offered. The same is true in collaborative relationships.

The experiences we have described with Benita and Annie, their particular ways of making sense of the journals, were by no means the experiences of every student teacher and cooperating teacher in the program. Others found their own unique ways to use the journals to ponder, wonder, and figure out together who they were as teachers and how their personal knowledge was made practical. For a few the journals never became the kind of reflective document that we had hoped they would. Looking back now we can see that the struggle over "what the university wanted" became an ongoing theme in these journals. For these individuals the journal remained a task assigned by the university; they never really owned the writing that was contained in their journals. They continued to write on the pages but never used the writing to explore, discover, or figure out their practice. Instead they reported faithfully on classroom events, on teaching strategies observed, and on progress made by children, but we had difficulty finding the writer in the lines on the page. With a couple of people, the journal seemed to be a "going through the motions" kind of activity where minimal entries were all they were willing to attempt. In some instances, students and even cooperating teachers were intimidated by the threat of evaluation. Students may have been cautious about revealing too much about themselves because the intimacy frightened them or because a grade was attached to the journals as part of each methods course. Cooperating teachers may have felt that their words or their practices might be judged if committed to paper. This led at least one student to feelings of defensiveness in response to each of our wondering questions. Our attempts to engage in "wondering with" were read as challenges and were met with certainty or silence.

We know that there is still much to be figured out about how to work with journals in the context of a university assignment. We need to find ways to make space for students to find themselves in their writing and to use writing to construct their own knowledge of practice. However, with students like Benita, we find a sense of possibility for what journals can be. She writes:

> Before this year, I had done journaling only once before. It was for a drama class. In the journal we had to describe what had taken place and comment on it. I found it difficult so when I found out that we had to keep a journal for our practicum, I was a little bit reluctant at first. I began my journal after my first meeting with Annie. Because I didn't know what we were supposed to write, I wrote how the day felt for me. Annie advised me to pick a book that I would like to write in; she had shown me some of her journals and allowed me to take one home to look through it. I struggled in the beginning in search of what to write. I think all of us questioned what we were supposed to be writing. We were used to being indoctrinated by the university as to what we should write. As time went on I found the journal easy to write in. Journaling gave me the opportunity to question things that happened during the day with the children or something Annie was doing. I was able to "wonder." The journal was a place for me to figure things out. I would write down my feelings about the day and focus on particular events. The journal was a place for me to express my thoughts and to gain voice.
>
> I gained voice through the dialogue that occurred between myself, Annie, and Pat. As I wrote about my experiences Annie and Pat were very supportive and positive. I was able to take risks about whatever I wanted. I never thought that I couldn't write about my feelings of uncertainty. But by writing about such feelings, I was able to get support and reassurance from Annie.
>
> I was curious and questioned Annie about her knowledge that she has in the classroom. By questioning her, she thought about her own practice and also gave me more questions to think about. The journal was a place where I could reflect and think deeply. It recorded my growth as a teacher and as a person. Through writing in my journal I used it as a tool to help me understand all of my questions and won-

ders. The journal is the development of my personal practical knowledge. (Journal response, July 10, 1990)

## REFERENCES

Byars, B. (1969). *Trouble River*. Toronto: Viking Press, Penguin Books Canada.
Hogan, P. (1988). A community of teacher researchers: A story of empowerment
and voice. Unpublished manuscript, University of Calgary.
Williams, M. (1975). *The velveteen rabbit*. New York: Avon Books.

# CHAPTER 6

# The Gift: A Story of Giving and Receiving

## Deb Lloyd Nettesheim and Sherri L. Pearce

Many years ago I recall watching my dad meticulously handcraft a beautiful pine rocking chair. It was a surprise present for my mom. I remember asking him why it had such big arms and, "Why was the cushion green?" "Because your mom likes to rest her elbows when she knits and reads and green is her favorite color," he answered. I could see this gift was lovingly and thoughtfully being created for one person only—my mom. When Christmas finally arrived I distinctly remember two things—the pride and excitement I had in being a part of Dad's secret and the look on his face when he presented this wonderful, wooden rocking chair to my teary-eyed mom. I suppose that is when I first became aware of the notion "it is in giving that we truly receive."

This chapter is about sharing the gift of stories. They are stories that have taken Sherri, my student teacher, and me on a journey of discovery and growth, a journey that is helping us to better understand ourselves and give value and meaning to what we know and do. It is in the giving of these stories—these gifts—that Sherri and I have truly received, for we get back pieces of ourselves that give us more insight into who we are. It is only a beginning.

Sherri and I met at a gathering for the alternative teaching program last June. This meeting was designed to welcome student teachers and cooperating teachers to a new and exciting program for student teaching.

As we sat around our table sharing bits of our stories, I recall telling a tale of my student teaching experiences 11 years ago. Back then, we were not encouraged to discover for ourselves what teaching was; rather we were given correct methods and theories and encouraged to apply them. I was aware of the need for change and expressed my hopes that this program might offer that change. It was this program that was going to allow us the freedom to take risks, make mistakes, learn from each other, and grow. It was this meeting and this program that brought Sherri and me together to be partners in learning for the school year ahead.

## THE BEGINNING OF OUR JOURNEY–SHERRI

I was very excited about this program. Many of my friends, after completing their practicum, felt unprepared to take on the task of classroom teaching. Their practicum had been similar to Deb's–modeling what their cooperating teacher deemed to be good teaching.

This program was giving me the opportunity to be in the classroom all year. I was going to learn about the rhythms and cycles of teaching and begin to understand what it takes to create a classroom community instead of arriving, as a student teacher, months after it has been established.

On the first day of school I entered "our" classroom before the students arrived. I felt touched because Deb had pulled up a table for me next to her desk. It was cleared except for a blue notebook and a brand-new sharpened pencil. I had been welcomed. On the first page of the book Deb had written:

To Sherri,
    as we travel on this road of
    discovery together . . . .
    We do not write to be understood,
    we write to understand
                            (Lewis)

This book was to become my journal. I did not begin to understand the meaning of this quote until Deb and I started writing and sharing our stories.

## OUR STORIES BEGIN–DEB AND SHERRI

Eisner (1988) believes that knowledge is rooted in experience. Sherri and I began to discover the truth in these words. Our first journal entries were personal pieces of writing about school experiences. Sherri wrote an insightful account of a speech she proudly presented in grade 6. I wrote a story called *The Mitten*, an incident in grade 8 where I hid in a classroom cupboard. As we shared our stories we were both amazed at the detail and images we could recall. Still, we wondered what purpose this first exercise in writing truly served. The immediate effect seemed to be that it provided a place for the trust to begin because we were willing to share bits of ourselves. We realized how important it was to establish trust, but what else? In sharing our stories we began to talk more about what we thought they meant to us. Our talk evolved into questions and wonderings about education and living and being. We were immersed in a mutual dialogue of inquiry. I recall thinking to myself how is it Sherri knows so much and how is it we are both sitting here like colleagues asking these questions when I am the one with 10 years experience, who is supposed to have all the answers. We began to understand Eisner's words that knowledge is rooted in experience. We further began to understand Jean Clandinin's (1986) writings about personal practical knowledge and how our past experiences can give us insight into our present ones. The messages of our personal stories began to unfold as we gathered threads and put pieces of our puzzles together to give more meaning to our experiences and our lives.

## Sherri

### SUCCESS

My first journal story told of a speech I presented in grade 6. I had no idea why I wrote the story. It was my first experience of being successful at school. I wrote about how the success felt to me and how the result of that success seemed to offer me acceptance from my peers. In retelling the story and discussing it with Deb, I — and she — began to realize the importance of the experience I chose to write about. Deb made a connection to this being the start of my practicum and how I want to be successful. I pulled the thread a little further and expressed my belief that success needs to be fostered in all our students. I began to see there was meaning in my story. I discovered a piece of myself that is part of my teaching philosophy. My first experience with success has stayed with me and I want to provide that same kind of experience for the students that I teach. I had no idea how valuable this sharing of my first story would be.

## Deb

### TRUST

My first journal story, entitled *The Mitten*, was a humorous anecdote about a time I ended up hiding in a cupboard in grade 8. I went on and on about my silly antics and those of my two friends. The story ended with our teacher discovering me hidden in the closet trying to dig myself out of this situation by pretending to be looking for a lost mitten in the middle of June. Like Sherri, I was not sure why I chose to write about this particular memory. Looking back, the idea of me hiding in this cupboard was pretty silly. Mr. Wright, my grade-8 teacher, didn't ask what I was doing in there, nor did he reprimand me as I thought he might. Instead, he gave me a warm, knowing smile. That was all. He didn't say another word. He kept this incident as our shared secret.

When Sherri and I talked about this story I remember telling her I thought it was about friends and the importance I place on them. It was about this, but with time we discovered even more. Another piece of my story was given back to me a few weeks later in the classroom.

I sat down with Jonathan,* a boy in our class, to discuss some behavior problems he was having. Jonathan has a tendency to get pretty silly in class. I remember telling him that I understood this kind of behavior because I too had done (and still do) some pretty silly things. I had played with the idea of calling Jonathan's parents, and told him so. Jonathan and I talked at length and set up a mutual contract. In the end, the contract did not include notifying his parents. We had set up a partnership of trust. After Jonathan left, Sherri, who had been in the room during this conference, came running over to my desk journal in hand. She sat down and compared this situation with my personal story of *The Mitten*. This story had a hidden message about shared secrets and trust. My beliefs about trust were coming through in my conference with Jonathan. I believe that trust is an important component in a caring, cooperative classroom community. The things we believe in are somehow in our stories. I was not aware until that moment to what extent personal practical knowledge and storying ourselves becomes a way of making sense of what we know. In the telling and retelling of our stories, new meaning is created and we experience change in more of the same in a different light (Coles, 1989). The threads from our own stories tie into our beliefs and give us more insight into who we are.

## Sherri

### ANDREA

At the university I was learning to listen to the children's stories, to listen and value their stories as being part of who they are. One afternoon I saw Andrea crying her eyes out at her desk. At first she blurted out her frustration about the glue on her artwork not sticking. As I listened to what she had to say, the meaning of her tears became clearer. Andrea's parents are divorced and it was her birthday on Saturday. She really wanted to have a party, but she usually spent the weekends with her dad. This dilemma was creating considerable stress for her. I too had grown up in a family torn by divorce and constantly spent weekends away from my friends. I shared this story with Andrea. We talked together about how it felt. She was no longer crying when our conversation ended. As Deb estab-

---

*The children's names have been changed to pseudonyms in this chapter.

lished trust with Jonathan, I had reached Andrea. Later in the afternoon as Deb and I cleaned up the room I mentioned the talk Andrea and I had shared. Such an important story! It was eye-opening for both of us. It reminded Deb to listen to the students' stories for the meaning they convey, and I made a connection between what I had been taught at university and the realities of the classroom.

## Deb

### KAMIL

For me, learning to listen to the students' stories is becoming an important part of my practice. The more I know about their stories, the more I understand about them.

I sat with Kamil's mom at parent teacher interviews. I expressed some concerns about Kamil's inability to sit still and attend to his work for any length of time. In tears, she told me the story of their escape to mountains in Iran 3 years ago. She told me about the fighting and struggling and hate going on in their country. She said Kamil was only 3 years old at the time but that he has vivid memories of this horrifying experience. Kamil's mom wants Kamil to be in a place where he is loved and where he knows he is loved. I look at Kamil differently now. Children's stories are so important. We need to know who they are so that learning can take place.

We had no idea how, through sharing a classroom, we would be sharing an experience that would begin to lead us inward, to question ourselves and why we do what we do. As we struggle with this discovery we are learning who we are as teachers and individuals. We are on this road of discovery together. The occasions are endless. We have shared, talked, laughed, and hugged our way to knowing. We know ourselves better and we know the students better. Our relationship as a team of learners grew from our stories.

## I KNOW THIS HAS NOTHING TO DO WITH TEACHING BUT ... —SHERRI

I had been faithfully writing about all of my classroom feelings and experiences for some time. Everything in my journal was specifically classroom related until one morning, nearly in tears, I wrote about an incident at work. I work evenings as a cashier. I had had a run-in with a very difficult customer. She had deeply upset me to the point where I could think of nothing else. I wrote about the experience to get it off my chest.

Deb's comments, crammed down the margin and over onto the next page, helped me see that everything we experience is part of who we are.

> I don't think this is just about teaching (our journals)—I think it's about our belief system and our values. Your story tells something about what you believe in—those beliefs are in your teaching too: It's all important and has relevance and meaning.

By sharing this story we had connected who I am as a person with who I am as a teacher. We teach what we are. Deb found another piece of who I am. Without her response, I would not have made the connection from an isolated incident at work to my emerging teaching philosophy.

## THE GIFTS WE RECEIVE ARE NOT ALWAYS WHAT WE WANT . . . —DEB

Sherri and I became completely immersed in our stories and in dialogues about our stories. Each day we seemed to find another connection. Our experiences together in the classroom were turning into a wonderful ongoing story as we collected more threads and pulled more meaning into our practice. I also started to realize some of the meaning in our actions was not what we wanted or what we were expecting to find. I had written to Sherri about the enjoyment I get from Halloween and about how the classroom is so busy and full of enthusiastic learners. I continued my writings with a personal account of my daughters at home. I had gone to great lengths to have very special costumes handmade for them. When Halloween rolled around neither of them wanted to wear the costumes. These outfits had cost a good deal of money, and I was determined to get my girls to wear them. In the end, my husband reminded me that this was their Halloween not mine. I wasn't concerned about them. I was concerned about how wonderful my children would look at the neighborhood Halloween party. This whole episode got me thinking about power and control. I wondered if I was dealing with the students in our class in the same manner. I began to re-evaluate some of my classroom management techniques, and Sherri and I began to consider ways to give the students more choices and more say in what they do.

Through this story I became aware of some of the things I want to work on. I believe in our classroom as a cooperative, caring community. If I believe in this idea of community so strongly then I feel it is important for all of us to be working together as a team. We are trying to empower the students and encourage them to take some ownership in their learning.

My beliefs as a classroom teacher and as a cooperating teacher began to emerge. I feel a tremendous responsibility to let others find the place from which meaningful change can be made, to lead others to their own discoveries, and to allow them to take ownership and pride in their learning. I believe that our reflective journals and our stories are the seeds for that growth. Through them Sherri has begun to believe in herself and feel that she truly has something to offer.

## I REALLY DO HAVE TEACHING KNOWLEDGE – SHERRI

"Deb is letting me develop my voice, and is listening." This is how one of my journal entries began. It was an account of an incident where an experience outside the classroom helped me make decisions as a teacher.

Deb was very frustrated and angry one day about having to raise her voice to gain control of the classroom. As soon as she was finished talking, the class would be out of control again. She was concerned that the students didn't know how to listen. Tentatively I told Deb a story. I say tentatively because she was the teacher. Who was I to tell her what to do? She let me talk and as I said, she listened.

During the summer I took my dog to obedience school. One day I expressed my anger over Jasper's behavior to the instructor. "Some days she is so good and others she is so bad," I said. The instructor's words ring in my ears every day at school.

My instructor replied, "She is not being bad. She just does not know. She is not breaking her heel position to make you angry. She is breaking it because she does not know that she has to hold it. You must teach her to heel, step-by-step."

Deb understood the analogy. In teaching the students, we began to realize that some things such as listening also need to be taught in a step-by-step manner. I had knowledge! I had an experience that I applied directly to teaching. From this story we decided to introduce a unit on listening. Most important, Deb, a real teacher, felt it was a credible story.

My anxieties as a student teacher have lessened. Deb has stretched her arms over her mother's chair. She has shared her class and herself. I have experiences and stories to take with me. I will not leave this program in April knowing all of who I am, but I will be one step closer.

As I write this chapter, in December, I have traveled quite a way. I have 5 more months to go. The journey has just started. I have experienced growth through shared stories. I have learned that everything in my life affects who I am as a teacher and as a person and I have learned that I can make my experiences meaningful in the classroom. Finally, and most important, I have been given the gift of voice. I have spoken as a teacher and been heard by another teacher.

Without this shared teaching experience with Deb, I too would have entered the classroom unprepared, without a voice, without knowledge of my stories and who they make me. I may take 10 years to discover who I am as a teacher. With Deb's gift of sharing, this "10-year" journey has begun. Deb has been like her father carefully crafting the chair. The chair is her teaching and all she believes, carefully being refined and developed. She has shared her experience and the notion that there are no answers, only better, deeper questions and stories, always stories.

## SHARED STORIES

Sherri and I give our stories to each other, like gifts, knowing that they are given with love, trust, and caring. Our relationship as a team of learners is growing from our stories. We accept the stories and the meaning we gain from them even if it is not the meaning we expected. From our stories we have gained more knowing about ourselves.

> Their story, yours, mine—it's what we all carry with us on this trip we take and we owe it to each other to respect our stories and learn from them.
>
> Robert Coles (1989, p. 96)

We are learning.

## REFERENCES

Clandinin, D. J. (1986). *Classroom practice: Teacher images in action.* London: Falmer Press.

Coles, R. (1989). *The call of stories: Teaching and the moral imagination.* Boston: Houghton Mifflin.

Eisner, E. (1988). The primacy of experience and the politics of method. *Educational Researcher, 20,* 15–20.

# CHAPTER 7

# Becoming

## *Angela N. Barritt and Kerry E. Black*

This chapter is about becoming—becoming teachers. It is a retelling and an interpretation of our year together as we worked and learned in the context of a shared classroom. Our stories are ones of becoming, a narrative of our experience.

This is a story of our journey. Along the way, we have examined our knowing. Our journey can be described as an interactive narrative of becoming through sharing.

This is not just a professional relationship we share. It is a supportive, caring, moral, honest, and respectful one. It is this relationship that has allowed us honesty with one another and our students and the freedom to take risks in a supportive community.

We have constructed this chapter as parallel stories told by Angela, the student teacher, and Kerry, the cooperating teacher.

### Angela

I have been a teacher for most of my life. I taught one sister to roller skate and another to sew. I taught my best friend, Margaret, how to back-comb her hair. I taught my husband how to cook and although it took years it was, I think, one of my finest efforts. I taught my children how to tie their shoes, how to read, how to fly kites, how to put on makeup, and how to drive a car. As a volunteer for Junior Achievement, I taught hundreds of high school students about business and the free enterprise system. I can't imagine why it took me so long to realize that I love teaching and that it is what I want to do for the rest of my life.

### Kerry

I have been a learner for most of my life. As I grew I learned how to walk, how to talk, how to make people care and smile and frown, how to please, how to read, do sums, and write. I knew all along I wanted to be a teacher. Learning was easy for me; I could make it so for others. Learning

72

to be a teacher through my coursework and practicum were just a few minor delays, necessary prerequisites.

## Angela

When I finally did decide to go to university to become a teacher, I had a very clear vision of what it would be like. I believed I already had many life experiences that would help me on this journey. It was simply a matter of amassing all of my knowledge, packing it all neatly so that it could be readily retrieved, and setting out.

I carefully packed all of my caring, my enthusiasm, and my determination, qualities I believed I would need to see me through. I packed everything I knew about schools, about teachers, about learning, and about children. I am a mother and so this information was especially cherished for it was full of laughter and tears, of hopes and dreams . . . and realities. I put my "mothering" experience with the rest and surveyed my inventory. My baggage contained the basic essentials for my journey; university would provide me with everything else I would need until my journey was over and I was finally a real teacher.

In my first 2 years at university I packed away more useful information. I was convinced that the more I accumulated on this journey, the better prepared I would be upon my arrival. I immersed myself in books, determined to learn as much as I could. Each course gave me items to add to my ever-increasing inventory of knowledge. I worked as a volunteer teacher, building relationships with students and teachers. I eagerly watched each teacher's every move, for each was a model of what I aspired to be, an expert teacher. I asked questions—"How do you know . . . ? Why do you . . . ? What's the best way . . . ?"—and added their responses to my now bulging personal baggage.

I looked forward to my practicum year with excitement and trepidation. I was excited because I would have an opportunity to try out what I had learned. More important, it would enable me to observe a master teacher and to have that teacher observe me and tell me what I must do to become a "real teacher." I was nervous because I like to take time to find my place in a new situation and I knew that practicum students were expected to "be" teachers almost from the start. How would I know what kind of teacher to be?

## Kerry

When I began teaching, I quickly discovered that no one had ever told me what to do on the first day of school. I was suddenly panic-stricken.

This was real. I was a teacher. And, for all my ease of learning, I was unprepared. There was so much I learned that first year. The most important lesson was probably humility. It was my most intense experience of not being at ease. I continued to learn from my students and colleagues who shared and questioned with me.

## Angela

The Alternative Program seemed like a dream come true. It would enable me to be in a school for 8 months with the same teacher and the same students. Eight months would give me time to find my place. It would give me time to try on different roles. It would give me time to learn to become a teacher. The 8 months are almost over and I have found my place. I am comfortable in this and I have discovered that "becoming" is not a state of being but a process of growing.

## Kerry

This year we have tried to approach teacher education from a new perspective. The Alternative Program has been a chance to look at teacher education as an ongoing process, which only begins with the practicum. In our year together, Angela and I have questioned and wondered about our practices and about how we affect the students who share our classroom community. As Angela joined my journey, each of us brought our hopes and dreams. Together we created new meanings. For me, this year was a year of possibility for learning, change, and reflection.

I am a seeker of knowledge. A few years ago I entered graduate school searching for more answers to my questions. I have come to see that there are no big revelations, no hard-and-fast answers to my questions, no big "Ah-has." There are only more questions. I have come to understand that answers to my questions are within, part of the knowing that comes out of my narrative. This year Angela's narrative and my narrative have been lived out together. We have worked, questioned, laughed, and doubted together. We have become this year. Our story is one of becoming.

## Angela

In my first year of university I was asked to write about teaching, what I knew of it and what it meant to me. I wrote of empowerment and voice and community. Although those terms were not then part of my vocabulary of knowing teaching, their meaning was deeply embedded in me. Part of my growing this year has been looking at my personal stories and learning from them (Coles, 1989). Through my stories, I am beginning to understand the "whys" of my beliefs.

For my practicum I was fortunate to be matched with Kerry, for whom community is the classroom, with empowerment and voice as its foundations. Together we have examined why we consider these things paramount.

## Kerry

It is my belief that children need to feel "part" of the classrooms in which they work. My notions of feeling "part" are deeply rooted in my personal narrative, in feelings of belonging and of not belonging to communities. Perhaps I understand the feeling of being "part" when I remember those times when my presence was marginalized and the way I felt when this occurred. I return to the experiences I had as a child, experiences of being "new" and feeling left out.

I experienced several new classrooms throughout my school career. Several school moves were unsettling. One move in grade 2 was particularly difficult. The children in the school were a close-knit group. They were not especially interested in a new girl from another part of town. I remember not having very many friends until another new girl moved into the classroom. She too was given the "silent treatment" from the class. We were drawn to one another like magnets. We remained friends. Neither of us was really accepted but we had one another.

## Angela

I started school one January at the age of 4 years and 9 months. I was not supposed to start until after Easter but I was an only child and terribly lonely because all my friends had been attending school since September. I wanted so much to go to school. I remember how grown-up I felt that first day. I was going to school!

The school I attended was very old and overcrowded. There were more than 40 children in the "infants" class and the desks were crammed tightly together in rows. Children's coats were hung on hooks along one wall of the room. Because there was not a spare hook for me, I had to hang my coat over someone else's. There was no desk for me either and so I spent my first day at school playing in the sandbox, tidying the dolls' house, and drawing pictures. I was not impressed! A few days later I went to school and hung my coat on Mary's hook as usual. The teacher came and took my hand and showed me how a new hook had been installed at the end of the row. The yellow label above it read "Angela." I had my own hook. Now I belonged.

Belonging has always been important to me and I have my own ways of sensing when I do or I do not belong. Because of my personal story of belonging, it is important to me that children feel a sense of belonging. They must feel comfortable in the classroom. It must be theirs. They must have their own hook.

We worked hard to ensure our students would feel they belonged in our classroom on their first day. On the Saturday before school began, we made name labels for each coat hook, a hook for every child. We wrote their names and ours on our classroom door.

## Kerry

I needed to feel I belonged on those first few days of school. As we planned and prepared for the arrival of our students, I was finding my way in a new school with new team partners. My concern is reflected in my journal entry.

> Somehow, this collaboration between Angela and me must be nurtured so we both feel equal as learners in this school and as our story of the year is enacted — it's probably a good thing that I'm also new here. We're both trying to make things happen. (Journal entry, September 18, 1989)

I had unpacked my color charts, alphabet, and calendar. Together, Angela and I came to our room the Saturday before school began. We made the classroom "ours" as we decided where things would go, how the desks would be arranged, and where the greeting area would be. I had begun to belong.

## Angela

When we were finished arranging, I looked around the classroom. It was as ready as we could make it. I hoped the children would see this place as holding a special welcome for them. On my first day at this school, just 3 days earlier, Kerry had welcomed me warmly and assured me I had a place here. I had wanted to believe her but I still felt like a visitor. Finally on this third day as I surveyed the preparation we had made for our students, I saw their names printed neatly on the door and I realized my name was there too. I was a part of this. I belonged.

We tried hard that first day to learn all the students' names. It is important to both of us that the children realize we see them as individuals. We wanted to get to know our students so we could begin to understand them. We shared our stories so they could get to know us. We were a community in the process of becoming.

We have tried to create for our students the warmth and support that we have experienced together. In our community we strive for a sense of belonging, purpose, importance, and validity that we feel when we are part of the group. It is important we have a place. Part of finding our place is recognizing the value of our individual and collective voice. It was a story written by Sherri Pearce, a fellow student, that helped me to understand my knowing of what voice means. Sherri wrote of giving a speech at school, which changed her life. As I read her story, I saw an image from my past, which continues to shape the stories that I live and tell.

When I was 14, my mother decided to send me for elocution lessons. She said it would give me confidence. I did not really understand how learning to recite poems would give anyone confidence but I went anyway and soon began to enjoy it. Each year my teacher staged a concert in which all her students participated. That first year, I practiced my piece for weeks. When my name was called, I walked up to the stage. All I could hear were my footsteps echoing around the cavernous hall and my heart pounding in my chest. When I turned and faced the audience my knees were knocking and I had to clasp my hands together tightly to stop them from shaking; I was terrified. I spoke the title of my poem but the voice I heard was not my voice. I was never going to get through this! I looked at my teacher sitting in the front row. She smiled at me and nodded encouragingly and raised her shoulders slightly, a signal to me to take a deep breath and begin. I began. My voice was thin and weak but after reciting a few lines, I began to realize that all those people were listening to me. They wanted to hear what I had to say. That knowledge gave me strength. I recited the poem with more feeling than ever before and when it was over I felt exhilarated. My mother and my teacher had known I could do it. Now I knew it too.

The strength I gained from that audience, so long ago, came from finding myself in a supportive environment where people wanted me to succeed. Their faith helped me learn to believe in myself. I learned to judge my audience and to sense when I am "safe." For when I feel safe, I feel free to be myself.

**Kerry**

In writing my papers in graduate studies, I included far more of myself than was ever possible during my undergraduate studies. However, I continued to cling to someone else's theory, which always sounded so much more powerful than mine. In writing this chapter and in telling Angela to look to herself for answers to the questions of becoming, I have begun to look for my own theories and answers. I am becoming, through trusting my own knowledge. This has allowed me to experience a sense of developing my own voice.

Our experiences of developing our own voices have had a powerful influence in how we live our lives. We want our students to experience this and so we are constantly seeking ways to help them tell their stories in our community. Our most powerful stories are ones in which we trust in our own knowing. We want to hear our students' stories. We actively seek ways to do this.

In our classroom, our students find their voices in many ways, but especially through their writing. For an hour each day, they write, conference, create, and share. They choose to work together, to work alone, to write, to conference, to create stories through pictures, to work in a quiet spot or a noisier one; to share stories in small groups or large groups. The children make these choices. They have the power to decide. We believe the children will make good choices. They rarely disappoint us.

Sharing is a special time in our classroom. All of our activities culminate in coming together to share and celebrate children's work. We have a daily Author's Chair where children share their stories and illustrations and then respond to questions and comments from the rest of the community. We celebrate achievements in reading as children read passages from books that they have enjoyed. We celebrate an understanding of math concepts as children share their strategies and thoughts with the class. The children know that they have nothing to fear through expressing their ideas because their audience is always attentive and supportive. This sharing and responding among the children and ourselves creates trusting relationships in which children feel safe to take risks. As we work together over time, a sense of community develops.

Early in the year, not all our students were ready to share their work. We were faced with a dilemma. We needed to hear each child's voice, including those students who were not yet ready to share their work. Our voices were connecting through our journals and we began to write to each other about student journals as a vehicle for every student's story to be told. Angela wrote:

> . . . there are children with whom I don't seem to connect for days, or even weeks at a time. I see them and talk to them, but not in any meaningful way and not enough to "hear them." It occurred to me that we, as adults, get to know each other and understand each other by socializing. I think I see journals as a way of "socializing" with our students. In the journals students will be able to "talk" to us about things that

are important to *them* rather than what we consider important. It will, I think, allow us to know our students better and perhaps allow them to know us in a different way. (Journal entry, November 20, 1989)

Kerry wrote:

> . . . this caused me to give more thought to the idea of the ways teachers know students . . . this (writing journals) is a way to "know students"—or at least, a search for understanding and hearing students' stories in a way in which we normally don't in classrooms. (Journal entry, November 9, 1989)

We also considered a message board that would invite students to communicate with each other. The children loved the idea. Angela created a tapestry of pockets, which the children were able to personalize by decorating them. Through this message board, the children were able to select their own audience. New friendships were initiated, old ones consolidated. We were included. We had another way to tell the children how special they are. They had a new way to tell us about things that were important to them. We became a stronger community.

**Kerry**

My journal is a powerful reflective tool that enables me to examine my practice in new ways. I write for enjoyment, for examination of the day-to-day happenings of my classroom, to capture ideas and work them through, and to think. My journal is me. When I offer my journal, I offer myself. To write and to offer the writing to another is a risk.

My first journal experience came when I participated in the Calgary Writing Project. The Calgary Writing Project is affiliated with the National Writing Project in the United States. Writing daily in my journal and having another respond allowed me to discover the power of written response. Each day I recorded my thoughts and ideas and handed them in. I could hardly wait for the next day to read the response to me, to my thoughts.

I learned about myself that summer through my journal. Two things became critically important in my process of writing: I had valid, worthwhile knowledge about teaching, *and* ownership for learning is a natural outcome of a caring, supportive community. My stories were listened to and responded to, on both a personal and professional level. I felt a responsibility to convey my message clearly to my audience. Because of my experience with journals, I hoped that journals would be a means through which Angela and I could examine our practice and learn together.

## Angela

When I first learned that journal writing was a course requirement, one that would account for a substantial amount of my grade, I was somewhat disquieted. I remembered my school days and having to write about such topics as "What I did over the weekend," and I wondered what I would write about. My first journal entries were somewhat stilted, consisting of linear descriptions of the day's activities. Gradually they began to include thoughts and ideas and hypotheses. They were filled with observations of children's behavior and ponderings on what that behavior might mean. My journal became a way for me to see my thoughts and, through seeing them, to begin to understand.

## Kerry

Together, Angela and I have become writers. Our journal topics are those events that strike us as important as we reflect on our day in the classroom. Often, these are the same; sometimes, they are not. We read and treat each other's writing with the care with which it is offered and respond in ways that we hope are supportive and meaningful.

## Angela

My journal is a three-way conversation among Kerry, Jean (my university teacher), and myself. We all write in it. It is really "ours." This is new ground for me. I felt uneasy sharing something that was quickly becoming so personal. But Kerry gave me her journal and asked me to respond to it. She was sharing her thoughts and feelings and uncertainties with me. She was trusting me. Kerry's trust enabled me to see the importance of being honest in my journal. I did not have to couch my words for fear of offending. I could say what I felt and know that it would be understood.

At first I was frustrated when many of the questions I posed in my journal were answered by more questions. "They are the experts," I thought, "Why won't they share what they know?" But now I can see how necessary their questions have been in the process of my learning to become a teacher. Their questions and observations keep me focused on what is really important and cause me to become more reflective. They have helped me see how I must look to myself for answers.

## Kerry

There are few "answers" to being a teacher. My journal notes:

> No wonder first-year teachers are so very vulnerable — perhaps they've
> never been given a faith in themselves, their personal practical knowl-
> edge. We don't set them up to feel confident in themselves as we
> model them in our images! This confidence in the self must be ac-
> knowledged. (Journal entry, October 18, 1989)

I want to nurture awareness of personal practical knowledge and re-
flection-in-practice. Belenky, Clinchy, Goldberger, and Tarule (1986) call
teachers who do this midwife teachers. They "focus not on their own knowledge . . . but on the student's knowledge" (p. 218). This metaphor of birth
as related to ideas recognizes that students have their own ideas that must
be brought forth and nurtured. We were struck by the appropriateness of
this metaphor to describe our experience.

## Angela

There is no manual of "How to Be a Teacher." In the first weeks of
my practicum I wished for one. I knew I possessed my own knowledge but
I mistrusted it. I wanted to be told what to do, how to "be." Kerry's gentle
insistence that I do things in a way that felt right to me allowed me to
understand that I have to develop my own ways of knowing and to write
my own manual. By answering my questions with more questions, Kerry
and Jean were my "midwife teachers." They encouraged my ideas, my
knowing. As I presented my ideas, they provided encouragement and support. As I become more confident in my knowing, I find I am more profi-
cient in my doing. This is an important part of my becoming.

I am a different person from the one who began this journey. My first
two years at university were not the start of my journey. My journey began
this year with my practicum. And with this beginning came the realization
that this is not a journey that ends with an education degree. The degree
will allow me the freedom to select my own itinerary as I continue to travel
and learn.

This year I have learned about school, about teaching, about children,
and about myself. I have begun to see myself as a teacher. I became aware
of this change when I visited the school where I volunteered last year. I
went to see Mary, the teacher with whom I worked. We talked about
students, how her year was progressing, and how much I was enjoying my

practicum. We talked about math and I spoke enthusiastically about how
we were teaching math in my classroom through manipulatives and games.
Mary was interested in this approach, which was quite different from anything she had ever done. I showed her a resource book that I had in my
bag. As we examined the book together, I was aware this conversation
would not have been possible even a few months earlier. I had changed. I
was no longer the eager student looking for answers; I was a colleague
sharing a professional resource manual. For the first time, I was aware of
my becoming.

## Kerry

As Angela gains a sense of herself as a teacher, I continue to question
my place in this process. I am learning not to be the expert. I wrote in my
journal:

> . . . the whole notion of teacher as expert . . . I'm often guilty here—
> though I wonder if I'm getting better. When I think back to my initial
> encounters with student teachers, I shudder at the amount of expert-
> ness I poured forth. Certainly, the more I teach, the less I feel I know
> as absolute—and I feel strongly that Angela must find her own way
> . . . but again, my practice is more than likely dragging behind my es-
> poused beliefs!! Giving answers is so easy and when your "expertness"
> is questioned so frequently by publishers, parents, students, other col-
> leagues, it is very flattering to have a disciple to spout wisdom to—to
> be a clone and stroke your ego! However, learning is making sense of
> yourself—making it your own. (Journal entry, October 24, 1989)

## Kerry and Angela

As we reflect on the year we have shared, our stories present themselves
in recurring themes of voice, belonging, and community. These stories are
intertwined with one another and with our students' stories. Our present
stories have become ones of the past for, once reflected on, they have
become part of the personal knowledge that forms the foundation of our
practice. Our stories are our future, our way of seeing our practice with
new eyes based on the knowledge we have come to hold from our work
together.

Writing this chapter has been an opportunity for us to examine the
journey that we began in August and that continues to unfold. We continue
to become teachers with a new narrative of experience from our year together. Our knowing is grounded in our shared belief in the importance of

community. We have built this community together. Sharing the community with each other and our students has allowed us to grow, to become. We have learned. We continue to learn. We continue to become.

## REFERENCES

Belenky, M. F., Clinchy, B., Goldberger, N., & Tarule, J. (1986). *Women's ways of knowing: The development of self, voice and mind.* New York: Basic Books.
Coles, R. (1989). *The call of stories: Teaching and the moral imagination.* Boston: Houghton Mifflin.

# CHAPTER 8

# Poetry: An Improvised Conversation

## Barbara Kennard and Lynn Johnston-Kosik

Lynn and I began to talk with one another in a small room, among friends in the Alternative Program part way through the year. As the evening began, we sat on opposite sides of the room, eyes averted from one another, searching painfully for a way to express the feelings of frustration and silence that had been building from the beginning. Paired as student teacher and cooperating teacher, we had come together in September. For both of us, the nature of our relationship soon emerged as extremely important, taking a central place in our thoughts. While we sensed that something was amiss, we were unable to find the words to tell each other that this was so, words that would help us to explore our worries together. Instead, through the days and weeks of the practicum, we gave each other time and space, maintaining a distance in which we hoped something would happen to bring us closer together. We shared our work but kept our more personal stories hidden.

Although we recognized a problem and were able to refer to it in conversation labeled as the expert–novice myth, we really had not begun to understand what was happening in our lives. Indeed, the label in many ways served to widen the gap between us, providing us with yet another hiding place. We found that we were exploring our concerns with others in the program, recognizing with them the tensions and pressures of the old myth in which we saw ourselves caught. However, even though we knew, on the surface, that we wanted to reject the ways of working with each other inherent in the myth, we had not begun to find new ways to replace them. We were unable to talk to one another, not having found the words. Thus we found ourselves sitting opposite each other part way through the practicum year, needing to reach out to one another, desperate to find a way.

That night, as we listened to other student teachers and cooperating teachers describe their work together, Lynn and I sat apart, wondering in separate ways about our experience and about the silence in which we were trapped. We needed to set aside our resentment and our fear. Both of us need to tell our stories and to be heard. We talked about our feelings, but our words, spoken softly, seemed to drift into the gap between us and were lost.

The conversation turned eventually to other stories and I found myself listening to Lynn talk about some writing that she kept at home. She had a collection of poems in which she had written about her experience and expressed her feelings. As I listened I heard her tell, for the first time, that she had many stories, many thoughts and feelings that she knew how to tell in poems. She spoke about the ease with which she wrote poetry. I heard her say, softly, that she would like to share them. I heard within her story, Lynn's cautious invitation to begin a conversation through poetry. I knew that I needed to respond somehow with an invitation of my own. We decided to write poems, tentative explorations of our experience, to share.

This moment was a beginning, for in Lynn's story we found a way to talk, an improvisation grasped in a moment of desperation. Through poetry, both of us found a way to know our own stories and to tell them to each other. Our poems freed us from the powerful constraints of the expert–novice myth and allowed us to begin to tell a new story with each other. They are conversations with ourselves, written for each other.

## Barbara

### FIRST DAY

I remember
The first day . . .

Stretching beyond myself
To smile and welcome others
Into a place that wasn't mine:
Too soon to belong, not knowing
Who we were.

You were a part of that welcoming,
A stranger: Student teacher.
Do you remember
The first day?

I remember wanting,
To ease your way, to leave you spaces
That you could define for yourself.

Expert!
your eyes dared me —
I was afraid —
What is it that you do? Show me,
Tell me
What is it that I should do?
You sat across,
The other, fifty pairs of eyes, the children
Watching.
I was afraid,
I couldn't tell you that I didn't know,
Was just beginning, as you were.
I didn't know what it was that we should do,
Together.

Now, I see
I left you
Abandoned in spaces already defined
Spaces that pressed, time welling up from the past,
Yours and mine, catching each of us
Within a different space,
Separated
Alone
Afraid . . .

## Lynn

### BEGINNING

Sleep does not come,
morning breaks at 3:00
sitting and waiting
the hours tick . . .
Life begins,
The clock turns slowly
the hands meet
and pass . . .
The key turns beneath
sweaty fingers
the car jolts
the adventure begins.

The car guides the mind
it turns
then straightens again
back onto the path.
the car glides
into an empty space.
I sit and watch
those looming walls.
Suddenly a scream pierces the air
slowly I realize . . .


THE BELL!
A rush of laughter fills the air.
Children fill the
sweating streets
and I wait.
The numbers roll slowly by
on the clock,
minutes pass and children
return to the street.
I sit, I watch as several children laugh
as they throw a bright circle
into the tree beside me.
A mother yells,
Children scatter to the grey snake
that leads to the mouth
of the school.


I too must run because behind the door lies another
the one I call COOPERATING
TEACHER.


I miss the main doors,
I'm trapped!
Frantically I search . . .
finally I'm guided towards an opening.
As I rush through the door,
a large sign reads OFFICE
this is where the beginning begins.
the P.A. booms

a familiar voice answers
I am asked to wait . . .

As I wait I notice,
my palms are cold and wet
my stomach queasy.
I hear people guessing about me
My nervousness grows.
Finally someone asks
what do I tell them? what do I say?
Answers race forth from a
rehearsed speech.
She enters . . .
I stand with shaky knees and
shreds of kleenex fall from moist fingers.
I want to bend — I can't.
then a warm hand reaches out to shake mine
as a calming voice answers all questions.
I follow her lead
through a menage of voices and laughter
and here another warm voice says "Hello."

A sudden rush of small bodies
cuts off all communication
all I can do is stare . . .

Our beginning contained the threads of our own personal stories of beginnings at school. While full of uncertainty and apprehension, we anticipated the year ahead as a time of exploration and of working together. Finding our way with each other was tentative and cautious, a playing out of the way that we knew the story of school in our own lives as we looked for ways to work together that would be new.

## Barbara

### FINDING A PLACE

I am silent.

I think
If I speak,
that is all that you will hear.

And yet, you are silent.
As if you do not want
To find your place, in your own way.

I think
that if I tell my story,
If I speak,
I think
that you will tell your story.

And yet, you are silent,
As if you are waiting
To hear something that I cannot say.

## Lynn

### WATCH AND WAIT

Through our first steps
We move alongside shadows,
hiding from the light we search for.
We watch ourselves in the mirrors of our minds.
slowly
yet
suddenly
We realize we are hiding
from ourselves — each other . . .
We notice our differences
forgetting we belong as one
creating silence
We watch and wait
hoping to see
shadows and darkness disappear
*We* see each other as separate
not understanding
yet
*We* ask to . . .

We thought that it would be so much easier to establish a new kind of relationship between us as cooperating teacher and student teacher. However, we continued to live out an old story, unaware of the plot line that had already been written for the story of teacher education and the ways that it influenced our actions and our way of being with each other.

## Barbara

### SILENCE

I wonder, when upon entering the room
Voices hush, the chattering stops.
What could you be saying that you don't want me to hear?
I smile anyway.

I wonder, when I ask for your journal
You forget, or leave it somewhere else.
What could you be writing that you don't want me to read?
I smile anyway.

I wonder, when you say I won't understand
I'm too experienced to remember.
What could you be feeling that you don't want me to know?
I smile anyway.

I wonder, when I try to see what you see
I don't recognize the mask.
What could I be hiding that I cannot show my tears?
I smile anyway.

## Lynn

### ME

Can it be?
Do I silence those around me . . .
Am I the creator of our silence
Does the strength of silence build
through that which I do not share

I sit and ponder —
The mystery of our silence
It builds
All is quiet . . .

Do I ask for quiet
Do my actions demand our silence
Do I see our silence as my refuge
Or is silence a gun ready to explode

BANG!
The silence is broken with conversation
Now silence is D E A D L Y!

Caught within our roles as expert and novice, we searched for ways to break the silence and to tell of the uncertainty and caution that both of us felt as we tried to explore our work together.

## Lynn

### THE FIRST STEP

Sitting and worrying are things I do
when it comes to taking the first step.
Will I fall?
The first step was like that of a toddler
it was shaky and scary, yet exciting.
Yet, would I fall?
But like the toddler I planned the steps
and the path I was going to take
to stop the fall.
And like the toddler I received lots of support
The furniture was close so that I could hang on
so I would not fall.
But like the toddler, one must stumble and fall
so that she may learn to walk and just like the toddler
I too had to fall.

## Barbara

### NOW AND THEN

Will you
Take my word for it?

You think that I am too far down the road
To remember how it used to be.
Beginning teacher, starting out.

Let me tell you,
I remember those beginning days.
The fears, the tiny steps are with me every day.
And every moment.

They are a part of me,
Although I feel them, now, at different times and places.

We had glimpsed the possibility for something new, but still we hesitated, unsure of what to do. Unable to communicate, unwilling to let go, we waited, giving each other time and space as we wondered to ourselves.

## Barbara

### WAIT TIME

We
are waiting.

Listening.
Learning to hear
Each other.
Ourselves.

Still
Silent voices.

## Lynn

### DANCING BESIDE

We sit and watch
We wait
Who is going to be the first to move?
What dance steps will she choose
Will she start with Right or Left
Do I follow
Will she continue to lead
Will the dance be Complicated or Simple
Will the pattern change
Will the song's rhythm be Continuous or Change
Will the words become altered
Will I hear the beat
Will she notice
Will our moves become separated
Will they ever join
Will the dance become a choreographed sequence of steps
Will we meet as partners and work together
Or will we always dance beside one another?

Not understanding the plot, we struggled to express our feelings to one another, puzzled by the fact that we were not being heard. We were expert and novice trying to work together.

## Barbara

### SMOKE SCREEN

Expert,
I make it look easy —
Expert ease. Ha!
Experience.
It's a smoke screen that hides
Uncertainty and doubt
As I feel my way along the daily maze
of decision.

## Lynn

### HIDDEN — THOUGH OPEN TO YOU

I run
I hide
I twist and turn when
trapped.

I know
I feel
And I cry in the darkness
alone.

I watch
I wait
For I need to hear the answers from
You.

I scream
I cry
Waiting for the moment when silence
bursts.

I sit
I listen
For the invitation into the
circle.

I smile
I laugh
For now I am looking out instead of
IN!

Poetry, an improvised conversation, a form of intensely distilled experience, gave Lynn and me the words to tell and know our own stories. As we came to recognize and understand them more clearly, we found more words with which to talk to each other. Within our poems we found ourselves and were able, then, to listen and to respond to each other, making space for both voices as we found our places beside one another.

## Lynn

### LOOKING ON . . . TOGETHER

Now Barb and I . . .
Stand side by side
Not separate
Nor apart.
We stand beside one another
so that we may look on
Together.

## Barbara

### TOGETHER

Space for voice:
Look for it in more than one place.
It must be found between us,
but also
Within my own heart, and yours.
I must make it, too,
By ignoring the press of space already defined.
Pushing back horizons defined by others, based
On their experience, the other practicum, time that wells
Up from the past in me, and you, and them.
Space for voice, carved out from what is known.
It requires that I, that we, push on, even with
Our uncertainty.
I feel quite brave, when I think of what we
Have done this year,
Together.

# CHAPTER 9

# Learning Planning Without Planning to Learn

## Annie Davies

As I tell these stories I am able to stand outside my experience as a cooperating teacher and look back to consider other ways I could have lived out the experience. Revisiting the experiences through journal records allows me to see other ways of making sense of the experiences, ways I could not see clearly while I was still working with Benita, my student teacher, in the classroom. The stories I tell here attempt to reveal tensions that exist within collaborative relationships.

I have learned that silence and tension often exist in our collaborative experiences. Now as I tell these stories, I see silence with new insight and know that in collaborative situations I may silence myself; I may unknowingly silence others; or others may silence me.

The stories in this chapter help me to see ways of thinking about my experiences with collaboration. In the first story I begin to understand how important it is to share with my team partners the ways in which we envision classroom lessons being lived out.

### LEARNING TO CONSTRUCT PLANS TOGETHER

The reality of planning in teaming situations is that it is often fragmented or done at the last minute. My partner and I prefer to plan outside the school building where we can work without interruption. For example, plans for a computer-poetry writing unit were made 2 days before the unit was due to start. It was a complex plan involving three groups of children who were to rotate through three different stations. While one group was on the computers, another would be painting and the third group would be engaged in studying the work and life of famous painters.

We were excited about the work ahead of us and we both felt comfortable about teaching in all of the areas. We decided that Helen and Benita, our student teachers, would look after the painting group. Helen and Benita had not been included in the planning session. We did, however, explain the plan very briefly to them. We carefully set up the group lists and explained things to the children. There was no time left to spend with Helen and Benita.

While Helen and Benita had previously experienced painting with the children, they had not worked with a three-group rotation. We had not talked about the careful organization that would be required within this complex plan.

The first morning I headed off to the computer lab with one group. My partner began the artist study with another group. Benita and Helen began to work with the painting group. Once the computer lab was underway I ran upstairs to where Helen and Benita were working. I found there were too many children painting. This meant some children must have been in the wrong place and I had to find out which children these were. I ran back down to check the lab and ran back up again to remind the painting group to clean up in good time. At the end of the morning the paintings from the three groups were mixed together. Somehow I had expected the student teachers to figure out how to keep each group's work separate. We were all silently frustrated and very tired. Helen and Benita had not been prepared for the organizational components. Benita wrote about the morning in her journal.

> Today I got the feeling of "disorganization." I was getting used to the flow of the classroom up until now. But today was total chaos for the majority of the morning. This is what real teaching is all about! Helen and I were both a bit unprepared for what to expect this morning. The children's excitement added to this. To me there didn't seem to be a lot accomplished but if you really look at it, there was. Maybe it seemed like nothing because of all the commotion. I sure hope that things get better. (Journal entry, November 3, 1989)

I responded:

> Perhaps all of this gives you an appreciation of the pressure that happens when one new thing (computers) is added. The planning and organization is critical to the success of the new thing. Kids will be successful . . . we'll just get more grey hair. I was in "cranky mode" because there is a lot of pressure when two classes are suddenly three and then the timing of the START/STOP has to be dead on. (Journal response, November 3, 1989)

I wish I had understood enough to say, "Look we really messed up here . . . we did not let you in on the planning . . . we did not give you any choice in this . . . it wasn't very collaborative, was it?" But at the time I didn't.

Amazingly Helen and Benita put that day behind them. Benita found her place in the computer lab, and Helen became more and more interested in the teaching of art. They showed us they could find their own rhythm in a place where they felt most comfortable. At the time I was not prepared to see another side of the story that might be different from my own. Benita continued to write in order to make sense of this experience.

> I think that when we change the organization the children lose some of their trust. And it takes time to work it back, just like it takes time to establish trust in the beginning of the year. (Journal entry, November 23, 1989)

At the time, I did not hear the message Benita was trying to tell me. Now I understand. In talking about the children, she was talking about herself. She had risked because she trusted us. Her feelings about that particular morning would not be forgotten, but fortunately they did not stop Benita from risking again. In living out and telling this story I understand a little more about my work as a cooperating teacher. I learned how to live a different story, a more collaborative story, as my journal entry shows.

> While my team partner and I are aware of "connections" it is hard for the students to know "entry points" and our reasoning. We'll have a BIG planning meeting on Friday. They need to feel the direction the class is moving in and be part of that story. (Journal entry, November 22, 1989)

Benita's response showed me that finally we were on the right track, living a story that we were constructing together.

> Today after school we had a planning meeting for next week. It was a pretty good meeting. It gave me direction . . . I am not sure what to do with art, but Helen and I will figure something out. The plan looks pretty good. I am pleased with it. (Journal entry, November 23, 1989)

In this next story I begin to understand my own planning process and how to share it with a student teacher.

## LEARNING HOW TEACHERS PLAN

It was November. Benita had watched my daily physical education lessons since school began. She was eager to try her hand and asked if she could teach the next unit, skipping, from my long-range plan. I was surprised when she asked me for written plans. She looked perplexed when I told her I didn't have written plans. I tried to explain that I don't write out a unit for skipping because I don't have to. It doesn't work that way for me.

As I drove home that night I thought about my sense of the skipping unit. How did I know what I knew? I realized my knowledge came from working with other teachers, from trying things out with a skipping rope, exploring possibilities for myself and watching children in action. It was knowledge gained over time that gave me something to work from. The sum total of all my experiences provided a language of possibility, a set of options that were available to me. I knew that from year to year the skipping unit was different and that each opportunity to work with the unit gave me a chance to shape it in new ways.

That evening I worried about my response to Benita and felt compelled to write her a letter. My letter was an attempt to explain what I'd figured out on my drive home. The letter opened up the space for collaborative planning. I talked about how I could help her with the sequence of steps that were essential and appropriate, but I remember saying, "But that's not enough, the whole thing is the timing . . . the feel for the lesson . . . the business of how you integrate the new learning with what they know and how you move them on. You have to feel it."

Writing and talking in this way reminded me of my first disastrous physical education lesson as a student teacher. I did not want Benita to experience that. I wanted her to be successful. I wondered if she was ready. My fears lessened as I watched her prepare. At the end of the school day she took out a skipping rope in the classroom and began to plan her lessons. She practiced the steps, finding an order that would work for her. Benita was working things out for herself. Her journal entry describing her lessons reveals how she saw herself making sense and how she was evaluating herself.

At first I was nervous. The gym is an awfully big place when you are up at the front and have over 50 little people looking at you. For a while I was at a loss for words and sometimes I felt that the people at the back couldn't hear me very well. The time flew by, 25 minutes really isn't a long time for physical education. The class worked hard today. After a while my nervousness went away and I became more relaxed. I began to have fun with it. (Journal entry, November 28, 1989)

As she taught I watched intently, scribbling pointers on a small sheet of paper. She pasted my notes into her journal and the following day I could see her trying to work in my suggestions. I knew Benita was beginning to understand the timing of a lesson. She was feeling her way. I realized my initial overprotectiveness of Benita had not been warranted. I'd let my own story get in the way. I'd also missed something important. She'd written in her journal in early November, "I'm ready to do more" and I had responded. "You need to tell me what you want to try." And what she wanted to try was the skipping unit. It was her choice and I'd missed her readiness to risk.

Now as I think about this story, I am more aware of the many ways a unit of study can evolve. I could have easily written a generic unit for Benita and, in so doing, have perpetuated her ideas about planning. The nature of our relationship, our conversations of practice, precipitated a sharing of experience and led to a different way of understanding the art of planning. Benita experienced "preparation" for teaching in the sense that Yinger (1987) describes it. She was able to construct meaningful and appropriate activities for the children. She experienced planning as a personally situated event that relies on context. Her experience allowed her to voice her knowing in other situations. Benita told me about her friend in the regular practicum who asked for a game she could do in physical education. Benita asked her a number of questions about the past experience of the children. But her friend repeated, "All I want is a game," and Benita told her, "It doesn't work like that. You don't just do a game." When she told me this story, I felt like cheering.

## CONCLUSION

In telling my stories of the practicum experience, I can feel the rough spots in collaboration. I have come to know that when voices fail to connect there are silences. As I continue to learn to plan collaboratively with other teachers, I know we must be willing to examine and question our practices. We must be willing to speak about uncertainty and confusion and to talk about the story that is being mutually constructed.

## REFERENCE

Yinger, R. (1987). By the seat of your pants: An inquiry into improvisation and teaching. Paper presented at the annual meeting of the American Educational Research Association, Washington, DC.

# CHAPTER 10

# Finding Voice, Finding Place

## *Pat Hogan and Carol A. Flather*

The story of Carol Flather, one of the student teachers, can be seen as a story of relationship as well as a story of how teacher education can be viewed as collaborative research. When I read Clandinin and Connelly's (1988) words about how collaborative research "requires a close relationship akin to friendship" and about how "the idea of friendship implies a sharing" (p. 281), I think about Carol and about the connections she made during her practicum experience.

Carol came to her placement a few days after the other practicum students at her school. I met her in those early days and was struck by her silence and her wide eyes as we sat in a classroom for our first informal meeting. The other practicum students were chatty and excited, but Carol seemed a little overwhelmed and she barely spoke during the hour we spent together. I thought at the time it must be hard for her coming in late. The others had already moved past initial awkwardness and had begun to form relationships with each other and with their cooperating teachers. Carol was very new to the situation and she coped with her newness by remaining silent.

Carol continued to be rather silent in our methods classes and in the small group Wednesday afternoon seminars for the first month of the school year. She did not seem to talk very much with anyone, including her cooperating teacher and the other student teacher assigned to her grade 2 team. But Carol's wide eyes were taking in a great deal and she began to write just a little bit about what she was seeing and about what she was trying to figure out. She began to make entries in her journal about Janice,* a troubled youngster, new to the school and experiencing difficulties at home and in the classroom. These entries constituted the beginning of my dialogue with Carol, and I sensed they also were the start of conversations between Carol and her cooperating teacher. Perhaps Carol felt drawn to

---

*Children's names have been changed to pseudonyms in this chapter.

Janice because of her newness to the school. Perhaps, I speculated, she saw Janice's struggle to find a place as parallel to her own negotiation of entry. Carol continued to write in her journal and to puzzle over what was happening for Janice. I invited Carol to talk about Janice in one of our small group seminars.

When I repeated this invitation in mid-October, I was surprised at how quickly Carol was moved to tears as she spoke about Janice's home situation and difficulties with her peers. The other student teachers in the group were also surprised by Carol's tears, but they listened hard to what Carol was saying and asked questions about the upset that Janice's story was causing for Carol. When Carol talked about her tears, it was as if she had found some of her story reflected in the gap that existed between Janice's family history and her own. She described Janice's troubled family and contrasted it with her suburban upbringing in a family that looked entirely complete and "normal." Carol's tears seemed to come from the realization that all lives were not like her own and that some of the children she would teach came to school with much more complex stories than the one Carol had lived. I felt Carol was weeping over the injustice she saw as she came to that realization.

Carol made some important connections during that afternoon seminar. She came to new understandings as she reflected on her relationship with Janice. She looked at Janice's life and used it as a mirror to think about her own. The discrepancies in the reflected image were deeply felt by Carol and she learned about herself and about teaching. Carol's story of Janice's abusive background also triggered tears for Benita, another student teacher, who saw a story of her own childhood in Janice's story and shared just a bit of how that felt with the group. Benita helped us all understand just a little better what it means to come from such a background. In response to Carol's question about what she could do for Janice, Benita replied, "Just be a friend and listen." Benita and Carol moved closer together through the sharing of stories, and Carol began to find her place in the seminar group.

Carol's connection with Janice continued as they lived out their stories in an ongoing experiential text in the classroom. From time to time Carol would write about Janice in her journal and talk about Janice with the seminar group, telling stories of how Janice was progressing in the classroom and in her life out of school. At the end of the school year, Carol remarked Janice was a completely different person from the one she had been at the beginning of September. She said, "Now Janice doesn't stand out from the group the way she did at the start. She is more part of the group . . . involved in teaching others." I commented that in some ways the same could be said for how Carol had changed over the course of the year and she agreed. But then she added, "I hope that Janice still stands out a bit so people will look out for her . . . so they won't forget her story." Carol learned about the importance of listening to children's stories, and I heard in her remark about Janice the echo of a plea for herself and the need to have her story remembered.

Carol's realization of the importance of story and of being heard surfaced through another connection she made with a little girl named Michelle. This is how Carol described Michelle in a paper at the end of her practicum.

> Michelle is a quiet, well-behaved little girl. She is one of those who would be easy to miss in your class. Michelle used to draw pictures of rainbows in her journal and the accompanying story was always the same. It would be about how much fun it was to play with her brother. Michelle was searching for a voice also and having a hard time. I think if we had told the kids what to write about in the journal we may not have noticed her search. Michelle, like myself, is good at writing about what others want to hear. I started to sit with her during some writing times to talk and write her ideas down for her. This seemed to help. The big breakthrough was in early February, when she wrote her "unicorn story." Michelle's story was about a unicorn who did not play with anyone because she could not fly. One day though the unicorn grew up and she was magic. She was bigger than her brother — she was as big as her mom and dad. Now she could fly like the other unicorns. Michelle's own story could be seen in the story she wrote. The unicorn had to discover herself before she could be a true part of the group. Michelle's unicorn story came not long after my own writing about voice. "Could it be that we all changed, reflecting each other?" (Bach, 1970; Flather, final paper, April 1990)

Carol's quote from Bach (1970) is especially insightful. In it she alludes to her own story of a personal struggle for voice and place through reflection on Michelle's story. The story of Carol's emerging awareness came to light following the Christmas break. During the first week of January, students in the Alternative Program spent a full week in the schools; for Carol, this week of continuity and almost full-time teaching was an important milestone. Following this week, however, the program reverted to the regular Monday, Wednesday morning, and Friday schedule for student teachers in schools. The change was a significant one for Carol although, at the time, the meaning for her was not clear. In January, right after the schedule change, an on-campus meeting of student teachers and cooperating teachers was held for the purpose of renegotiating assignments (see

Chapter 19). At that meeting, Carol was very tearful and unable to articulate the cause of her upset. I spent most of my time at the meeting trying to talk with her and her cooperating teacher. Carol talked a little bit about Michelle through her tears and I encouraged her to think about why Michelle's story was so important to her. As we talked, I think Carol began to see connections between her story and Michelle's story but the connections were tenuous. Carol left the meeting, however, and wrote the following letter, which she brought to a lunch meeting with me a few days later. Carol's letter eventually became a journal entry.

> In one of my own journal entries I came to a self-discovery. I need to write things down in order to sort them out. So I decided to sort something out. I used to think that for some things there are no answers, no reasons, they just are. Kids are starting to teach me that there are reasons — reasons that come from stories — stories that come from our lives.
>
> In my class Michelle has struck a chord within me. Why is she so closed up? Why does she write the same story every day in her journal? These questions led me to wonder what is her story? Does she have voice? Can she share her stories? So I decided that maybe I could help her relax enough that she could find her voice and tell her stories. Then a big obstacle loomed ahead. Can I help someone find their voice if I cannot find mine? Can I ask someone to share their stories if I cannot share mine? So now I have to do a hard thing. This hard thing is to figure out my own place and why I have such a hard time finding that place. The hard part came when I asked myself this question. Can I find a place if I do not have a voice? I think I could fit in but this would not be a place — my place. First I need to discover my own voice.
>
> This has led me to discover why I always enjoyed English. I always thought I was an open person who had thoughts and opinions. If I wasn't I would enjoy the classes that had only black and white answers. It was a good trick — I even had myself fooled. I think that I have always enjoyed English because I have always been good at figuring out what people want to hear — what they want me to say. As long as I can figure out what they want me to write, I can write a good paper.
>
> I wonder if Michelle's story was praised and now that she knows the "answer," she knows what to say/write. I know how Michelle feels about not knowing what else to write. It is a risky thing to do — to write something new. To tell a story is to take a risk. But to find that story and that voice is a part of finding that place.

I am starting to understand why some people are hung up on titles. Titles partially describe your place. About 3 months ago I broke up with a guy I had gone out with for 2 years and 2 months. Even though it had been a mutual agreement (mostly), I felt lost. Here I was going to school to learn how to teach but I didn't feel like a teacher. I was going to the University of Calgary only 2 days a week so I didn't quite feel like a student. I wasn't a teacher or a student or a girlfriend. If I wasn't any of these, what was I? I was no longer sure of what to call myself. So now I had to find out who I was—without anyone to define myself by. It is hard to tell what has to be defined first. Who am I? What is my place? They are very mixed up in each other. I sometimes wonder why I have a hard time finding my place.

We have learned in our class that one way to discover your stories is to look back over your experiences to see what stands out. I wonder why I am not an open person. I always thought that kids who had a "normal" childhood wouldn't have problems later. If anyone ever had a "normal" childhood it was me. Married parents, small town, backyard, station wagon in the driveway, two-car garage, dog, tent-trailer for summer vacations, two younger sisters. These are all the ingredients, so what is my problem? I shouldn't be having any problems. Maybe a list of ingredients isn't what is needed to ensure voice and place.

My family has never been one to have long or deep discussions. I used to wonder when people said I was part of a close family. Because we used to go camping every summer—we were close? I used to think, "Big deal; now instead of sitting in the living room staring at a book or the television set, we sit around in lawn chairs staring at a book or the campfire." Sitting in the same room does not make people close. I come from a family where solving your own problems and working things out was done by yourself. I do not know my parents' stories as to why this was encouraged. I know even as very young children our parents didn't yell or lecture or discuss—they always told us to go to our rooms until we were ready to act properly. In the lower elementary grades I was one of those students whose report card always said "tends to be chatty." In grade 3 I had a teacher who stressed individual work and not helping each other. I remember getting in trouble for talking and helping. It didn't seem quite right that we weren't allowed to talk or help. It took that teacher a while but she finally convinced me to keep quiet and keep to myself. I do not know if it is only this incident that shut me up but I do know that it is a clear memory. I also know that after grade 3 I didn't get any more comments about being "chatty." Luckily she didn't stop me from feeling that helping people is right. Now to go back to Michelle. Right now all I can do is tell her that it is okay to talk and help people. It is alright to help yourself. I cannot ask her to write her own stories until I tell her that it's okay to talk first. To feel safe enough to write it down. Writing is even more scary than speaking. It makes it, somehow, permanent.

It is important to find a voice in order to find a place. But no matter how important it is, it is also risky. As a teacher and a person I cannot ignore the risk, with myself or my kids. I understand how risky it is for Michelle to write a new story. What if Michelle's/my story isn't a good one? What if no one wanted to hear Michelle's/my story? What if the risk becomes so great that Michelle/I cannot reach past it for the story deep inside? "The voice is very fragile and it doesn't take much to shut it down." (Davies, 1988; journal entry, January 23, 1990)

Again Carol uses a quote, this time from Annie Davies, a cooperating teacher, to punctuate the insight she has gained through reflection on how Michelle's story became a mirror for thinking about her own story. Carol's awareness of the fragility of her voice leads her to further insights about how she might find her place in the classroom. In the following epilogue to her letter, Carol writes with a sense of personal power and awareness of self, voice, and place:

I am going to write an epilogue to my story about Michelle/myself. I realized, as I reread the story I had written, that I have always felt that I had to work things out by myself. I cannot easily change how I feel and I cannot change the past. But! I realize it is me who can change what is yet to come. I do not have to sort things out for myself. I do not know why this feels like such a revelation — people have been telling me this for a while now. The person most responsible for finding my place is me. During that week of teaching I had found a place. After that week I felt I had lost that place. Now I realize that I lost that place because I gave it up. I backed off. It was like I said, "I did a week — so now what do I do?" I should have hung on to that place instead of stepping back. It was like I found myself backing off from the place I had found. It had nothing to do with anyone else in the room — it was me thinking, "Now I am not teaching full time — I can't keep that place." *But* I can. I don't know why this was so hard to see — I guess we often overlook the obvious. So now I know I can have that place — because it was mine anyway. What a lot of deal over an obvious (obvious now anyway) solution!

Maybe this is part of why I was upset on Tuesday. Maybe part of me knew already that I needed to move myself back to that place I had found. (Journal entry, January 25, 1990)

In Carol's writing we see her working out some important ideas related to the nature of growth and empowerment. She saw that professional and personal growth are individual accomplishments that occur in the context of meaningful life experiences and relationships with others. She came to see that she needed a sense of her personal power and voice in order to grow. Power is not given by one person to another. It develops in the context of a relationship. Empowering relationships develop over time, and it takes time for participants to recognize the value that the relationship holds. Personal power may be taken away in circumstances that are oppressive or given away in circumstances that are intimidating. Carol was intimidated at the end of her week of full-time teaching when she lost the continuity of being at school on a daily basis. She backed off from her place in the classroom. Yet Carol was involved in relationships with children that afforded her opportunities to reflect on her story and to be responsible for her actions. With help from her cooperating teacher, from members of her seminar group, and from me, Carol was able to reflect on the meaning she was making as she learned to teach. Carol used her reflections to become aware of her knowledge and her strengths. Her relationships were empowering ones.

These empowering relationships involved feelings of "connectedness." As Carol developed her relationships with children in the classroom, as she came to feel connected to those children and their stories, she came to know herself better and to better understand what it is she knows. As she came to value her own knowledge, she became an active learner and researcher of her own practice. Teaching became an ongoing inquiry for Carol and empowerment came from within. As she came to respect and value the knowledge, experience, and stories of the children in her classroom, she began to see those children as colleagues, and a trusting, caring community developed. She was able to talk and write about her classroom experiences, and her thoughts and feelings engendered response from her cooperating teacher and from me. Our response helped Carol to go further with her thinking and to figure out more about herself and her teaching. Teaching became a collaborative inquiry for Carol and empowerment came from collaboration.

In April 1989, when Carol completed her application to be placed in the Alternative Program, she wrote, "I want to learn about myself, define a teaching philosophy, learn about children" and "really get to know the routine and the children, which is not always possible in the traditional practicum." She has come to know more about herself, about her personal philosophy, and about children. She has begun to see how the inquiry is an ongoing one. The following comes from a paper Carol wrote at the end of the practicum:

> I have bought myself a hard-bound notebook and decided to use it as a journal. I feel like I need to keep writing or I will lose touch with myself. I think it will be hard to keep a journal that does not get response — but I need to keep writing. I do not want to fall back into silence. I am learning about myself and I feel like I am finding my voice. I know that writing helps me with this so I need to commit myself to keep writing my thoughts and feelings. I need to keep discovering myself and through this my voice will become stronger. "I keep discovering things inside myself. I am seeing myself all the time in a different light." (Belenky et al., 1986; Flather, final paper, April 1990)

I marvel at how Carol chose this particular quote from Belenky. She uses it to capture her sense of how she experienced the year. In the same paper Carol created a metaphor to try to describe how she sees learning to teach.

> Maybe it sounds corny to compare this to skiing but it does relate. You go up the lift to the top, knowing that you can't stop halfway. When you get to the top, the bottom looks so far away — sometimes you can't even see it. You start out cautiously making your way down the slope. If you are lucky, you have people with you to help and encourage. There are other people on the slope too — some are nervous like yourself. There are others who are braver and have done the slope before. Don't let these people discourage you — they started out like yourself. There are times, on the way down, that you will ask yourself why you are doing this. Yet there is a longing if you sit at the bottom and watch. There will be times when you want to give up and sit at the side. This is okay — we all get tired sometimes. Just make sure you get back up and keep moving. Let your friends help you — they understand. When you see the bottom, you get excited — you feel that you have accomplished something. When you get to the bottom, you go back up. Each time you go back up, the journey is different. It will become easier and more comfortable. If it gets too easy or too comfortable, move on to the next level of difficulty. Look out for people who are nervous beginners — as you once were. At the end of the day you may be tired, you may even hurt. You will, however, have a sense of contentedness and satisfaction with having tried your best, taken a few risks, and experienced success. (Flather, final paper, April 1990)

# REFERENCES

Bach, R. (1970). *Jonathan Livingston Seagull*. New York: Macmillan.

Belenky, M. F., Clinchy, B., Goldberger, N., & Tarule, J. (1986). *Women's ways of knowing: The development of self, voice and mind*. New York: Basic Books.

Clandinin, D. J., & Connelly, F. M. (1988). Studying teachers' knowledge of classrooms: Collaborative research, ethics and the negotiation of narrative. *The Journal of Educational Thought, 22*(2A), 269–282.

Davies, A. (1988). Two caring communities: A story of connected empowerment and voice. Unpublished manuscript, University of Calgary.

# CHAPTER 11

# Not Finding the Connections

## Pat Hogan

When Joanne* came to visit with me in my office several days after the end of her practicum experience, I was struck by the story she told. It seemed to be an important story constructed out of her personal experience, a restorying perhaps of her involvement in the Alternative Program. Joanne told a story of going out for dinner with friends. She told her friends that she really didn't think she wanted to be in a classroom again and that she doubted she wanted to be a teacher. The most interesting part of the story to Joanne was that no one wanted to hear it. Her friends couldn't understand why she didn't want to teach after spending 8½ months involved in a practicum program. Joanne and I spent a little time talking about why people might find it hard to accept this story, but I encouraged Joanne to keep on telling her story until someone heard it. I saw this story as one Joanne composed herself rather than having it told for her, and I saw it as an important milestone in Joanne's struggle for voice.

It took almost the entire year for Joanne to begin to tell her own story. As I look back now on the time she spent in school placements, in seminars, in classes, and alone with me, I think about the many stories that all of us who came in contact with Joanne constructed to try to understand what we were experiencing. From the beginning of the year, Joanne told us very little of her story and very little of what she thought or felt. She seemed unable or unwilling to find words to describe her experiences. She answered questions with minimal responses or she simply stated she "didn't know." In the absence of information from Joanne, her cooperating teachers and I constructed stories about Joanne. In a sense we were trying to make meaning of our experiences with Joanne by "constantly telling and retelling stories . . . that both refigure the past and create purpose in the future" (Connelly & Clandinin, 1990, p. 4). I begin to wonder how our stories might have got in the way of Joanne's story or how our telling of them might

---

*Joanne is a pseudonym requested by the student teacher.

have produced some of the conflict we felt during the year. But perhaps there is a need to try to go back to something of a beginning as I try to reconstruct this story for myself.

In June 1989, Joanne was matched with Carol, a grade 2/3 cooperating teacher. Carol had served as a member of the program's steering committee and was looking forward to having a student teacher. During the spring and summer prior to Joanne's placement, Carol's teaching assignment had been changed so she found herself in a teaming situation with two teachers who were job sharing. This meant that Joanne's placement was really with three teachers instead of the one she had expected. It also meant Carol was working hard on establishing good working relationships with her two new teaching partners as well as taking primary responsibility for working with Joanne and for responding to Joanne's journal. I think Carol expected Joanne to become an equal member of the teaching team and anticipated a student teacher who would engage in an active relationship with her, the other teachers, and the children, and with what was going on in the class-room. Instead she found Joanne to be somewhat closed or distant and uncommunicative both verbally and in the journal. I, too, found difficulty in communicating with Joanne either in writing or in our times together in class, in seminars, or in one-to-one visits. She said she found it hard to get to know Carol and that she had difficulty talking to her. But Joanne seemed unable to explore those problems or to take steps to try to overcome them. She did not seem to be making connections with children and remained largely silent at school, in the seminar group, in classes, and in one-to-one conversations. As time elapsed, both Carol and I experienced some frustra-tion with this young woman who just did not seem capable of opening up and who did not seem to put much of herself into her relationships. So, in the absence of very much from Joanne, I think both Carol and I began to construct our own stories about what was going on for Joanne.

Carol, I think, attempted to fill the silences with directions and sugges-tions about what Joanne ought to be doing in the classroom and in her writing. Often Joanne became tearful or defensive about what Carol was telling her. When Joanne failed to respond to these directions and sugges-tions, Carol tried other ways to engage Joanne. She attempted to tell her own stories of struggle and uncertainty in the classroom. Still Joanne did not seem to respond. When Carol tried to give Joanne more and more in the way of tips and ideas for teaching, Joanne seemed to read these sugges-tions as criticism. Joanne became even more silent. Carol agonized over what to do about Joanne and eventually, through her frustration, began to story Joanne as lacking initiative, commitment, energy, and even perhaps the ability to learn to teach. This is not to say that Carol gave up on Joanne, for she continued to try, but she was becoming discouraged.

I, too, began to try to construct a story around what was happening. I was puzzled over the differences between the way Carol told the story of the relationship and what I sensed was happening for Joanne. During a meeting with Joanne and the three cooperating teachers, I witnessed their attempts to fill what they perceived as a void with suggestions about more structure in the practicum and more attention to format for lesson planning and reflections in the journal. The relationship between Joanne and the three teachers did not look very collaborative at this point. As I look back now, I can see how the relationship might have evolved, but at the time I felt silenced and began to see how Joanne could feel silenced by this group of competent, dynamic teachers. I started to think of Joanne as being overwhelmed and unable to fulfill the expectations set up for her. The story I was constructing seemed to be validated when I learned more about Carol's vision of team teaching and her expectations for Joanne as a member of that team. Perhaps I needed a story that would reduce my frustration with Joanne's silence and allow me to see some future for her. By this time Carol's frustration had led her to consult with her principal regarding Joanne's apparent lack of progress. The principal had a talk with Joanne and storied the possibility of her failure in the practicum. This seemed to prompt Joanne to request a move to another placement. So despite some reports of recent progress from Carol, I saw Joanne's request as a possible way to manage the dilemma and I arranged to move her to another school. Carol, I know, felt many emotions in response to Joanne's move. She felt that somehow she had failed with Joanne and that her story with Joanne lacked closure.

Joanne, on the other hand, seemed to approach the move with enthusiasm. She said she thought she had learned a great deal about the nature of the practicum and about herself and she looked forward to a fresh start. Up until this time, Joanne had avoided talking about her practicum experiences with the seminar group. Just prior to the move I pushed a little for Joanne to tell the other student teachers what was happening for her. As I think back now on how Joanne presented her situation to the others, I hear echoes of the story I had constructed in what Joanne told her peers. She told a story of feeling silenced and overwhelmed and a story of lack of collaboration. Now I recognize that Joanne seemed to be giving back the story I had been telling about her practicum experience. It was a reflection of my story, not her own story. Joanne received support and encouragement from the members of her seminar group. They heard the story Joanne was telling and agreed she needed a fresh start.

So, by December, we had several stories going: Carol's, the principal's, mine, and an echo of what I now see as my story reflected back through Joanne and the seminar group. It was not until the end of April that we read Joanne's own storying of her experiences in that initial placement. The following is an excerpt from a paper she wrote:

> I was asked recently if I thought this year had been a good year for me. Technically the results are not good and emotionally I have struggled but despite this, I have come out with some positive benefits. Was it worth it? I am not sure. I took the most difficult route this year, nothing came easily or with joy. I experienced different feelings and thoughts during the year. I have written an account of the Alternative Practicum for me, describing how I felt at the time.
>
> . . . So each of us was placed in a classroom to discover the secret of effective teaching. We were not given specific tools, just a blank piece of paper to fill. I lacked the confidence to fill my paper. I was a productive teacher's aide cutting and pasting. This is how I was first useful in the classroom. I began my experience in the classroom sitting in the far corner cutting letters as I watched the real teachers get to know their students and set up their classroom. I felt inadequate. Where was the knowledge I needed to know how to teach? Where were the rules? I wanted to do it perfectly. I knew nothing and I was seeing in the distance a classroom forming. My sense of awe and inadequacy left me questionless. This was not my classroom, I was just filling a space in the corner.
>
> Finally I was to step in and pretend to be a teacher. I was given a topic and a time to do my show. I was excited, I had been in the classroom almost a month and was tired of cutting things out. The ideas I was to teach were all laid out; I just needed to present it.
>
> After the lesson I read the comments of my cooperating teacher. I was devastated. The words were filled with what I should have done and a comment that we will discuss it Monday! I sat there and pondered. I was at a loss because there was no definite path. I struggled with this on my own. Monday brought a brief statement and I moved on. I discovered something about myself; I do not like criticism. I did not know how to take the criticism or where to go with it. I had begun my journey of being silent. The definite feeling I had in the classroom was not having a place. Where did I fit? I had not become a part of the teachers' discussions on students, units, or future plans. Why had I missed out? I was there in the corner. I discovered something else about myself, that I am silent in situations that are unknown, that I do not feel safe in. (Final paper, April 1990)

This was a difficult paper for Carol to read. It did not connect with the story she had constructed. Carol had been looking for initiative on

Joanne's part. She had also been waiting for signs from Joanne that she was ready to become more involved with the teaching team. When she did not find these, she storied Joanne as less than able.

At the same time, Joanne had storied herself as an outsider. Joanne, too, was waiting behind the "wall of silence" she had constructed. She was waiting for someone to bring her out of her corner and into the group. Carol's and Joanne's stories and lives failed to connect or intersect. They built individual and separate stories without a mutual construction of a shared narrative of experience.

When Joanne began to work with a new cooperating teacher, Tony, everyone had high hopes. Tony began the relationship with the story I had constructed about what had happened for Joanne with Carol. He was determined to work collaboratively with this young woman. Problems began to surface, however, when my story proved to be too simplistic to explain Joanne's behavior in relationships and in the teaching situation. In time, Tony started becoming frustrated with Joanne. He found her lacking in initiative and unwilling to commit herself to the hard work he saw as necessary for teaching. Again Joanne was closed and silent. It became apparent to me that Joanne's story was more than one of being a silenced, overwhelmed young woman. By the time 6 weeks had elapsed, Tony was thoroughly frustrated and told Joanne to leave the school. At this point I started to wonder if my story had been all wrong and if Carol's story had merit. I started to doubt myself, then I found myself confused and finally angry. I was angry at Joanne because I saw everyone involved trying very hard to make this practicum work and I began to doubt whether Joanne was ever going to become really involved in a practicum experience.

When Joanne and I met in my office, I had a feeling that Joanne thought I would once again rectify the situation for her. She tried to tell me she had "learned her lesson" and she now knew what it was she needed to do to have a successful practicum. I heard, in her words, echoes of what she had said at Christmas. I wanted more from Joanne, more involvement, more participation in figuring things out. We talked for a while and I sent Joanne away to do some thinking and writing. When she returned a day or so later, I again saw in her pages an echo of my own words. At that point, I think I made a decision to stop constructing stories for Joanne and to push her to construct her own. I sent her away again to think and write her own story of what had happened. When she returned, her writing had a different tone. Joanne had begun to see she had not given her "all" to the practicum and she expressed a sense of how that had shaped her experiences with Carol and with Tony. When I suggested that Joanne might return to Carol to complete the practicum and finish their story together, she initially appeared a little shocked but agreed to go back to her original placement. I admired Joanne's courage. It would not be easy to return. I also admired Carol's willingness to take Joanne back. But she did return and together they finished out Joanne's practicum.

Joanne continued throughout the year to struggle with a way to tell her own story. Her story is still very different from Carol's. In this piece from one of her final papers, I see a small hint of Joanne trying to move toward an understanding of Carol's story.

> My cooperating teachers have felt it was necessary to have a common front when dealing with me. This is easy for me to see now but I have not always felt this way. I saw me knowing nothing and lacking confidence against a self-assured team. Recently I have seen that their collaboration involving me is not always the same. Seeing their uncertainty, though not intended, helps me to understand that I am not alone in being confused. This also shows me that forming a team is not easy. (Final paper, April 1990)

Joanne is right. Forming a team is not easy, teaching is not easy, and learning to teach is not easy. Trying to accomplish all of these in the context of a collaborative program that constitutes a new story for teacher education is not easy either. But Joanne, Carol, and Tony help me to better understand something of the relationship between story and collaboration. I came into the program with some kind of understanding of how people tell stories to make sense of experience. As I try to look back on the stories Carol, Tony, I, and finally Joanne constructed and at how these stories failed to connect or intersect, I begin to understand how important the connection or intersection of stories is to the idea of collaboration. For without the connection, there does not appear to be any way to construct a shared story of experience. And somehow, in my mind, collaboration means a mutually constructed narrative, a living out of a story together.

The idea of mutual construction brings me to another insight about stories. I have learned this year how easy it is to construct a story about an individual who remains silent. I have also learned how in constructing those stories out of silence, I set myself up to become "cranky." For when the character in the story I have constructed fails to live out the story I have come to believe, I begin to doubt myself. In the face of a story that no longer "works," I can become resistant to hearing a new story and even angry. Perhaps this in itself is good reason to avoid constructing stories for a silent individual. But I think there is an even greater issue at stake than my crankiness. When I construct a story for another person, I am scripting a life for that individual and in doing so I am faced with a moral issue. I cannot write a life for someone other than myself. I believe that each individual needs to write her own life, be her own self, find her own voice.

When I encounter a silent young woman like Joanne again, I will try to avoid constructing a story for her. I will need to remember Joanne's story and think about other young women who allow the people around them or society in general to construct stories for them about what they will be like and about what they will like to be when they grow up. These are the young women, I think, who learn to get along in the world by being pleasing and conforming and by doing what they feel is expected of them. They remain silent and let others construct stories for them. By living out the stories constructed for them, they drift through life, never really finding voice or themselves.

When I encounter a silent young woman like Joanne again, I will need to find ways to still my own story-making and help the silent other find voice and construct her own story. I hope that Joanne will, in time, look back on this practicum year and decide that it was "worth it." I hope she will come to see she started to find her voice this year and began to tell her own story of not wanting to teach.

## REFERENCE

Connelly, F. M., & Clandinin, D. J. (1990). Stories of experience and narrative inquiry. *Educational Researcher, 19*(5), 2–14.

PART THREE

# RESTORYING OURSELVES IN OUR WORK WITH STUDENT TEACHERS

The chapters in Part Three of the book are stories of our learning as teachers through our work in the Alternative Teacher Education Program. Frequently teachers say that working with student teachers is their most significant professional development experience. They rarely, however, take the time to write about why their experiences are so important to their ongoing professional growth. Perhaps it is because working with student teachers is not usually considered a recognized and valued form of professional development. It is more commonly seen as service to the profession.

We have chapters from five cooperating teachers and one university teacher in this section. In Chapter 12, Garry Jones and Gary Godfrey write about their experiences in the Alternative Program. Garry Jones wrote the paper as he read and reread his journal dialogues with his student teacher, Gary Godfrey, and talked about significant moments. In Chapter 13, Deb Nettesheim uses the idea of moments to structure an account of how she has learned through her work with Sherri Pearce. For her, "moments" are those times that give meaning to their experiences. Moments are what we might have called images in the language of personal practical knowledge. In Chapter 14, Lori Pamplin constructs a metaphor of dusting to illustrate the way she has storied and restoried herself as she worked in the Alternative Program. In Chapter 15, Kerry Black explores how her experiences in the Alternative Program have helped her to restory her personal practical knowledge and the ways she sees expressions of her images in practice. In Chapter 16, Jean Clandinin makes new connections between her work as a teacher educator working with young women and her experiences as a young girl in school. She identifies as important the need to construct spaces for young women to question the cultural and institutional narratives in which they live in universities. In Chapter 17, Barbara Kennard examines her experience as a cooperating teacher in order to raise questions about how she has come to know teacher education.

While many of the chapters touch on the narrative themes laid out in Chapter 1, each story allows us new insights into the ongoing storying and restorying of our educational lives.

CHAPTER 12

# Points of Entry:
# A Cooperating Teacher Learns by
# Seeing the Lessons in the Stories

*Garry Jones and Gary Godfrey*

I haven't written down much about my experience with Gary Godfrey
because we talk to each other constantly and he wrote everything
down. I didn't recognize the importance of his entry into my life until
after Christmas. I have learned a lot about me. I've seen what I do. He
provides a mirror reflecting me back to myself. (Journal entry, February 7, 1990)

Gary and I met on the first day of the school year and worked together
with the children of room 18 until the following April. We walked, talked,
laughed, worked with children, and talked some more. We wrote a paper
together (Godfrey & Jones, 1990) documenting the experience, attempting
to capture the uniqueness of this practicum. The paper emphasized *his*
learnings, *his* journey of experience because it was *his* practicum in a program that placed student teachers in "contact with phenomena related to
the area to be studied—the real thing, not books or lectures about it"
(Duckworth, 1986, p. 481). The 8 months provided him with a successful
and joyous teaching experience.

   Now that the program is completed and the classroom is "mine" once
more, I am haunted still by that phrase, "I've learned a lot about me."
What exactly did I learn? What do I now know that I would not have
known if he had not been there? If he is a mirror, what was reflected back?

   I began to restory the year searching for points of entry into the experience. I, as a writer in the present, recollected the past, the stories in which I
played a part, in order to gain new self-knowledge (Crites, 1986). I reread
several articles that had been assigned in various courses during the past 2
years of my graduate studies. I met with a small group of teachers who also
had student teachers in the Alternative Program. I still was unsure of the

direction for this chapter until I met with Gary. We taped our discussions and reread our collaborative paper and journals.

This chapter will tell the stories that became my points of entry. They led to my own self-knowledge, through a constant interweaving of articles, journals, courses, meetings, and conversations. I can now voice some of what I learned.

## "I'LL HAVE TO WAIT AND SEE?"

Gary and I met on the first day of school, about an hour before we were to meet the new class. After hanging up our jackets we headed down the hall to the classroom. Within 5 minutes of meeting he asked me a question about teaching, and I could not find the words to answer the question. Gary retold this incident during our conversation in May.

> My first worry was classroom management. I said to you, "I've got something that is really bothering me. How do you maintain discipline? How do you keep control of everything so they don't go crazy?" You said to me, "That's a very good question. I don't know how to explain this to you. It's a little bit of this and a little bit of that. You'll just have to wait and see." I remember thinking, "I will have to wait and see? This is no answer!" (Taped conversation, May 19, 1990)

In September, I had felt guilty for giving him a nonanswer, and stupid for not being able to express myself quickly and easily. Why couldn't I answer his simple question?

Now that I have taken the time to reconsider, I can see the meanings that were hiding within this story. My understanding begins with Gary. In the same conversation in May I wondered how he decided that I did indeed have answers to his question. How did he know I was a competent teacher, even though I said, "You'll have to wait and see"? What was his proof? Gary responded to my questions.

> I watched the way you brought those kids around (on the first day). You said to them, I guess we have to establish some sort of bathroom and water routine. What did you do last year? Some kids put up their hands and answered and you said, "Okay, that sounds fine to me." I didn't know at the time that you were building community and I didn't know that the kids would have a voice in this community. But it was then that I noticed that you knew what you were doing, you had confidence. It was a different you. It was not the you I had walked down

the hall with, the undecided you, the unsure-of-how-to-answer-the-question you. In front of this audience you were a different person. (Taped conversation, May 19, 1990)

He saw my knowledge was manifested in my actions. This took me back to Schön (1983), who writes about professional knowledge.

> When we go about the spontaneous, intuitive performance of the actions of everyday life, we show ourselves to be knowledgeable in a special way. Often we cannot say what it is that we know. When we describe it we find ourselves at a loss, or we produce descriptions which are obviously inappropriate. Our knowing is ordinarily tacit, implicit in our patterns of action and in our feel for the stuff with which we are dealing. It seems right to say that our knowing is in our actions. (p. 49)

This helped me to recognize that much of my knowing is submerged, like fish swimming unseen in a dark, green sea. Gary's question on the first day was only one of the thousands he was to ask throughout his time with me. These questions forced me to search for these fish, to yank them out for inspection. I understand what Schön (1983) means when he describes the reflective practitioner as one who "reflects on the phenomena before him and on the prior understandings which have been implicit in his behavior" (p. 69). While in the past I have used a journal for some of this reflection, Gary became my living, interactive learning log. As I struggled with the answers, I learned to put words to my knowledge.

But I also learned that so much of what I know and feel deep inside about teaching cannot be put into words. So much of who I am as a teacher is only evident in my actions and in my relationships with the students in my class.

Britzman (1986) brings another perspective to the same story. When she says that student teachers "bring to their teacher education a search for recipes and often a dominant concern with the methods of classroom discipline" (p. 446), I can fit Gary's question into that larger picture. She also writes that, for student teachers, knowledge is often "reduced to a set of discrete and isolated units to be acquired" (p. 450) and that the experienced teacher, as expert, is presumed to have this knowledge. It "resides between covers of textbooks and presumably becomes familiar after many years of use" (Britzman, 1986, p. 450). This view of knowledge does not fit with mine; thus my answer to Gary's discipline question was consistent. I could not repeat a list of rules for discipline because for me, classroom management is tied to classroom community, my relationship with the students, the particular individuals in the class, their histories, and many other fluid, changing issues. In June I could tell someone what works for me with the individual students in the class because by then I know.

If I had given Gary a list of rules and techniques, it would have "answered" his question and might have closed off his search for further answers. My "you'll have to wait and see" forced him to search for his own answers.

He had noticed that my approach to the bathroom and drinks routine was the first step in building community and allowing each child to have a voice. In the same way, my approach to his questions allowed him to have a voice and helped build our trusting relationship. And the act of restorying these events at this time has helped me to see what it is that I do when I deal with people, whether they are the adults or the children in my care.

## "NEVER DO THIS WITH GRADE 2s"

Another first-day story became a point of entry. We were an hour into the first day. Before school I had written the day plan on one chalkboard, instructions for an activity on another, and a passage of handwriting on a third. I used the day plan to explain the activities, their order of completion, and follow-up work. As I pointed to scribblers, construction paper, and chalkboards all around the room, I realized that Gary, my new student teacher, was seeing a grade 5 classroom at work. With many years of primary experience in my mind, I wanted to clarify that while grade 5 students can usually follow a series of instructions, younger children cannot. I turned to him and said, "Never do this with grade 2s!"

As I elaborated, my comments connected for him with his own experience as a summer computer camp instructor. He had worked with a group of children of ages ranging from 8 to 12. His usual routine had been to begin in the classroom with a lecture-style explanation of the day's work, then to move to the computer lab. Invariably the younger students needed a great deal of help. His reaction ranged from anger at the students for not listening, to frustration with himself for not teaching adequately. However, he did not know what was wrong.

When I turned to him in that first hour and said, "Never do this with grade 2s," he saw the connection with his summer camp experiences. Of course the younger students had been listening to him; they simply could not retain everything he had said without more hands-on experience. As he said to me in May,

I probably had a psychology course somewhere along the way where someone explained the abilities of kids at certain ages. But it didn't mean anything until you pointed it out in the classroom. (Taped conversation, May 19, 1990)

This is theory in ordinary language, connected to experience. Just as the younger students needed to touch the computers to understand the instructions, Gary and I needed to be surrounded by students to understand our knowing-in-action, our theories-in-use.

Indeed I needed to be surrounded by students in order to put words to the theory. In November I pointed to one of our children's stories (Marianne's*) and said to Gary, "This is brilliant." Marianne had written a detailed detective story with an intricate plot and wonderful character development. Gary examined his own thoughts about the meaning of my excitement.

> For me it didn't seem like such a big deal at the time. Ya, okay, so she did that, great, good for her. But you kept saying that most kids weren't capable of doing this. That's when I would have to examine what you were saying and ask, "What does he mean? Am I missing something?" Then by watching these other kids and seeing that they didn't produce stuff like that and comparing what they did with Marianne's, then I could see it. (Taped conversation, May 19, 1990)

Gary and I were dealing with learning theory and the writing process, but in ordinary language connected to experience. My words helped move his thinking along and forced him to observe the students.

Britzman helps clarify these stories when she writes that student teachers usually discount the value of theory. They are concerned with survival and want to know what works, rather than why it works (Britzman, 1986, p. 446). This view is based on images of learning "cultivated in their school lives," where learning takes "the form of a concrete product, something acquired, possessed and immediately applied" (p. 447). In our case, Gary used a first-day experience to reconsider the previous computer camp experience, to see it again in a new light. Gary learned so much on that day and throughout the year, because I encouraged him to "interrogate school culture, the quality of students' and teachers' lives, school knowledge and the particular role biography plays in understanding these dynamics" (Britzman, 1986, p. 454).

While Gary interrogated, we both learned. I came to see theory *is* important to student teachers as long as it is meaningful. I now see that

---

*The children's names have been changed to pseudonyms in this chapter.

one way to bridge the gap between theory and experience is to question and examine, as Gary did with the computer camp and Marianne's story and as I did while attempting to explain the classroom to him.

## "THIS IS A LESSON PLAN?"

Gary and I were in the staff room discussing the next day's writing lesson. I explained a very simple acrostic poem in which the students could use their own names. I pulled a paper towel out of the dispenser by the sink and wrote a poem as an example. He looked at the paper towel in his hand and said, "This is a lesson plan?"

By the next day he had an overhead prepared, and the students created published copies of their acrostics, which were displayed on the wall. A student remarked, "This wasn't poetry, this was art!"

Gary was heavily involved with students from that moment onward, but more often as my team partner than as a student teacher. I knew student teachers usually wrote detailed lesson plans, carried them out in class, and were observed by the cooperating teacher. In our case we talked about the coming days, wrote short notes in my day plan, and worked as a team. We took turns performing the various tasks of the classroom such as record keeping, checking homework, instructing from the front, and helping individuals. On the one hand I believed he was gaining valuable experience just by being there in the midst of all the action, while on the other hand I worried.

By January 22 I was doubting the appropriateness of the way I had structured Gary's student teaching experience.

> I worry that I haven't done a good job, that I've done it wrong, since I did not write pages of notes in his journals or get him to write lesson plans every day. I wonder if he's taught enough or planned enough. . . . Have I observed enough? (Journal entry, January 22, 1990)

I felt better about what I had done when I thought about the variety of planning strategies, including long-range planning, revising plans from past years, planning untried units, following guide books, and thinking about lessons, both inside and outside of school. Gary experienced these with me, as well as the planning that two teachers do verbally. His planning ranged from the paper towel lesson described earlier to month-long units that he planned and implemented on his own. We discussed some activities in detail; others he wrote out formally.

Because of his classroom experience he was able to predict student reactions and plan accordingly. He made decisions that would not have been possible if he had only written formal plans in university courses disconnected from a particular context. For example, when preparing the first day of a new science unit, he knew he needed to set up equipment and rearrange the classroom during the noon hour. A plan written for a course would not likely have included this preparation.

Now I see our days, weeks, and months in the classroom as so prepared, organized, and orchestrated that I can no longer see the planning involved. Like fish in the sea, unaware of water, I am unaware of the planning. Seeing Gary's growing awareness helped me see my own unconscious, intuitive planning.

## "YOU ARE NOT SEEING WHAT I'M SEEING!"

As a teacher I suffer from a consistent and persistent case of uncertainty (Jones, 1988). I worry about opposing issues simultaneously. I am too rigid here and too lenient there, not teaching enough and teaching too much, not creative enough and too creative, not demanding enough and too demanding, too concerned about the curriculum and not concerned enough. I am often confused about the best way to teach, to discipline, to encourage, to control, to care for, to enforce, to demand, to assist. I try to do Everything, to be the Best, and, of course, in my own eyes I usually fail.

The all-school assembly Gary and I organized partway through the year was a moment filled with success, a moment when I could step out of the way and give it all to the students. I wrote about the assembly in detail in my journal.

> The kids got into groups and worked on it Monday. The assembly is tomorrow (Thursday). It won't be a polished production . . . it will be kid made. Amazing things have happened.
>
> Roxy and Charmaine simply took the job as co-hosts. They talked to other teachers who are involved, set the program, and wrote the introductions. Charmaine NEVER reads to the class and tomorrow she'll read to 500 kids! Roxy just told her, I guess.
>
> Vivian has organized a wonderful fashion show. The script has the right tone, mood, it sounds right. She trained all the girls (and two boys) and taught them how to walk. Vivian said that her mother is coming . . . for the first time ever!
>
> Erica, Cynthia, and Amelia are doing a dance. They worked on this for many hours at home. Like, is this homework? Did I have to check it on a class list?

John is reading a poem which Jeffrey wrote, while four kids act it out.

All these leaders are NOT kids I would have chosen as leaders. They have shown abilities I did not suspect. (Journal entry, February 13, 1990)

Every child was involved in the assembly and it came off without a hitch. I was out front operating the tape recorder and Gary was backstage surrounded by cardboard props and kids wearing too much makeup. The assembly stands alone, one tiny piece of the total school year, a success story. It was one time I knew they would come through. This was tacit knowledge, deep inside of me, knowing I could not voice. I knew.

So why am I telling this story here? When Gary told me what he had told his friends about the assembly, he helped me see another view of my work with children.

I'd say to my regular practicum friends, "You guys are not seeing what I'm seeing! You should have seen this assembly!" Three days before Garry said to them, "Okay, guys, it is all yours. Break up into groups and do your thing!" And be damned if they did! And it was Wonderful! But it would not have worked if he had been authoritarian all along because they would not have had confidence in themselves to do anything. This other way he was saying, right from the first day, that he had confidence in them. As well they have done a lot of group work. (Taped conversation, May 19, 1990)

The assembly was successful because of my work with the class, which began on the first day. Until I heard Gary's words, I had not seen my place in the assembly. I had only seen that children can do amazing things when I get out of their way. I had seen a moment when the students were empowered to lead, to create, to share, to celebrate, to perform. I believed it had little to do with me.

Over the year, while Gary and I talked about the classroom and our work, we failed to see the significance of the assembly. It was a few hours of nonteaching in which the kids had fun. Now I see that while it had little to do with the official curriculum, it had a great deal to do with the real curriculum.

As Roxy, Charmaine, and the others took on their tasks, they worked as a community toward a common cause. They used their skills in reading, writing, dancing, singing, acting, storytelling, speaking, listening, and art to cooperatively produce a program that received rave reviews from teachers and students. I have learned I set the atmosphere for these results.

Teaching looks easy when children are working productively and independently. I step back and follow the lead of the children, but the atmosphere of trust and confidence has been built in countless tiny actions. By listening to Gary talk about his experience with me, I have been able to determine what some of the actions have been. The discipline question, the first-day bathroom and water routine, Marianne's detective story, and the assembly all have a common theme. As a teacher, I consistently try to encourage others to find their own answers, to follow their own pathways, to search for their own truths.

But therein lies a source of my uncertainty (Floden & Clark, 1987). While I had no uncertainty discussing the assembly with Gary, I often felt uncertain about the mandated curriculum, rules, routines, and expectations. It has been difficult to encourage others to find their own answers. Partly I have come to see that evaluation makes me feel uncertain.

I have learned I cannot truly evaluate children. As an adult, I cannot easily define and evaluate my learning this year. It has taken the interweaving of courses, articles, conversations, writing, and much reflection to describe in this chapter these few thoughts about my own learning. So how can I evaluate the children? Perhaps if I could spend hours with journals, taped conversations, and group discussions, perhaps then I might know what an individual child has learned. Perhaps.

Just as Gary watched me working to see my knowledge expressed in actions, so I need to see the children in action to obtain clues to their tacit knowledge. I need to allow the assemblies of life to be as important as the mandated program.

I am learning to seize opportunities to capture the classroom action, to freeze it and analyze it. By looking again at the first-day questions, Marianne's story, our paper, and the assembly, I have been able to re-examine those events and discover new meanings.

I am learning to trust my own answers. Sometimes "you will have to wait and see" is the best answer of all.

## REFERENCES

Britzman, D. (1986). Cultural myths in the making of a teacher: Biography and social structure in teacher education. *Harvard Educational Review, 56*(4), 442–456.

Crites, S. (1986). Storytime: Recollecting the past and projecting the future. In T. R. Sarbin (Ed.), *Narrative psychology: The storied nature of human conduct* (pp. 152–173). New York: Praeger.

Duckworth, E. (1986). Teaching as research. *Harvard Educational Review, 56*(4), 481–495.

Floden, R. E., & Clark, C. M. (1987). Preparing teachers for uncertainty. Occasional paper, Institute for Research on Teaching, Michigan State University.

Godfrey, G., & Jones, G. (1990). Learning to teach. Unpublished manuscript, University of Calgary.

Jones, G. (1988). An inquiry into uncertainty in teaching. Unpublished manuscript, University of Calgary.

Schön, D. (1983). *The reflective practitioner: How professionals think in action.* New York: Basic Books.

# CHAPTER 13

# Moments in a Year

## Deb Lloyd Nettesheim

Every morning I head out the front door and get in my car to go to work. I always look over at our living room window because my 3-year-old daughter is there waving her little hand and smiling. That, for me, is a moment.

My 8-year-old daughter is learning to play tennis. Recently, she began connecting with the ball and we would have real rallies. I would hit; she would hit; I would return; she would return. I remember that beaming smile on her face, that proud glow of success. It was the same face I saw her make when she passed her red badge in swimming and the same face when her Oma and Opa arrived from Toronto for a surprise visit on her birthday. These, for me, are moments.

I remember thinking what beautiful pictures these moments would have made and I felt a little sorry I had missed the opportunity. But, I suppose I didn't really need a camera to remember them — I obviously do!

Moments to me are gifts. They are captured pieces of time we somehow hold deep inside and treasure forever. Sometimes they are unique; other times, they are connected with a story, moments that when revisited trigger stories connected with them.

I like to think of them as pieces of a puzzle about myself, precious pieces of my life that give me more meaning and insight into who I am and help me to value that. Times I have taken to smell the autumn leaves, absorb a summer sunset, hear the laughter of children's voices, see a caring look in someone's eyes. To me, they are my personal moments of truth. It is not just the moments, but the meaning they represent to me — an ethic of caring and taking the time to care, an ethic that has "fidelity to persons and the quality of relationships at its heart" (Noddings, 1986, p. 496), one that is compassionate and understanding of self and others.

This year has been an incredibly intense one for me. It is full of moments. Moments of growth, moments of seeing, moments of joy and pain. This chapter is a reflection on some of these moments — the meaningful, important times that for whatever reason reached out as truths to me. It is about my year with Sherri Pearce, my student teacher, and how the journey we took together offered new meaning to my way of seeing things.

Our year together was an exciting and, at times, an overwhelming adventure. There was so much that happened. Perhaps that is why I have chosen to focus on the moments — the times that gave some meaning to all the things we were doing and experiencing. It is only a glimpse of our year in action, but it is hoped that through this glimpse, a sense of the whole story shines through.

## THE END — A MOMENT FOR THE BEGINNING

It is the end of June. The students have been taking all their work and displays off the walls. The last thing to come down is the monthly weather chart and the graph of this year's weather. I stand quietly immersed in a moment — looking at all the little rain umbrellas, snowmen, clouds, and sunshines. I think about all the hours Sherri must have spent coloring, cutting, and laminating all those pieces. I think about how proud she felt when she came to me with this idea for the weather chart and graph in September and how she went home one weekend and came in on Monday with everything ready to go. I recall her telling me how she got her whole family involved in the project (grandmother and boyfriend included). Sherri's chart and graph were a part of our classroom the whole year. Every day the students put up the picture on the graph and calendar. It was so much a part of our daily routine and it, like so many other things, played a special part in our year together.

It is interesting to me that this moment at the end of the school year allows me to see meaning in our beginning.

Sherri and I kept a journal together. We wrote daily about our feelings, questions, and concerns. I am drawn to an entry Sherri wrote early in September, which relates back to this moment at the end and the development of the weather chart.

Do I need to take more initiative? I'm very sensitive to ownership and what belongs to others, i.e., supplies. I always have been — even at work or at church. I don't want to get in the way but at the same time I want to be involved. (Journal entry, September 7, 1989)

I responded:

Sherri, I'm glad you mentioned this and I'd like to talk more about this idea of ownership. I really want you to feel like we are a team — this must feel awkward for you right now but as you start to feel your place and a level of comfort I'm sure it will feel easier to take this initiative you talked about. Please feel free to use whatever you want, Sherri. You don't need to worry about what belongs to whom — it's all there for the taking. I can understand your feelings. Thanks for bringing this up. More talk, o.k.? (Journal response, September 8, 1989)

This entry, like many others that followed, was a catalyst for our dialogue. So much of our talk came out of concerns we had written about first. In this instance, it was Sherri's need to share a concern. As we talked I began to understand Sherri better. She had wanted to feel a part of "our class" — to belong — but did not want to be intrusive. I, on the other hand, had never even thought to tell Sherri about all the supplies in the room and took it for granted that she would know to help herself. I understood Sherri's concerns because I had lived a similar story, one of wanting to belong but not get in the way. That moment helped me to restory my experience.

A few days later, Sherri arrived at school with the handmade weather calendar and graph. She put it up on our bulletin board. She belonged.

In our year together, the ideas of collaboration, finding voice, and empowerment came to have new meaning for us both. We lived out a change regarding our roles through our teaming experience where fears of the unknown were shared. No longer was there a feeling of isolation. Our learning to care about each other made our experiences special. We embarked on a journey together.

## GUMMY BEARS (COLLABORATION)

Once a month our staff enjoys a luncheon together. A few of us have made a tradition out of giving gag gifts and golden awards to our colleagues at this time. At our April luncheon we celebrated our student teachers. Sherri received the Golden Gummy Bear Award complete with a bag of gummy bears. As I presented this award to Sherri, our tearful eyes connected. That, for me, was a moment. Both of us knew the significance of this award and the many stories associated with gummy bears. For me, they are a symbol of collaboration. This way of doing things with another is part of what made my year with Sherri such a powerful one. When we shared a bag of colorful gummy bears during a conversation early in September, I knew Sherri was someone I was going to like. We attempted to figure out a teaming relationship while sharing gummy bears. Sharing gummy bears represents how Sherri and I connected and how connecting and sharing helped our paths to converge. We learned to collaborate through our journal.

## OUR JOURNAL AS PART OF COLLABORATION

A year ago I used a journal with another student teacher. It was a beginning and I valued the experience. In the summer, I participated in the Calgary Writing Project and learned how journal writing could help me figure out my teaching.

I bought two large notebooks in September and presented one to Sherri. I hoped she would want to share in my enthusiasm for exploring this way of learning. Sherri did and our shared journey began. Questions, wonderings, and hours of talking emerged from our entries. And throughout there was the consumption of gummy bears!

While Sherri was involved in her practicum in our classroom she was also at the university doing coursework. I, too, was at the university each week taking a graduate course. Our paths crossed again as we both took classes with Jean and Pat. Our collaboration on a paper evolved as we connected our experience in the classroom with our learning at the university.

Our first paper, entitled *The Gift* (see Chapter 6), came out of our journal dialogue. In our classes we learned to value our personal practical knowledge and use our past experiences and stories to construct new meaning in our present lives (Connelly & Clandinin, 1988). This notion was very intriguing. We were exploring together. We learned to value our personal stories as a means of helping us to make sense of why we do what we do as teachers.

This paper was my first experience of writing with someone.

As Sherri and I searched for answers to our questions, our relationship grew stronger. Caring and trust were important to our growing friendship. That, and a big bag of gummy bears. Whenever we engaged in conversations, it seemed we always had a bag of gummy bears at hand. They became a symbol of our sharing. We listened to each other's concerns. We wondered about things together. We shared articles, we wrote, we talked, we listened.

We worked together easily as a team. We planned together and divided the work load so that we each designed learning centers. In the classroom we both shared in the work with the students. After school we sat down together and marked their folders and talked about the day. Sometimes we ate a few gummy bears as we talked.

There were times when I felt guilty about the way we were doing things. In the past, I had spent more time observing student teachers' lessons and evaluating their progress. Yet, working collaboratively seemed more realistic. I hoped Sherri was learning who *she* was as a teacher and that she understood that the knowledge she was constructing was her own. I didn't want her to think that my way of doing things had to be hers.

I came to find new meaning in my role as a cooperating teacher as Sherri listened intently to my dilemma. I shared the ideas of Deborah Britzman (1986), who refers to the need for change in student teaching. I told Sherri of my student training days and how imitating my cooperating teacher, doing everything in mirror image, was my way of passing. I wanted Sherri's experience to be different.

I began to feel a weight lift from me as I developed the courage to admit that I do not have to know all the answers. In September Sherri told me that she envisioned her practicum as an experience that would "teach her how to teach." She thought she would come out of it with a neat little package that she could open, follow the instructions, and be a teacher. As we worked together, she told me she was coming to view teaching as personal and that there did not seem to be a "right" way of doing it. I wondered if a weight had been lifted from Sherri too.

Our collaboration intensified. We found ourselves looking at issues I had not examined as carefully in other years. Looking closely was easier when I had someone with whom to view the problem. Sometimes, just seeing the problem through someone else's eyes gave clarity. Other times we put our heads together to brainstorm solutions. And often, just offering or being offered a shoulder to cry on was helpful. Sherri and I wrote a second paper about how we managed our inner city classroom (Nettesheim & Pearce, 1990). As we collaborated on the paper we looked at our concerns about this classroom community and how we went about working in the classroom. I believe it was the support we gave to each other that added another dimension to our special way of connecting. And it was that support in questioning, in wondering, in trying, and sometimes in crying, that helped us learn more about ourselves, about taking risks, and about solving problems.

The gummy bear consumption on that paper was massive. I'm sure we devoured enough to be major shareholders in a large sugar company. I can no longer look at gummy bears without secretly valuing their importance in collaboration.

## SAD MOMENTS

Sherri finished her practicum at the end of April. I will always remember the intensity of our last moments in our grade 2 classroom. The students had all gone home after giving their hugs and crying their tears. The room

was empty. All I remember was the silence. I got busy and started changing
the displays on our bulletin boards for the new units I would be attempting
alone on Monday. Sherri sat down and marked math. We could not speak.
What could I say that would possibly express what this year, this journey,
had meant to me. It had been so wonderful, such an exciting adventure. I
sensed endings were just as difficult for Sherri as they were for me. We
could not bring ourselves to say goodbye. I handed Sherri a new hardcover
journal for her next journey. In it, I had written a poem.

### MOMENTS IN A YEAR WITH YOU I'LL CARRY FOREVER

That wide-eyed look on the first day of school
sitting with Amanda as she cried about glue
a blue polka dot clown on Halloween
and you, writing in your journal
a note on my desk to have a good day
a cup of Mac's coffee
an African violet
chicken pox and a jiggling camera
you, and that half-beaten journal

Britzman and Paley
Jean and Pat
a tear in your eye (mine too)
teddy bear picnics
a table full of junk food
and still there's you writing in your journal

computers and salt and vinegar chips
The Gift
Tough Love
laughing
you and the journal

the look on your face as you marched Jeff to the time-out room
power walks and car rides
talking, talking, talking
Diane, Don, and Jasper
you and that dog-eared, weather-beaten journal
the hospital on a cold, snowy day
you touching Jason
the how to's, the wonder if's

the why bother, the questions
the vision of you figuring it through
all in that tattered blue journal

We both knew the special significance of each and every moment mentioned in that poem. I suppose it said more than spoken words could. We hugged and she was gone. That for me was a moment. A sad moment.

## CROW BOY: MAGICAL MOMENTS

My story seems to have come full circle, where I am back to the ending.

Sometimes moments are like a light that goes on in my head. I can experience something all my life but it is not until that moment of connectedness, that moment of seeing, that I come to value and hold onto its importance. Rare moments like that seem so magical to me. As if some pixie came along and blew fairy dust all over me, so that I magically came to know a deeper meaning, a truer meaning, to what I had been experiencing all along.

It was the last week of June. I was reading a Japanese story called *Crow Boy* (Yashima, 1955) to the class. I have read this story before but never has it brought tears to my eyes. Its message was so simple, yet so powerful to me. It is the story of a young Japanese boy who lives on a mountainside. He goes to school in the nearby village. He feels very different from the other children and tends to keep to himself, never valuing who he is or what he could be. One year, a new teacher comes to the school. He is so unlike the other teachers! He takes the time to sit down and talk to the children, to listen to their stories and care about their feelings. He spends time with the little Japanese boy and helps him discover something special about himself. The boy makes many different crow voices. The teacher encourages the boy to share his special talent at an assembly. All the other children are awed and amazed at his talent. The story ends with the boy growing up believing in himself and owning a sense of pride and self-respect. All because someone cared!

When I finished reading the story I glanced up at the students, tears welling up in my eyes. I talked with them about this powerful story. I told the children how important each one of them is and how each one is special in her or his own way and each one has something to offer. I remember my deep-felt desire to encourage them never to stop trying, never to give up. I wanted them to know that making mistakes is alright. I wanted them to know that I cared. I remember the room being quiet and I remember looking straight at one of the children, Lisa. She had tears in her eyes. That was my magic moment. It gave some of my story back to me about this year of growth and discovery.

These moments, so transitory and yet they live in our hearts and minds forever. They are those rare times in our lives that allow us to see just a little differently, just a little more clearly.

The moments in this chapter tell only a small part of my involvement in this Alternative Program. It is these special times that shine most in my year of wondering. A year of discovering what it means to care.

## REFERENCES

Britzman, D. (1986). Cultural myths in the making of a teacher: Biography and social structure in teacher education. *Harvard Educational Review, 56*(4), 442–456.

Clandinin, D. J. (1986). *Classroom practice: Teacher images in action*. London: Falmer Press.

Clandinin, D. J., & Connelly, F. M. (1990). Narrative and story in practice and research. In D. Schön (Ed.), *The reflective turn: Case studies of reflective practice* (pp. 258–282). New York: Teachers College Press.

Connelly, F. M., & Clandinin, D. J. (1988). *Teachers as curriculum planners: Narratives of experience*. New York: Teachers College Press.

Kennard, B. (1989). Moments of seeing: Parallel stories of narrative change in collaborative relationships. Unpublished manuscript, University of Calgary.

Nettesheim, D., & Pearce, S. (1990). Tough love. Unpublished manuscript, University of Calgary.

Noddings, N. (1986). Fidelity in teaching, teacher education and research for teaching. *Harvard Educational Review, 56*(4), 496–510.

Yashima, T. (1955). *Crow Boy*. New York: Viking Press.

CHAPTER 14

# Dusty Images

## *Lori Pamplin*

The sun shines. It cheerfully lights up each room in the house. I notice the dust that has accumulated over time. I feel a little overwhelmed. Where to begin? I decide to take it one room at a time.

This year has been a journey of possibilities for me. I was very fortunate to have the opportunity to be a cooperating teacher for the Alternative Program. This program had, at its foundation, the desire to look at student teaching in a collaborative way. By design, theory and practice were closely related as cooperating teachers, student teachers, and university teachers worked together over a period of 8 months. We were a team of colleagues searching for a clearer understanding of teaching and learning.

I have learned a great deal about the power of collaborative relationships. These relationships require commitment. They are not always easy. They must be nurtured over time and treated with care and respect. They can be frustrating as similarities and differences are honestly shared. Yet "differences, viewed positively, provide more food for thought . . . we discover more about ourselves through each other" (Pamplin & Payne, 1989b, p. 26).

We also learn about ourselves through our stories (Clandinin & Connelly, 1992; Coles, 1989). I have come to know myself better as a teacher and a person, if these terms can be distinguished from each other, through learning to listen to the narratives of experience that are within me. My stories are important; they are part of my personal practical knowledge (Connelly & Clandinin, 1988).

I wonder about narrative inquiry. I am just beginning to understand it and its power. Connelly & Clandinin (1988) define narrative as "the study of how humans make meaning of experience by endlessly telling and retelling stories about themselves that both refigure the past and create purpose in the future" (p. 24). This sounds rather simple but it is not. "Constructing a narrative account of oneself . . . is difficult, rewarding work" (p. 25).

I have come to realize that mine is a complicated story. The plot is complex, the characters abundant. In trying to make sense of my world, I am reminded of the feelings that I get when I dust. Sometimes, I just do a cursory job with the feather duster as I move quickly through my days. Yet the feather duster has only limited effectiveness. It doesn't get the dust that is hiding away in the corners. Further, as I am in the act of dusting, more dust is accumulating.

There comes a time for me when I need to take time to dust thoroughly. In writing this chapter, I have dusted some of my stories with the care I would give to a delicate ornament. My stories are fragile. They have the ability to make me feel frustrated and sad, hurt or overwhelmed. Yet, my stories are also strong. They have great power in shaping how I see things. They can make me feel free and happy, confident and clear. My stories are precious to me. I have wiped the dust away from my stories, some of which have rested undisturbed, in the corners of my mind, for a long time. In so doing, I have only learned to wonder more about narrative inquiry; what it means to me, how to understand it better, and how to figure out the complexities inherent in it.

I am in awe of the wisdom that can be found in stories. So often, though, I miss it. I see only the dust and not the treasure that is underneath.

At times, I feel a sense of losing the story. At other times I wonder about so many of the things I know. Schön (1983) explains that "often we cannot say what it is that we know. When we try to describe it we produce descriptions that are obviously inappropriate. Our knowing is ordinarily tacit" (p. 49). I care so much about what I do. Why then is it so difficult at times for me to explain why I feel what I do — why my practice looks the way it does? Sometimes, the wisdom is hidden beneath the dust.

In trying to tell the story of my growth through working with my student teacher, I discovered that it was really messy. I wonder further about the temporal and social qualities of the nature of narrative.

> One of the primary questions for anyone undertaking a narrative study is to design a strategy for continually assessing the multiple levels (temporally continuous and socially interactive) at which the inquiry proceeds. . . . A person is, at once, then, engaged in living, telling, retelling and reliving stories. (Clandinin & Connelly, 1992, p. 260)

How could I explain all that I've learned this year? How could I, when the lessons continue? How could I say that my learning was a result of any one thing? Why could I imagine many of my experiences in a multitude of ways? Why did I keep jumping from the present to the past, from the past to the future, and so on? Why did my story lack coherence? I realized with mixed emotions that my journey is not a linear one, not at all. It is unnerving at times not to be able to explain in a sequential order a life that has always seemed to flow smoothly one day into another. I try to understand my stories so they can inform my future.

As I gently wipe away the dust of untold stories, I see possibilities. There are several possible beginnings to this story, each one legitimate. I do not choose one but share two of them. I decide to take it one beginning at a time.

## BEGINNINGS

### Beginning One

I lived in Paris once. It took a while for me to feel at home in this city renowned for its history and romance. I needed time to learn to negotiate within the "City of Lights." It took me several months to see its beauty.

I remember feeling very alone and scared. At times I felt like I was on a marathon run. I needed to register at the university, learn how to use the subway, find a family to live with. I had to do it fast. What if the course I had come all this way to take was full? What if I got lost? What if there wasn't a family for me? I felt tired after a while, disoriented and confused. The finish line seemed so far away. Would I ever make it? Why were there so many detours along the way? Couldn't anything go smoothly?

The car rides were exhilarating. I sat bolt upright in the backseat and sped around the traffic circle surrounding the L'Arc de Triomphe. I hung on for dear life. I wondered what I had got myself into. I felt energized and excited. I felt like I could do anything.

Each sightseeing tour taught me something new. I learned about the French people, their land, and their culture. I never knew what to expect from each trip but I paid my fare and took a chance.

I especially enjoyed the walks in the park. I felt peaceful then as I soaked up my surroundings.

When I first arrived in Paris, all I wanted to do was go back home. I wanted what I knew. But I ventured out with small, tentative steps that gradually became more confident. I found my place within a magical city and began to run.

### Reflections

My student teacher and I worked together for approximately the same amount of time that I lived in Paris. I use this beginning because it serves me with a parallel as I think about the journey that we have been on. New stories lived out this year took on meaning in relation to old stories revisited.

Our journey found us moving tentatively at first. The pace was slow and careful as we came to know each other and our surroundings. The itinerary was sketchy, the destination unknown.

As our relationship developed into one of trust and respect, the pace quickened. Our dialogue became open and honest. As Joan, my student teacher, wrote, it led us on a "journey of two friends, and colleagues, discovering, experiencing and learning" (Payne, 1990, p. 2).

Again it felt like a marathon run. I expected the busy times as we lived out the rhythms and cycles of the school year (Clandinin & Connelly, 1986). These were times when I wanted to let the dust just settle. The daily demands did not provide the tranquil time needed for reflection. It is an issue for me to find this time, to seek a balance in my life. Dust never settles for very long. The slightest touch or the whisper of a breeze can produce patterns that evoke thought. There is no way to prevent it. There is no way to stop it. One could ignore it, I suppose, if one wasn't endlessly curious.

At times I thought of the car rides in Paris. There were times when my student teacher took the steering wheel and I was a passenger. I found myself feeling some inner tensions. I had conversations with myself: "Should I tell her how to do it? No, that wouldn't be fair. She needs to find her own way of being in the classroom. But it wouldn't hurt just to give her some hints. Yet, I know that she can do it." When I sat back and relaxed, I began to enjoy the ride. I was always amazed when she did something in a way that I would never have thought of. I felt energized and excited. I learned.

Joan took me on many sightseeing tours this year. She acquainted me with green water (chlorophyll added to water), assuring me that it would be good for my health. She demonstrated to me that making my own compost at home would be good for my garden as well as the environment. She shared her stories and let me see how she was making sense of things. She reminded me that "the ways of coming to knowledge are as varied as the people who live and tell stories of their lives" (Kennard, 1989, p. 3). I learned as she showed me pieces of her world.

There were times when I felt contented. They were the times that I remember being glad that we had this opportunity to work together. I remember our early morning breakfast meetings and our chats at recess. I was so happy to have someone who wondered about the same things that I wonder about. We were involved in a unique kind of exploration.

Over a period of 8 months in Paris, I learned to walk more confidently. There is no exact moment when confidence struck; in fact it came and went. Knowing what I know now, I would find it easier to go and live in another foreign country. Over a period of 8 months in our classroom, Joan and I learned to walk more confidently. I wonder what Joan's first year of teaching will be like. Will it be easier because of her experience this year?

## Beginning Two

In June 1989 I realized there would be two new things in my life. I was going to have a student teacher who was involved in the Alternative Program. I was really thrilled about it. I was also going to a new school. I had so much to look forward to. It would be an exciting, challenging year!

In mid-August as the new school year approached, I began to think about what it would mean to have a student teacher for 8 months while I found my place in a new school. I still felt excited. There were so many possibilities, but I also felt anxious. This combination of feelings was not new. I experience it each summer as I speculate about the year to come. I plan and ponder, wonder and worry. These mixed emotions, I understand, accompany me as I do beginnings. But this year I was to have a student teacher. Suddenly, I had so many questions. How was it that I felt so confident and sure in June? How could I work with a student teacher, help her rehearse for her chosen role, when I didn't even know where the pencils and erasers were kept? Who was she? Who would "we" be? How could I answer the questions she would undoubtedly have when I might not have the answers myself? How could I presume that I would answer her questions in meaningful ways? What had I got myself into?

Joan arrived at school to meet me in late August. As we organized our classroom we began to share our stories. We began to think about what we could do throughout the year. We agreed early on that we were well matched. I wonder how we knew. What made us feel connected from the very first day? With my new travel companion, a journey of connected knowing began.

## Reflections

Despite a fear of the unknown, I take chances. My participation in the Alternative Program was a way of trying something new. I had no idea what to expect but I knew I would learn. I was sure it would be a positive experience. I wanted to be a part of it. I was a member of the steering committee that met to discuss possibilities. It sounded wonderful.

Then August rolled around and with it my yearly dose of pre-first-day-of-school nerves. This year, though, I had something additional to worry about. THE STUDENT TEACHER. When I reflect on what I was insecure about it relates, I think, to two things. Beginnings are hard for me. I never really know what to do, what to expect. With each change I experience, I am learning to relax and to trust that the anxiety will pass. I feel a strong need to belong, to be a valued member of a community.

Then there is the notion of the expert–novice relationship between the cooperating teacher and the student teacher. I had never had a student teacher before. My own experiences as a student teacher were not too far in the past. I had moved into the world of the expert and I suddenly felt like an imposter. Could I do it? Did I know enough?

I have learned this year that I will never know enough. I believe that we learn all the time. I know that, with each experience and with each swish of the dust cloth, I will learn new things. I have also learned what it means to collaborate.

## COLLABORATION

Britzman (1986) describes the "teacher as expert" as a cultural myth. This view of the teacher implies that "teachers seem to have learned everything, and consequently have nothing to learn; knowledge appears as finite and unchanging" (p. 450). Many of my insecurities about having a student teacher were related to this myth.

I began to dispel the myth and to learn about collaboration as Joan and I worked together. We became a team of teachers working hard to do the best we could for children. We talked endlessly and we wrote in a dialogue journal. We asked questions and we wondered. We taught the children independently, we taught them together, and we taught each other. I discovered that in a collaborative context the roles of expert and novice interchange.

The Alternative Program was collaborative. Cooperating teachers, student teachers, and university teachers met to discuss how the assignments could be made individual and relevant to the situations within which the student teachers were working. The students were allowed to decide what they needed and wanted to explore. Joan and I also wrote a collaborative paper that reflected on our shared journey (Pamplin & Payne, 1989a). The evaluation process was also collaborative in nature. It was very difficult for me to imagine writing a formal evaluation for someone who had become a team partner. We talked about the things that Joan was learning and she told me the areas in which she felt she had really grown. She identified areas in which she wanted to grow further. Using her input, I wrote an evaluation. She read it and we discussed it before it was submitted.

We can learn so much through collaborative relationships. I know that I will continue to learn. I will try new things. I also know that as I continue on my journey, I will not travel alone. I have met, and will meet, many people who will travel with me.

Collaborative relationships are challenging. There are times when differences require time and attention. There are times when the desire for solitude is strong.

I remember several times throughout this year that I wanted to be left alone. I wanted the dust to settle for awhile. I learned that within collaborative relationships we cannot always decide when to let the dust settle. The journal that Joan and I kept was a prime example. There were times when I felt overwhelmed. I did not want to hear any more questions, wonders, or thoughts. Did I have to figure all of this out right now? From time to time, I relented somewhat and got out my feather duster. I responded with a comment like, "This is something I need to think about some more. Let's come back to this." I knew that I could not stop and ignore the world as it went on without me. But I could take a rest, couldn't I?

Although I could control my response, I could not control the response of others. With one question or comment, one tiny movement of a finger, Joan could wipe the dust away. I remember wondering if I was ready for what was uncovered. Sometimes, I wasn't. Most often, though, my journey was enhanced by what I found.

A lot of dust accumulates in attics. "I guess wonder and awe and joy are always there in the attic of one's mind somewhere, and it doesn't take much to set it off" (Fulghum, 1988, p. 89). It takes only one swish of the dust cloth.

## ENDINGS

I do endings a lot like I do beginnings. They are hard for me and there have been several in this practicum program. I decide to take it one ending at a time.

### Ending One

During the last week of the program, the student teachers were in the schools full time. I tried not to think about their leaving. I could not talk about it. Joan and I turned back to our journal that week. It allowed us to figure out how to say goodbye much the same way as it helped us to say hello. We had come full circle and the journal symbolized our journey.

The children needed the opportunity to say their farewells so they wrote personal notes to Joan. I collected them and put them into a scrapbook that the children presented to Joan.

Joan and I needed to say goodbye. We met for breakfast and lunch that day. We wanted to spend more time together. Later she packed away her things. She cried as she saw the children off after school. Now it was my turn to say goodbye. It was very difficult.

I wondered about why this ending felt so strange. When June arrives,

I am ready for the end of the year, but when Joan left at the end of April, it upset my way of knowing the school year. It was not the end of the school year yet. Where was she going? There were still so many places that we could travel together.

## Ending Two

I went into the classroom on Monday morning realizing that Joan was gone. It felt strange. The charts that she had made still hung on the wall but she was not there except in our memories. The ending had felt wrong so we needed to do something to make it feel better.

We got together at my house with our good friends from the program, Deb and Sherri. Here was another ending of sorts. Our relationships, as we had known them, were changed. We talked for hours about many things, although we tended to avoid the topic of school. Perhaps it was just too soon. But we talked as friends. As I sat with my colleagues, I looked at the fireplace and noticed the dust that was forming. On the fireplace sits a school bell that I got when I left one of my first schools. Whenever I dust that bell, it brings back good memories. I gave Joan an engraved school bell when she left. I hope that when she dusts it off she will remember the many special experiences that we shared.

## WITH THE SECOND ENDING THERE CAME A SECOND BEGINNING

In completing this chapter I feel like I have dusted very carefully. Certain memories were evoked as the cloth connected. As the dust accumulates again, I know that there are people who I will still invite into my house. These people are my collaborators and they are an important part of my life.

Furniture polish adds a shiny glow when you dust. You look down at the surface and you can see yourself looking back. The image is clear. I wink at it.

When I dust again, I wonder what I will learn.

## REFERENCES

Britzman, D. (1986). Cultural myths in the making of a teacher: Biography and social structure in teacher education. *Harvard Educational Review, 56*(4), 442–456.

Clandinin, D. J., & Connelly, F. M. (1986). Rhythms in teaching: The narrative study of teachers' personal practical knowledge of classrooms. *Teaching and Teacher Education, 2*(4), 377–387.

Clandinin, D. J., & Connelly, F. M. (1992). Narrative and story in practice and research. In D. Schön (Ed.), *The reflective turn: Case studies in and on the educational practice* (pp. 258–282). New York: Teachers College Press.

Coles, R. (1989). *The call of stories: Teaching and the moral imagination.* Boston: Houghton Mifflin.

Connelly, F. M., & Clandinin, D. J. (1988). *Teachers as curriculum planners: Narratives of experience.* New York: Teachers College Press.

Fulghum, R. (1988). *All I really need to know I learned in kindergarten: Uncommon thoughts on common things.* New York: Villard Books.

Kennard, B. (1989). Moments of seeing: Parallel stories of narrative change in collaborative relationships. Unpublished manuscript, University of Calgary.

Pamplin, L., & Payne, J. (1989a). Someone else's eyes: Personal inquiry, teacher education, and collaborative relationships. Unpublished manuscript, University of Calgary.

Pamplin, L., & Payne, J. (1989b). Aware of wonder. Unpublished manuscript (within unpublished manuscript, Someone else's eyes: Personal inquiry, teacher education, and collaborative relationships), University of Calgary.

Payne, J. (1990). This magic called real. Unpublished manuscript, University of Calgary.

Schön, D. (1983). *The reflective practitioner: How professionals think in action.* New York: Basic Books.

# CHAPTER 15

# Restorying Ourselves Through Working Together

## *Kerry E. Black*

Why are we worrying about how much these students are teaching?
Let's worry about what is really important, the colleagues we'll be
teaching with. We should start thinking about the kind of experiences
we want these students to have; they are our future colleagues. Think
about being with them as your team partner, in the next classroom,
teaching your children. This is what we need to think about.

These words, spoken by a colleague with a passion that cannot be
conveyed in print, call us to examine teacher education in a new way. It
calls for the examination of our practices as teacher educators as we work
with student teachers in practicum situations. My colleague's question is a
good one, and it is from this perspective that this chapter looks at my
experience as a cooperating teacher. In order to explore this perspective, I
begin with a brief examination of current teacher education practices.

In the traditional practicum, students are temporary visitors in a classroom. Gradually they are given increased responsibility and authority by
the cooperating teacher. Many student teachers view this experience as a
means of applying theory to practice, in much the same way as one would
apply paint to a building. Student teachers quickly learn that theories are
not easily applied and that students are not what they expected.

In the way the traditional practicum is lived out, student teachers often
seem to be the last consideration of the system, which founds the practicum
on convenience for schools and the university. Student teaching is seen as a
necessary inconvenience. The timing is such that it occurs during preparation for holidays in schools, and at the completion of a university semester.
Yet, the practicum is viewed by both teachers and student teachers as the
most important part of their teacher education.

Universities prescribe the standards: teaching load, lesson and unit
preparation formats, and appropriate supervisory models for the cooperat-

ing teacher to follow during the practicum. The message to student and cooperating teachers is strong: By following these steps, in this way, student teachers will acquire the necessary skills to teach.

In order to examine teacher education from a new perspective, it is necessary to uncover the assumptions that lie behind traditional practices. They are revealed by questions such as: What theories can one apply in practice? How much can the university teach the student teacher before she or he is able to succeed in the practicum? What is the "right" way for a student teacher to prepare lessons and unit plans? How should student teachers be evaluated? Which evaluative tools and standards predict successful teaching? What training do cooperating teachers need to assist their evaluation of student teachers? How quickly can decisions be made about who is suited for the profession and who is not?

When these are the questions in the traditional practicum, we place our energies in a technical rational mode of preparing teachers for classrooms (Schön, 1987). The language we use to talk about student teaching is testimony to this observation. It is the scientific language of preparation, application, evaluation, standards, success and failure, speed, correctness, and suitability. This language is not part of what I imagine as the work of teacher education.

I do not suggest we disregard standards. However, the traditional standards for teacher education are not the standards of which I speak. As my colleague so passionately stated, we need to stop looking at the lesson plan, the supervisory model, the "right" way to prepare teachers. Our focus needs to turn to the conscious examination of teacher preparation during the practicum as a way of working with our future colleagues, examining our practices as we do this.

We need to work collaboratively with student teachers in ways that help them to imagine possibilities for education. Drawing on the experience student teachers bring to teaching, while recognizing our own experiences, and those of our young students, we can begin to create new conceptions of education. In our collaboration, we begin to look anew at the institutional narratives that continue to shape the stories of students and teachers. What follows in this chapter is my story as a cooperating teacher in this inquiry into teacher education.

My story began with the first day of school, when I met Angela, my student teacher. We did not have a tidy package of answers, prescribed lesson and unit plans, supervisory models, or a beautiful handbook from which to seek answers. We created our experiences during the practicum in the situated context of our unique classroom and school. Uncertainty and improvisation were part of our exploration of the question: What kind of experiences do we want our future colleagues to have?

## RESTORYING MY PRACTICE AS A TEACHER EDUCATOR: WORKING WITH ANGELA

In this narrative inquiry, I am aware that my student teacher, Angela, and I both have unique narratives. As our narratives interconnect in our classroom, I examine the meanings made of our classroom experiences.

In examining my practices with Angela this year, one way of making sense of my experiences is by seeing them as expressions of images of practice. In my images, personal knowing is expressed. Images of belonging and questioning are found in my narrative of teaching. It is from these images I understand school.

I have found my journal to be an important reflective means by which I can view my practice. My journal writing is for enjoyment. It helps me to re-view the day-to-day happenings of the classroom, capture ideas, and work them through. This year, my journal became a dialogue among myself, Angela, and Angela's university teacher, Jean. The stories that are told in the dialogue are glimpses into my world of practice, connected by my images of belonging and questioning.

### My Image of Belonging

One of my images is of belonging; that is, everyone has a place. Part of my story tells of instances when I did not belong and of the discomfort I felt. Similarly, Angela's story included her struggle to find her place in school. We saw our stories reflected in the stories of each other, remarkably similar in the sense of needing to belong. Our shared stories were of seeking belonging, based on past stories of not belonging. In Chapter 7, Angela and I discuss, in more detail, our stories of needing to belong, stories from our own experiences of childhood.

When Angela became part of my year, I sought ways to welcome her, to show and tell her that she too had a place. After our first meeting, we planned the first day of school. I wrote:

We've really taken Angela into the fold — I hope she's not overwhelmed by it all. I wonder — we've just said in a way — you have a place here . . . you can contribute to this teaching that we do; as an equal. . . . That puts a new sort of pressure on. (Journal entry, August 29, 1989)

Angela responded:

It thrilled me that you and the team want me to function as a teacher. It does impose a pressure, of sorts; I can't allow myself to let you down. But this only serves to give me more confidence. I can do this! (Journal response, August 30, 1989)

By belonging in the class, we both shared a responsibility, a sensitivity to one another. The image of belonging was expressed through collaboration. It was up to us to make the classroom a place for everyone to belong. We needed to do this together.

My image of belonging is expressed in the arrangement of the classroom and preparations for students. I try to model my care (Noddings, 1986) by making the classroom a welcoming place for students. The desks are grouped, group areas and quiet areas are designated, names are displayed on coat hooks and in other places in the room, and student work is displayed.

These are ways my image is expressed in practice. I needed to talk to Angela about this. I began to understand my experiences as we talked and continued to write in journals. We became collaborators, as we explored the ways in which we could make an image of belonging apparent in our practices.

Belonging is an image that seemed to guide our practices throughout the year. One of the obstacles to Angela's belonging was the structure of the program. Angela was in the school Mondays and Fridays all day and Wednesday mornings only. Trying to find a rhythm in the expression of the image became a challenge for both of us in teaching and planning. Angela noted:

I am beginning to feel like a commodity. I want to be a team member, to the best of my ability, but only being there half time makes full participation impossible. (Journal entry, October 24, 1989)

Part of my image of belonging included working with Angela as an equal. When we planned, we did not always know how things would turn out. In preparation for Thanksgiving, we planned to make muffins, each of us with half the class.

We both gathered the kids around and had everyone involved passing the bowl, stirring, chopping, grating. Our area was organized chaos — everyone busy, busy. We hadn't previously discussed how the experience would be structured. (Journal entry, October 4, 1989)

What struck me was how similarly we worked with children, how similarly our images of belonging were expressed, and how important belonging was in our practice. Yet, this did not always happen. When we found ourselves working with children in very different ways, we reflected, improvised, and grew as a team.

We sought ways to establish relationships with our students that would encourage them to feel they belonged in our classroom. Judy,* one of our students, chose to write a story that she called "My Clas" (sic), which shows how she experienced belonging in our classroom.

> One day it was the first day of school. Some of my best friends were there. There names wer: Kenny Tina Larissa Karen. The techers were nice techers. They looked like nice techers. Then they began to tech they said: "on the pieces of paper on your desk put your name." So I went to my desk and wrote my name on a piece of paper. The next day she learnt our names. She taught us some songs and poems. . . . Then it was the last day of school. I cried. I liked the techer so much that it was the werst day of my life. (June 10, 1989)

In Judy's story, the importance of learning names, having a desk, and learning poems and songs were the things she remembered, the way she wrote her story of the year. Similarly, the community of friends was tantamount to understanding a new situation, with new teachers who looked nice . . . but were they? Judy's lived experience of belonging was evident in her sadness at the end of the year, as she calls the last day of school the worst day of her life.

Many of our concerns centered on children who did not appear to feel a sense of belonging—those who did not make any friends and appeared withdrawn; those who seemed to drive friends away through a confrontational manner; those who would only connect with one other friend and not seek others in the community. We continually looked for ways in which we might help them find a connection in the community.

## My Image of Questioning

As I reread our journal dialogue from the year, I became aware of another image, one of questioning. This year, I was struck by the depth of ongoing questioning of our practice. Angela's questions caused me to rethink my practices. I noted this in my journal.

> Angela's questions and comments really cause me to closely examine my practice and beliefs—multi-age grouping, "team" teaching and

---

*The children's names have been changed to pseudonyms in this chapter.

what that is; contrived lessons for units, etc. This is good stuff — and I need to be mindful of it. Who is being educated as reflective practitioner, anyway? Angela? Sort of. Me? Definitely YES . . . I accept that I continue to be a learner in this process. I hope that I portray this. (Journal entry, November 2, 1989)

Angela's experiences as a student led her to seek answers to the questions she posed. Gradually, she moved away from a vision of me as the source of answers to her questions. The way in which she was living out her story changed. Initially, Angela was frustrated by what she sensed as an apparent withholding of knowledge. She wrote:

At first I was frustrated when many of the questions I posed in my journal were answered by more questions. "They are the experts," I thought, "Why won't they share what they know?" But now I can see how necessary their questions have been in the process of my learning to become a teacher. Their questions and observations keep me focused on what is really important and cause me to become more reflective. They have helped me see how I must look to myself for answers. (Barritt & Black, Chapter 7)

Answering questions with questions is not part of my knowing. I struggle to change the knowing that comes out of the traditions of teacher as "expert." My questioning evolved as I made a continuous attempt to answer Angela's questions with an openness that indicated a changed lived story. I hoped that Angela would look within for the answers she sought. Answering Angela's questions with more questions, I tried to model questioning.

My reflections this year were also a restorying of past practicum experiences, in my work as a student teacher, cooperating teacher, and practicum advisor. These stories of the past connected me to the present Alternative Program. The differences caused me to feel uncertain, for there was no story of this year for me to follow. For Angela, there was no previous story of student teaching. This was the experience for her; she knew no other. For me, past stories of student teaching gave me a place to begin to rethink and learn student teaching anew. I knew where I had been, the past story of student teaching. I looked for new expressions of images of myself and my practice. As the year progressed, my questions became more numerous and difficult to address. An image of previous practica illustrates this point, as I reflected on the comparison of teaching young children and student teachers and the support we give unquestioningly to young children.

For the beginning learner such as the grade 1s, we support, nurture, encourage risks, accept failure as necessary and desirable, and keep on trying. The idea of student teaching used to be/still is: toughen 'em up for the real world? Let's not toughen them too soon — maybe not ever. Angela is so observant and enthused about her teaching and sensitive to the kids — those are qualities I value more than unit plans, standing alone, and toughness. (Journal entry, October 2, 1989)

How does this knowing find expression in my practice? This question is not readily answered. These are qualities that I value. They are not visible in ways such as the arrangement of work on a bulletin board. I recognized, in this reflection, that Angela already possessed ways of knowing that were valued by me in my moral ideals of a caring classroom community. In my responses to her journal entries, I acknowledged our shared knowing and how much I valued the moral stance it represented. In our dialogues together, written and spoken, there was a respect for the other's voice. This respect became our means of interacting with our students when they wished to convey a message to the class.

## RESTORIED NARRATIVES THROUGH IMAGES OF PRACTICE

Once again, I examine the question posed at the onset of this discussion. What experiences do we wish our student teachers to have? I cannot prescribe the experiences that we should provide for student teachers. It is important, as I look at teacher education, to know my own moral stance as it is expressed in my images. In seeking to know my images of practice, I can begin to examine the experiences in which I engage with students.

## REFERENCES

Noddings, N. (1986). Fidelity in teaching, teacher education and research for teaching. *Harvard Educational Review, 56*(4), 496–510.

Schön, D. (1987). *Educating the reflective practitioner: Toward a new design for teaching and learning in the professions.* San Francisco: Jossey-Bass.

# CHAPTER 16

# Creating New Spaces for Women: Restorying Teacher Education

## D. Jean Clandinin

I felt tears spring to my eyes as I heard Carol Gilligan (1990) tell a story of a young girl, a story that sounded much like one I could tell. As Gilligan told the story, I heard a way of telling my story. Gilligan spoke of a young girl silenced by the power of the cultural myth that we live out in our Western society, a myth within which perfection is defined for women and girls as a particular kind of physical, social, and emotional perfection. The view is one in which girls are to be surrounded by friends in order to fit within the image of perfection held up by our society. Their thoughts too are to be beautiful: thoughts without anger, without conflict, without negative emotions toward people.

As Gilligan spoke, my story came flooding back. I remembered myself in the grade 7 classroom of Mr. Cymbol. It was lunchtime. I was there with a small group of friends, girls with whom I had played in elementary school, girls with whom I had shared happiness and sadness, anger and fear. The conversation was about another of our friends and our thoughts about some action she was taking. The action is forgotten. It will not come back, but my words do. "We should tell her that we don't like what she is doing." My friends said, "No, that wouldn't be nice." And moments later when she appeared, no one mentioned it. I remember now a sense of puzzlement but I knew then that it would not be the popular or socially right thing to do to continue to speak out, to give voice to my concerns. The incident has remained, tucked neatly away, a story not given voice.

As I heard Carol Gilligan speak about young girls and resistance and loss of voice, my story came back. Gilligan (1990) spoke of adolescence as "an especially critical time in women's development because it poses a prob-

An earlier version of this chapter appeared in the 50th anniversary issue of *Phenomenology and Pedagogy*. Reprinted by permission of Publication Services, Faculty of Education, University of Alberta.

lem of connection that is not easily resolved. As the river of a young girl's life flows into the sea of Western culture, she is in danger of drowning or disappearing. To take on the problem of appearance, which is the problem of her development and to connect her life with history on a cultural scale, she must enter — and by entering disrupt — a tradition in which human has for the most part meant male" (p. 4). When Gilligan read these words in that crowded conference ballroom, she allowed me to begin to explore my own story of beginning to lose voice, of beginning to learn to know myself in silence, of drowning and disappearing. Gilligan's words about how Western culture excluded young girls' and womens' stories reminded me that the story given back to me in junior and senior high school by friends and teachers was one in which I was to be "perfect," without bad thoughts, with no voice for my experience but silence when my thoughts were negative. I learned to live out that story, which silenced the possibility for giving voice to my experience.

This story became my lived story until, angered by the educational structure years later, I began to find voice to tell of my experiences. I became aware, I think, of the conventional quest plot designed for men when I found myself blocked from living it out as I had imagined. I had learned in junior and senior high school and in undergraduate university days to live out the quest plot, a plot in which I set goals and achieved them and moved ahead. I began to teach. I returned to university to do graduate work. Each thing I did moved me ahead. It was when I was prevented from entering school administration that the first glimmers of anger began to emerge. I became aware that the quest plot was written differently for women and men. Carolyn Heilbrun (1988) writes about "a phenomenon evident in the lives of accomplished women who live in a storyless time and are either trapped in, or have wasted energy opposing the only narrative available to them . . . for women who wish to live a quest plot, as men's stories allow, indeed encourage them to do so, some event must be invented to transform their lives, all unconsciously, apparently 'accidently' from a conventional to an eccentric story" (p. 48). And when the conventional quest plot was blocked, I began to become angry, to hear my voice again as I had in my childhood and to imagine other possibilities. At first, I tried other possibilities within the quest plot. Gradually I began to be aware of the ways that my story was shaped by being a woman. Cautiously, with good friends, I began to tell my stories and then to retell them in ways that offered more possibility for living. Gilligan's work gave me words in which to give voice to the ways I had first been silenced.

Gilligan, Lyons, and Hanmer (1990) in their research see adolescence as the time in which young girls are caught in what becomes a dilemma for them and for women, that is, "was it better to respond to others and abandon themselves or to respond to themselves and abandon others? The hopelessness of this question marked an impasse in female development, a point where the desire for relationship was sacrificed for the sake of goodness or for survival" (Gilligan, Lyons, & Hanmer, 1990, p. 9). My anger at being blocked in the traditional male "quest" story marked the time at which I began to be aware of the dilemma to which Gilligan makes reference. I was able to name the dilemma our culture and institutions posed for me and for other women, that is, how to include both oneself and others. I began to understand how, confronted with the dilemma in junior high school, I had chosen to live within the myth of perfection, of caring for others and abandoning self. As I realized this dilemma in my own story, I, like Gilligan, began to wonder about the role of education in my experience of this crisis.

I had learned to silence my own voice, to become a "good" student and to live out the quest plot. I learned to keep silent and to give back the stories teachers and professors wanted to hear. Silence and received knowing became my ways of knowing. I began to awaken as I became angry at what institutions demanded of me as student, as teacher, as teacher educator.

My work in an alternative program in teacher education, an exploration of teacher education as narrative inquiry, offered new ways of thinking about my story as a teacher educator and as a woman working with other women. In our program we wanted to explore the ways in which university teachers, student teachers, and cooperating teachers live out their lives in school. Questions about how we learn to tell our stories and then to retell them in our practices guided the central story (Clandinin & Connelly, 1990). Our task was to learn to see ourselves as knowing persons, as persons whose knowing is expressed in our practices and embodied in us (Connelly & Clandinin, 1988). We were all engaged in becoming attuned to hearing our own stories as they were lived out in our practices, to hearing others' stories as they were lived out in their work, and to hearing our own stories as they were given back by other participants in the program in order that we might all see possibility for new stories of classroom practice and teacher education. We knew as we lived out those practices in this new program that we would be learning to live new stories.

And so my story as I had lived it out as a teacher educator was one I was trying to speak of, trying to learn how to give voice to the knowing, to the new stories, to the sense in which I now saw my story as having been bounded by cultural horizons of knowing. Even as we worked in the Alternative Program, I had found it hard to tell my stories, stories that had begun to be lived so long ago. And so in the spring of the Alternative Program year, I came to Gilligan's session with a wordlessness I had not felt for some time. My own memories of being a young woman had been pushing into my thoughts, formless and wordless, all that spring as I read the papers of the young women who were our students. They had written papers in which they came to understand their stories as they were learning to live them out in practice. Their stories were of the children in their classrooms. Many wrote, as Jean Fix (see Chapter 4) did, of children such as Michael and Tom, two children in her class. She wrote about her work with Michael in math seeing the connections between her story and his in these words: "I smile to myself, aware of the classroom once again. It was good to explain patterns to Michael. Maybe my connections are not his, but if I do not share mine, perhaps he will not recognize his own." Jean's words emphasize the importance of making connections between her own story and the child's story and of sharing those connections in dialogue with the child. Her words highlighted, for me, a similar connection between my story and the stories of the young women in our program.

Many of their stories were stories of struggle as they tried to learn to live new stories of teaching and learning where they were teachers in relation to children. As they lived out and wrote their stories, they saw their stories in the stories of the children. I heard in these young women's papers their struggle to hear their own voices, to be aware of themselves as knowing people rather than as receivers of knowing. They had begun to question the view that all knowledge "originates outside of the self" (Belenky, Clinchy, Goldberger, & Tarule, 1986, p. 48). As they began to question, they were trying to hear not only their own stories but the stories being lived and told by the children with whom they worked. As I worked with them, I was also becoming aware of my untold stories and of the possibility of telling them in order to allow me to engage in more thoughtful practice as a teacher educator.

In our work as teacher educators we were attempting to construct situations that would allow university teachers, cooperating teachers, and student teachers to establish relationships that would provide all of us with "experiences of mutuality, equality, and reciprocity" (Belenky et al., 1986, p. 38). We wanted these relationships to allow possibility for each of us to disentangle our own voices from the voices of others. "It is from just such relationships that women seem to emerge with a powerful sense of their own capacities for knowing" (Belenky et al., 1986, p. 38).

Gilligan (1990) reminded me, as others before her had (Grumet, 1988), that young women in their silence have learned to take everything they really care about out of their relationships with knowledge, with institutions. Working with young women and their stories had awakened in me a sensitivity to my own stories as a young woman. Gilligan's words gave me new ways of making sense. Her words also helped me see my own story more clearly and to mark the moments when I too had learned to take what I cared about out of my relationships with institutions, when I began to live my story as one of received knower. The moments such as the one in grade 7 began to crystallize into stories, into understanding myself as silenced. Gilligan's words created a space for me to begin to tell my story as a young woman and my story as a teacher educator with these young women.

I think of Lynn, a young woman who has struggled to trust us enough to look at herself, to look at herself as a knowing person. Lynn too has lived the cultural myth that I lived: the myth of perfection, of trying to live up to what parents, teachers, and society believed women should be. Beautiful to look at, bright but not too bright, hardworking but caring of others, and without bad thoughts. She had learned to be what Belenky and colleagues (1986) would call a received knower within our institutions. She knew how to reflect back to us what we had said, what the textbooks said. I saw Lynn as living out a story of my story. She too had given up her voice, her acknowledgment of her knowing. And she had not yet learned to allow me, someone who belonged to the institution, to hear her voice, her story. I wondered if I could find ways to help her begin to trust me as a woman and a teacher living my life, not someone living the institutional story.

I think of Hedy, another of our students. She too had learned to be a received knower, to give back to her teachers and professors the stories they wanted to hear. Stories of theory, of their words, of their silences, of their omissions. Hedy began to wonder, to speak, to tell her story, and as she spoke and wrote her life, she gave back my story.

My grade 7 story, my story of writing papers to give back professors' words, mingled with the stories of Lynn and Hedy as I sat with tears running down my cheeks in Gilligan's session. I began to understand the possibility for restorying when our stories as women are given back, of the possibility for new stories we have when others allow us to hear their stories. I speak particularly of my experience as a woman teacher with young women learning to be teachers. I sensed, as Gilligan spoke, that what we were trying to do in the Alternative Program was to allow these young women to tell other stories, not the stories they had been taught to live and tell by our culture and institutions. I came to understand our work in teacher education as, in part, a way of authorizing their own knowing, which had, for some, been denied. It was an awakening of their voices that had been silenced or sent underground at "the edge of adolescence" (Gilligan, 1990).

I knew that learning to listen to these young women's stories had helped me to see my own story better. I heard in their stories of learning to be teachers that they were learning to hear themselves speak, struggling to look at themselves as knowing persons, as people with stories that they were living and telling. And I heard in their stories the struggles to speak after years of not speaking with their voices but giving back the voices of teachers, theory, and institutions. Through their stories, I saw a way of telling my own story with new insight. It allowed me the possibility of restorying my own story and my way of working as a teacher educator. I saw that I could live and tell my story as a woman and a teacher educator in a way that did not merely replicate my own story of learning to teach. When I began to retell those stories, my story as a woman also was called into question. I learned again as we worked together to feel angry at the way the institutional stories silenced me and I felt new resolve to change the spaces created for women in our teacher education programs.

As we worked together in the program, teachers and learners all of us, story livers and storytellers, I came again to understand that I needed to look with others in order to see the ways in which I had lived out my stories. Collaboration seemed very important to learning to live and tell new stories. Initially, I needed to sense a space, a gap, a place where perhaps my words might be heard. I felt anger at having been silenced for a long time, at having not found those spaces into which to tell my story. Heilbrun (1988) speaks of the obstacles women face as they speak their anger. "The first was the ridicule, misery and anxiety the patriarchy holds in store for those who express their anger about the enforced destiny of women" (p. 125). And so I came to understand I needed to feel safe enough to speak those words, to feel that anger, to feel the possibility of being heard. That was partially what I sensed. Once having spoken, I needed to know that my story had been heard. But even more this year I have learned that someone needs to give back my story (Connelly & Clandinin, 1985). I needed to be "looking on with someone" (Kennard & Johnston-Kosik, Chapter 8) so they could help me see what I had said and could give back the story in order that I might see new possibility in what I had told and lived. I needed to find a space to say the story, to have the story heard, and then to be with someone who could give the story back, someone who could offer me a response of possibility for living and telling a different story. I valued the time that my collaborators in the program made for me to tell my stories. They waited quietly as I hesitantly told my stories, as I tried to give voice to what had been untold stories. I gave up the voice of expert, of teacher educator, of researcher, to tell stories of myself as a young girl, as a wife, as a mother, as a woman. They listened and gave back my stories in confirming ways, in ways that let me know that they were with me in trying to imagine new possibilities for living my life. As I thought about my own restorying, I saw new possibilities for working in teacher education. I saw new possibilities both for the substance and method for giving back women student teachers' stories.

As I look back on my experiences of this year, I wonder why both the young women and myself as a teacher educator have learned to speak, to hear the stories that we live out and that we are beginning to tell. What have all of us done as educators, as practitioners, to help ourselves and these students learn to tell their stories into practice with children. We have no answers but perhaps we can begin to speak tentatively about ways of storying the experience. We had made the spaces, listened, and stayed open to what they said in their writing, in their talk, in their lived practices. We stayed silent so they could speak. We made spaces for their voices. We gave them possibility. And we tried to tell our stories so they could hear our stories. We wanted them to hear women teachers speak of their experiences rather than of the cultural myths. For me this was a particularly difficult task. This telling and giving back of stories was a mutual process for as we told our stories, they gave back our stories with new insights. We read writing; we shared our favorite books; we read and talked about theories and research that resonated with our knowing. We told our stories in the margins of their journals. And as we heard their tentative voices, we tried to let them know that we had heard. In our responses, as we gave back their stories, we asked wondering questions about the meanings they had for their stories.

We too had learned to see and tell our stories differently. Our stories were set within a conversation of caring (Noddings, 1986). As we wondered about their stories, they allowed us to see our stories in new ways in a mutual giving back of story. I learned to see new possibility in my story, in my knowing. Our lived and told stories came back reflected from children, from student teachers, from cooperating teachers. They were not always the stories that we wanted to hear but, because they came from within relationships we cared about, we listened and tried to make sense of them.

My own struggle reminded me that we need to nurture all these fragile voices, those of ourselves as practitioners, as women, as young women learning to tell their stories into practice. I came to know the crucial importance of each of us learning to tell our own stories, as women and as practitioners, that acknowledge our conflicts, dilemmas, and struggles. I came to know in telling my own stories that it is only in telling our stories that we speak authentically of our experiences, that we acknowledge how we have each made sense of the cultural story, and that we can help create spaces in which young women can tell their stories. We need to provide other kinds of "role models" for young women — not ones of "niceness," or ones of playing the system's games, but models of collaboration with them as we join together in a kind of resistance to being silenced.

I now understand this resistance as one in which we acknowledge the dilemma of how to listen to both ourselves and the cultural stories in which we are embedded. In my experience I had come to know and name the dilemma of how to care for myself as well as for others. I now understand why others see the importance of this naming of our experiences as women. This helps us learn to tell new stories of possibility in which we neither, as Gilligan (1990) reminds us, deny our difference by living out the male cultural story in the name of equality nor deny self in the name of caring. Our new stories must be stories in which we find ways of knowing ourselves in the midst of a rhythmic tension that enables us to change our knowing, our stories as they are expressed in practice.

The process of learning to hear my voice and then to still it so I can hear others' voices and then giving voice to my stories as I respond to theirs in a conversation shapes all our stories. Neither my stories nor the stories of the young women like Hedy and Lynn remain the same. Thus, I must acknowledge that in my work as a teacher educator I am trying to reshape the ways in which these young women will live out their lives both in and out of classrooms. I shared this chapter with Lynn and we talked about how she sees herself as beginning to live out her story differently. That conversation reminded me with new force of the moral work of education and the moral part we play in reshaping our world and the ways we live within it.

As I wrote this chapter and gave voice to the stories I live out and tell as a teacher educator, I see new possibility in how I might tell my stories in ways that point to changed future possibilities not previously imagined. I see new ways to live and tell my story, new beginnings in the many beginnings that have marked my life.

## REFERENCES

Belenky, M. F., Clinchy, B., Goldberger, N. & Tarule, J. (1986). *Women's ways of knowing: The development of self, voice and mind*. New York: Basic Books.

Clandinin, D. J., & Connelly, F. M. (1990). Narrative and story in practice and research. In D. Schön (Ed.), *The reflective turn: Case studies of reflective practice* (pp. 258–282). New York: Teachers College Press.

Connelly, F. M., & Clandinin, D. J. (1985). Personal practical knowledge and the modes of knowing: Relevance for teaching and learning. In E. Eisner (Ed.), *Learning and teaching the ways of knowing*. Eighty-fourth yearbook of the National Society for the Study of Education (pp. 174–198). Chicago: University of Chicago Press.

Connelly, F. M., & Clandinin, D. J. (1988). *Teachers as curriculum planners: Narratives of experience*. New York: Teachers College Press.

Gilligan, C. (1990, April). Invited address. Paper presented at the annual meeting of the American Educational Research Association, Boston.

Gilligan, C., Lyons, N., & Hanmer, T. (Eds.). (1990). *Making connections: The relational worlds of adolescent girls at Emma Willard School*. Cambridge, MA: Harvard University Press.

Grumet, M. (1988). *Bitter milk: Women and teaching*. Amherst: University of Massachusetts Press.

Heilbrun, C. (1988). *Writing a woman's life*. New York: W.W. Norton.

Johnston-Kosik, L., & Kennard, B. (1990, February). Looking on together. Paper presented at the annual Calgary Teachers Convention, Calgary.

Noddings, N. (1986). Fidelity in teaching, teacher education and research for teaching. *Harvard Educational Review, 56*(4), 496–510.

# CHAPTER 17

# Restorying the Expert–Novice Relationship

## Barbara Kennard

While there are many beginnings for any story, words written on the pages of my graduate papers mark this story's beginning. They are words that described my coming to know and understand something of the nature of collaborative relationship and its importance in change and growth. Together, those papers are a story of my learning. This chapter is also a story of learning. It tells of my efforts to translate words on a page into a lived experience. As an account of my struggle to learn ways to live a new story, it tells of the ongoing process of change and growth and reveals the connecting threads of my narrative as I continue to make sense of my experience.

As I began to tell this story, indeed, as I searched for words to tell it, I was afraid, for I was only just beginning to understand it. As I searched, the memory of one particular desperate morning tugged at my thoughts. I remember, as I drove to school in my car alone, hidden from view, that I cried. It was the morning after a meeting with Lynn, the student teacher who had been paired with me. It was there, at that meeting halfway through the year, that I began to acknowledge the source of my feelings of frustration and the sense of silence that I had experienced as a cooperating teacher. That night, Lynn said that I had frightened her. She asserted that had I placed our chairs side by side in the room and looked with her, instead of looking at her, watching, her experience would not have felt so threatening. "We need to be looking on together," she had said. I was staggered as I saw the simplicity of what it was that we had been unable to speak of and the clarity with which it had been revealed in her statement. I listened quietly, smiling on the outside, but inside I was in turmoil, reeling from the shock of her statement: sitting side by side, looking on together, collaborating. I felt that I had made a mistake, or worse, I had been blind, unable to see. I had no answers. I had not known what to do. I wasn't so smart, after all. And yet, I felt that Lynn, that everyone, had expected me to know about collaboration and now they could see that I didn't know and hadn't understood this simple thing. Lynn's metaphor of looking on together, now that it had been said, was a perfect way to express the feeling of collaboration, a way to talk about how to live a collaborative story. It explained that she understood collaboration as I did and that she had been wondering, as I had, about an experience of dissonance as we struggled to work together.

And so, despite the teasing words from others that night, words that tried to help me see that it was okay not to know, I cried, in anguish, dreading the moment when I would have to look at Lynn and say, "I'm not an expert. I don't know, after all." Now, as I remember this, I wonder: Who storied me as expert? Had I, after all, told my own story of myself as Expert, keeping distance between us, making things difficult? Was it that we were caught in a myth, the myth that a university education and being named a teacher confers authority and status as one who knows, that without that rite of passage one cannot be expert, one cannot know? This myth lived out in practice constructs a particular relationship between cooperating teacher and student teacher. It constitutes the old story of the practicum. Were we merely caught in the plot line of this old story?

It is so easy to write words on a page once they have been found, words that tell the story of one's experience, reflections of what has been learned along the way. Once written, however, those words frozen on the page can conceal the ongoing nature of change and growth and mislead one into thinking that one knows how to act in a new way. I have learned that it is not so easy to do, despite words on a page, words written eloquently about another experience. An explicit statement of change, those words lie on the page, a moment of seeing, marking a turning point in the ongoing narrative of one's life. My experience in the Alternative Program has been one of learning to live the story that I was telling in words, one of carving a space for a new story from what was known in an old personal and institutional one. Above all, it is an experience in which I learned to tell and to live a new story in a collaborative relationship that began to develop over time, with Lynn.

Just prior to beginning the Alternative Program, I completed a graduate program in education. During this graduate work, I discovered what it means to learn, experiencing firsthand the exhilaration of being able to think deeply and reflectively about my teaching and about my life. It was an opportunity to experience myself as a knowing person, someone with knowledge of value. As I wrote and received response and support, I developed a sense of voice. I felt the power that comes with making my own sense of the things that I was studying. These experiences profoundly changed the way that I understood education and my work as a teacher.

While I had recognized the story I had told of myself as a received knower and had begun to tell a new story of myself as a knowing person, I needed to have the opportunity to learn new ways of working that incorporated those ideas that I was learning to tell so well in words. I wanted to continue to restory myself and to learn to live that new story in my practice. The Alternative Program held as important many of the ideas that I found essential in my own learning and growth as a graduate student: ideas about the importance of collaboration, of community, of relationships, of caring, and of voice. Part of my motivation to participate in the program was the opportunity, as I saw it, to continue my own ongoing story of change and growth in my practice.

Although I was excited about returning to the classroom to figure out how all of this was going to become part of my work as a teacher, I also knew that it would be a less rich experience without continuing my relationships with other people who were working in their own ways on similar ideas. I had known Jean and Pat during my days as a university associate involved with the supervision of practicum programs and, later, as a graduate student. I had felt empowered through my collaborative relationships with Jean, who had been my program advisor, and with Pat and others who had been research participants. I was interested in their ideas about teacher education. Part of my desire to participate in the Alternative Program included the opportunity to maintain my relationships, my connections, with a community of friends, for it was through these relationships that I had come to understand the need to dismantle old ways of acting in my own teaching practice. These ways were part of an old story, one that I have come to call the expert–novice myth. This story tells of my attempts to dismantle that myth in my practice throughout this past year with the Alternative Practicum.

The rhythm of the new school year was just beginning under the blue skies of late August when Lynn first contacted me by telephone. She introduced herself as my student teacher, worried a little about the distance from home that she would need to travel each day, and then explained that she would be unable to come to school during the initial days set aside for organization and planning. She would see me on the "first" day of school, when the students came. I recall my sense of disappointment with that first contact by phone. I was filled with the excitement and sense of expectation that is part of my story of each school year's beginning. This year, I felt an even greater sense of anticipation because of my involvement with the practicum. I looked forward to getting a new adventure under way, to sharing the work of beginning with this person who would be with me for 8 months. Thus, my disappointment was acute. I said goodbye to Lynn on the phone and proceeded with a busy school beginning, swallowing my disappointment and planning with my teaching partner, without Lynn. But all the while, there was a tiny, nagging doubt, a suspicion of trouble that arose from images of a certain kind of student, a student not quite committed who had been in the stories from the days when I had been involved with another kind of practicum program. I felt disheartened and unwittingly translated my disappointment into fears that she was going to be a student who would be cutting corners, avoiding the hard work of teaching and withholding serious commitment.

At the time, I chose to ignore these feelings. I agreed with the notion that the student should be able to negotiate the time for beginning depending on personal circumstances and that such negotiations should be made without fear of recrimination from me, the cooperating teacher. I wanted desperately to make the story of collaboration that I had told in my graduate papers become a part of my practice. I tried, in earnest, to put my feelings of disappointment and annoyance aside. But despite my good intentions, with this introduction my story as a cooperating teacher had begun with an unforeseen, yet predetermined, plot line belonging to an old and familiar story — of a student lacking commitment. It was with this predetermined plot line that I met Lynn the first day of school, welcoming her into my life along with the 50 children that arrived in the classroom in a swirl of excitement.

I had thought that it would be easy to live out a changed story in practice. The ways that this program might provide an alternative experience had been explored in countless discussions in steering committee meetings. My ideas were clear, or so I thought. Of great importance, as I saw it then, was the need to leave a space for Lynn, a space that would let her find her own way into the classroom community and our teaching team during the first weeks of school. Thus, I waited, responding as best I could to her queries and her tentative explorations of her place with us. I invited her to become involved wherever and whenever she felt comfortable, telling her that I believed that I had no expectations for what it was that she should do, that I believed that she should do whatever it was that would be meaningful for her as she tried to make some sense of classroom life as she saw it. However, those were my words telling of my own story of change and reflecting the exhilaration I had felt the previous year as I learned to make sense of my experience. I didn't realize at the time that my waiting was indeed filled with enormous expectations. In fact, I had anticipated that the students in this Alternative Program would be full of initiative. Supported by their teachers at the university, I expected that they would be ready with plans and intentions for their experience in the classroom and, more significantly, able to voice them with confidence. Once again, I was unaware of the powerful plot line that influenced the story that I was beginning to try to live and tell in my practice as a cooperating teacher.

As I waited for Lynn to take the initiative, to give me a sign that would let me know how it was that she would like to become involved, I encouraged her to write of her experience in her journal. I hoped that, in writing, she would discover for herself and, at the same time, reveal to me some direction for her practicum. I encouraged her to write and reiterated my offer to read and respond whenever she felt ready to share her journal with me. I understood from my own experience the powerful part that writing and receiving response played in the process of making sense. But while I could say these things to Lynn with some confidence, I felt a nagging suspicion that the idea of figuring things out for herself held very little meaning for her at this point. Still, I knew of no other way to proceed, at least, no other way that seemed to provide any alternative to the old practicum with which I was familiar. I trusted that our difficulty in talking together was merely a matter of time as a relationship of trust developed between us and that, soon, things would begin to fall into place.

Talking with Lynn was very difficult for me from the beginning. She shared stories of her teaching experiences, in another classroom and in programs for kids, that were full of confidence, telling of her successes and of the many things that she had learned already. In our conversations and planning discussions, these stories became ways for her to tell me what it was that she knew. She seemed to be storying herself as confident, knowledgeable, and ready to continue her learning. My first feelings of dissonance came as I began to see how hesitant Lynn was to participate freely in either planning or teaching. Discussing this with her was hard because I didn't understand why it was, given her stories of herself. I was unsure how to interpret this apparent contradiction since, at the time, I believed that simply by giving her some space undefined by my explicit expectations for what to do and how to do it she would easily find a place for herself within the classroom. Now looking back, I see that she was trying very hard to be a good student teacher, modeling her behavior after mine, sharing stories of the whys and wherefores of things that she had done in the past as I was doing, waiting to be told just how it was that she should participate. I failed at that point to see that the story being given back was really my own. In Lynn's hesitation could be found the threads of the expert–novice story that I was inadvertently telling in my practice, despite the story that I talked, the one I wanted to be living.

An important aspect of the practicum was the opportunity to record thoughts and responses in a journal. This represented a departure from the expectations for traditional logbook records of lesson plans and observations. Lynn was reluctant to write in her journal, or at least to share what she had written with me. She often asked what it was that she should be writing or how it should look, wondering what it was that I wanted her journal to be. She looked to me for advice on what it was that I thought the university teachers wanted it to be. Her apprehension, an apparent lack of confidence, puzzled me and heightened my own uncertainty about how to interpret what was unfolding. I encouraged her to find her own way. We talked about how important it was for her to reflect on and write about her current experience regardless of what it was. I believed that I was trying very hard to listen for her story.

The story that I thought I heard, as I struggled to listen carefully, puzzled me. I didn't want to interpret it as the story of a student who was trying to slip through her practicum doing as little as possible. I was unaware of a reason for my hesitation, thinking only that perhaps it was intuition that signaled the folly in that interpretation. I did not see that our relationship required that we find a place within each other's story. Thus, at the time I could think of no other interpretation. As my uncertainty and accompanying frustration grew, I began to talk with other teachers and administrators, people who had had student teachers in the past but who were not a part of the Alternative Program. I wanted to know what they thought, hoping to find in their responses some guide for what to do, a way to unravel the puzzling dissonance that I felt.

My discussions with colleagues served only to increase my frustration. They reiterated the stories from the old practicum, stories that spoke of the need for proving oneself independently. While I appreciated that hard work and an intense involvement in teaching were part of my own way of working, at the same time I was willing to accept that they might not be part of the story that Lynn wanted to tell of her own teaching. Their observations provided no satisfactory answer as I searched for new ways to respond. Thus, I continued to wait, listening hard, locked inside my own stories and not understanding hers. My inability to talk easily about these things with Lynn continued and my anxiety and frustration grew.

During the first term, there were one or two opportunities to meet with other cooperating teachers working in the Alternative Program. There, we had time to discuss our experiences and find a way through our uncertainty. As we spoke and listened to each another, we felt reassured. It was clear that there were a variety of experiences, some smooth and others not. However, even though I realized that each of the stories was unique, I was unable to find in any of them a possibility for another way to tell my own. Those who were most excited about what was happening seemed to be telling the same story of initiative and confidence that I had expected to see from the outset. Thus, while I was encouraged and supported in my decision to let things unfold, to wait for the meaning of our story to emerge, I grew more anxious. While I could speak about listening hard for Lynn's story, I did not recognize that the expert–novice relationship was reflected in her silence and her hesitation. I see now that hers was a hesitation laced with fear, a fear of failure magnified by her belief in the expert–novice myth. Then, still influenced by the same myth, I interpreted her hesitation as a lack of interest and commitment.

Thus, I grappled with how to share stories of my daily classroom experience, a sharing that would serve a twofold purpose. I wanted to provide Lynn with possibilities for her own story of teaching but without telling her what to do. I hoped that through this sharing Lynn would be encouraged to share her experience with me. Then we could explore classroom teaching together, collaborating in the way that I had come to understand it as a graduate student in my relationship with Jean. However, Lynn seemed to hear my talk as criticism or as instruction, directions for what she should be doing and how she should be thinking. Looking back, I understand that she was listening hard, looking for clues in what I said that would ensure her success as a practicum student. At the time, however, Lynn seemed only to be echoing my voice and ignoring the opportunity to find a voice of her own. I was baffled by such an apparent lack of commitment from someone in the Alternative Program and by this waste of opportunity. I began to wonder if she saw her practicum in the classroom as a lab, another course to pass, one more thing to do in order to graduate.

My thoughts were full of concern that centered on this experience of dissonance as I struggled to learn to talk openly with Lynn. As old practicum stories echoed and re-echoed in my mind, I found myself considering more serious action. While I recognized but as yet did not understand my disappointment stemming from my frustrated expectations for exploring practice with Lynn, I was unable to give voice to the worries that lurked in my mind, the nagging doubts and suspicions that had plagued me almost from the beginning. I wondered if I should be getting tough, laying down the law and demanding a specific performance. There had been the suggestion in some of the stories and advice I had received that perhaps so reluctant a student should be asked to withdraw, being unable to prove herself suitable to the hard work and commitment of teaching. So intense was my uncertainty, I found myself trying on a variety of cooperating teacher behaviors, behaviors that I am now able to see as a desperate attempt to fill the void that seemed to exist in my experience. I was, after all, the cooperating teacher. I was supposed to be doing something. I began to observe lessons closely, making notes and providing feedback tinged with evaluative tones. I made suggestions for improvement and requested more detailed day plans accounting for her time. I made tentative, yet suspicious, inquiries as to the status of her university papers. If this was a student attempting to pull the wool over my eyes, I was determined not to be fooled.

And yet at the same time, I found that I was able to step back a pace or two and recognize that Lynn was exploring many important and valuable ideas, ideas that I knew were fundamental to a teaching practice that was child centered, caring, and responsible. I saw that she worked well with our students, was thoughtful and concerned about the effect of her actions on their growth and well-being. When left alone, away from my watchful eyes, Lynn worked well, seemed more relaxed, and was increasingly more willing to write about and discuss her experiences. This, more than anything, underscored the sense of dissonance that had become such a part of this experience for me. I found myself at the end of the first term poised in mid-air, one hand on the ejector button and the other reaching for a hold in an intangible dream.

I began to see, if only dimly, that much of my concern arose from the fact that the time for evaluation was upon us. The puzzling contradictions and discrepancies of my experience as a cooperating teacher began to distill into an overwhelming dilemma. I had participated in the evaluation of student teachers many times before but only within the old story of the practicum, one that turned on the measurement of performance and judgments of success. Within that story, my choice of action seemed clear, but it was a choice that was inconsistent with the alternative ways of acting that I sought to learn, ways that would be caring and responsive to the real person that Lynn was, a person that I did not believe I had seen yet. I had no words to describe the experience that we had had, Lynn and I, nor could they be found on the official forms we were to use. I was almost paralyzed by this unavoidable requirement, caught by fear between making a mistake and taking the risk that finding new words seemed to entail.

Lynn, too, was aware of that story of evaluation and had spoken often and in many ways of her fear. I knew that she was very nervous, that the specter of evaluation served to silence her, to make her wary of what I might be thinking as I watched and listened. However, I had not understood the serious part that her fears played in her ongoing story. Had I listened more closely, I might have heard the story of our relationship as expert and novice. I might have understood that I too was caught as a cooperating teacher within the same institutional story. Seen through Lynn's student eyes, I held power, a power that she had learned many times in her educational experience could and would be wielded through evaluation. Was it any wonder that she hesitated? She too had no words with which to speak. And so, silenced and separate, we faced the unknown, wanting to act in new ways, feeling afraid and uncertain.

Fortunately, I was not really alone as we struggled with this experience. Despite the frustrations and fears that both of us felt, I had glimpsed the possibilities for a new way earlier, in my own story as a graduate student, and was unwilling to give up. I began to talk with other cooperating teachers and with Jean and Pat to find a way to write the evaluation. As I did so, I became acutely aware of a sense of isolation and realized that I had been trying to figure out what to do alone. I began to understand that part of my frustration arose from the lack of talk with others, that it had been talk that had helped me to find the words to tell a new story before. I guessed that if this were true for me, perhaps it was true for Lynn as well. As we dealt with the requirements of an evaluation, Lynn and I began to talk, attempting to suspend our fears and apprehensions as we discussed her work.

In these discussions, I wanted to provide an opportunity for Lynn to comment on her own progress. I wanted, if nothing else, to hear how she viewed this experience, to see if her perceptions corresponded in any way with mine. I hoped, at the very least, to enter a dialogue in which I could begin to express my concerns and my uncertainties. Lynn was very reluctant to voice her feelings. I could see how difficult these conversations were for her and, at the same time, I was able to admit that they were equally difficult for me. I didn't understand that the nature of the difficulty was similar for both of us. We were caught within a powerful but as yet unnamed story, and self-evaluation by the novice was not a part of the plot. Despite my assurances to the contrary, I was the cooperating teacher, the expert in a familiar relationship in which she continued to remain the novice. We had not yet developed the trusting relationship that a genuinely collaborative way of working requires. I held power and I needed to let it go. I had no guide, no new story, that could provide a possibility for the story that we were attempting to live and tell, one in which both persons have voice.

However, those tentative discussions that centered on Lynn's first evaluation marked a turning point in my experience of dismantling the expert–novice myth, underscoring as they did the radical nature of our struggle. During those discussions, I began to hear an old story of myself as student echo in my mind. I began to remember what it was that I needed to hear. I began to remember that reflected in Lynn's story as she wrote it, not as I tried to write it for her, would be the key to the puzzling discrepancies I felt. I would find her meaning, her voice, in that story and that would help me to know what to do. For the first time, I began to hear the real story that was unfolding. I began to understand the powerful influence of the institutional story that I had experienced in the past and of the personal story with which I had begun to write the plot for this current story. Those stories, invisible and as yet unnamed, had affected my ability to listen, had interfered with the sound of Lynn's voice as she struggled to make sense of her experience.

I returned to our work in the classroom and our daily discussions listening as hard and as carefully as I could. I began to hear from a new perspective Lynn's apprehension about burdening me with questions and her reluctance to ask me for help with her assignments. I began to recognize a profound sense of separation between events in our daily classroom life and the work that she was doing for her university teachers. I heard more clearly her silence, her lack of voice as she worried about how to figure out what it was we wanted her to say. I began to perceive that her hesitation and reluctance were not a sign of her lack of involvement and commitment to classroom work, that she was not a student taking the easy way, attempting to collect credits without working too hard. Rather, I saw that she was living out the traditional story of the novice, hesitating to participate for fear that her ideas might be unsuitable, knowing her place as that of one who does not know, one who is there only to learn the secrets, the tricks of the trade. I understood that I too had been locked within that plot as expert. I was the one who was supposed to know, the one who held knowledge, the key to Lynn's success. Her job was to find out what it was.

Although I was now able to name the story that had so powerfully influenced the way that I knew and understood my role as cooperating teacher, change was not immediate. Indeed, I discussed these insights with Lynn and while they eased our frustration and enabled us to talk with greater trust and less suspicion, echoes of the old story continued to shape our actions as we worked together in the classroom. I saw that Lynn was beginning to take a more active role as a member of our teaching team, that she appeared confident in her work with students and that her university assignments were taking shape as reflections of her work and her growing knowledge and understanding. However, I continued to feel anxious, to experience the dissonance that I had felt all along. I worried that something was wrong. I suspected that Lynn continued to struggle with the meaning of making her own sense of her experience in the classroom, that she remained self-conscious and concerned about my opinion of her work, fearing response that might be judgmental or evaluative. I did not understand that while we were by then able to frame our experience in a new way that provided possibilities for restorying our relationship, we continued to play out the old story that was so much a part of the way that we both knew education and learning. I did not understand that I needed to shift the spotlight that I had focused on Lynn for so long, to shine it on my own actions to see the ways that I continued to play out the role of the expert.

Instead, I focused on listening for Lynn's voice, understanding more clearly that hers was an emerging and fragile one. In an effort to encourage her further, I offered to share my journal with her and invited her response. I wanted her to know that I also struggled with uncertainty as I made decisions in my work. I assumed that she would see in my reflections some similarity with her own and that this recognition would encourage her. At the time, however, I read her responses as justifications of her actions that I had recorded and reflected on. It seemed that she had not heard my struggles or caught the sound of my uncertainty and pain. I was disappointed, failing to see that the voice with which I spoke and wrote was a powerful voice, one that needed to be stilled for her voice to be heard. In my disappointment, I failed also to see that we were not ready yet for the dialogue, the conversation of practice, that I so desperately wanted. Instead, we continued to live and tell our separate stories, sensing new possibilities for our relationship but unable to break free. It was at this point, halfway through the practicum, that Lynn and I met that evening to discuss our experiences with others in preparation for a presentation.

Although unaware of it at the time, that meeting became another important turning point in my experience of dismantling myth, of disentangling myself and my actions from the powerful influence of other stories and the stories of others. Lynn's eloquent statement of desire, that I look on the classroom experience with her instead of looking at her in the classroom experience, served to shift the spotlight, highlighting my own story for my attention. Face to face at last with knowledge of Lynn's story of her experience, I began to examine more earnestly the meaning of my actions and feelings. I saw that I had indeed storied myself as expert, fearing the loss of authority and stature a different story seemed to threaten. While I had attempted to redefine the role of the cooperating teacher, to back away and to provide Lynn with space in which she could begin to find her own place in the classroom, I had, in effect, abandoned her. In my eagerness to find a partner with whom I could engage in learning, I failed to support and nurture the emergence of a teacher's fragile voice. Lynn's unexpected actions served to underscore my own enormous expectations, revealing the plot line that I had predetermined for our story, a plot line that interfered with the careful listening and responding required for the development of a trusting relationship in which both of us had voice.

I felt disappointed and resentful as I recognized the silence that had surrounded us both, stealing our voices and distancing us from ourselves and each other. In desperation, I struggled with the need to forgive myself: Still influenced by the expert myth, I perceived my actions as inadequacies. I needed help to recognize the nature of our experience, help that I found as I turned to friends who were a part of the Alternative Program. As we talked, I began to understand our struggle as a restorying and a learning of new ways. There were no ready answers. I saw that we were finding our way, as if in the dark, gingerly feeling for the spaces ahead, without guides, arms outstretched for protection. I found, however, that in the company of friends, Lynn and I could, and indeed had begun that night, to listen and to respond to each other with new understanding and wonder. Stepping outside the stories from the past, we found new ways to begin to share our stories, exploring our experience in tentative ways through poetry. Entering into a more honest conversation, we began to build a relationship of trust. We've continued this conversation, developing a friendship that has lasted beyond the practicum.

# EXPLORING THE INSTITUTIONAL NARRATIVES OF OUR WORK

In Part Four, we turn our attention away from the stories of individual participants in the program to the institutional narratives that shaped both our individual narratives of knowing and the ways the Alternative Program was experienced. We have included three chapters in this part.

Chapter 18 written by Jean Clandinin is a story that explores issues as the university teachers worked together in the program of teacher education undertaken collaboratively with teachers and student teachers. Chapter 19 written by Annie Davies, Barbara Kennard, and Pat Hogan is an account of our attempts at changing the relationships among university teachers, cooperating teachers, and student teachers as we negotiated the assignments and the evaluation of students in our program. In Chapter 20, Jean Clandinin and Pat Hogan explore ways of giving accounts of individual participants' stories. Here, we frame the accounts as trying to live stories of connected knowing within institutional narratives where received knowing has been more valued.

CHAPTER 18

# Learning to Collaborate at the University: Finding Our Places with Each Other

## D. Jean Clandinin

In this chapter I give an account of my experience as a university teacher in the Alternative Program in teacher education. As we planned and worked in the program, I became aware of the institutional narratives that shaped our experiences in the program. I began to see the ways in which the university and the schools relate with each other as institutions and, as a consequence of the institutional narratives within which we are embedded, the ways in which our relationships as school persons and university persons are usually constructed.

## PROFESSIONAL EDUCATION

Schön (1983, 1987) notes that what is valued in our modern research universities shapes the ways in which the professional schools engage in professional education. He writes that technical rationality is the epistemology of practice built into the very foundations of the modern research university (Schön, 1987). Technical rationality holds that practitioners are instrumental problem solvers who select the technical means best suited to particular purposes. Rigorous professional practitioners solve well-formed instrumental problems by applying theory and technique derived from systematic, preferably scientific, knowledge. Schön sees professional education as founded on the premise of technical rationality, the result of a kind of bargain between the universities and the professions. Professional education is based on a curriculum that first offers "the relevant basic science, then the relevant applied science, and finally a practicum in which students are presumed to learn to apply research-based knowledge to the problems of everyday practice" (Schön, 1987, p. 8). As Schön develops his argument he makes the point that the "greater one's proximity to basic science, as a rule, the higher one's academic status" (p. 9). The knowledge that is most valued in our professional schools is derived from the basic sciences where knowledge, the product of inquiry, is fixed and unchanging, not dependent on person or context. What Schön helps us see is that the knowledge that is found in practice, that is, professionals' tacit, uncertain, and contextual knowing, is not valued as knowledge in our research universities or in the professional education programs based on the premise of technical rationality.

Even within each professional school in the university there is a kind of hierarchy of status that comes from the relation between the university professors and the professional practitioners. As Lanier and Little (1986) have noted for education, the closer one is to practice, the less status there is associated with the work. The highest-status knowledge is located furthest away from practice. The knowledge that is valued is the knowledge of certainty, not the tacit, uncertain knowledge of the practitioner. However, as many researchers now recognize (Eisner, 1988), our work must be situated in practice and with practitioners as we try to understand practice, teacher knowledge, and the ways in which teacher knowledge is constructed and expressed in practice. University teachers and researchers in education are faced with a dilemma created by the institutional narratives in which we work. As researchers in teacher education, we see the importance of collaborative projects undertaken with teachers in their schools and classrooms even though these projects do not result in the kind of knowledge valued by universities.

Standing immersed with teachers in their lived worlds is not the usual way that researchers have stood in relation to practice. It is a new way of constructing our work with teachers and it is a way of working with teachers that is not valued in the universities where we work. This collaborative agenda shared with teachers is not our taken-for-granted way of pursuing our work as university professors. It is not our lived stories, not what we have, in other places, called what is bred in our bones (Clandinin & Connelly, 1992).

Some of us are beginning to work against the pressure of the bargain made between the professions and the modern research university and are trying to construct new ways of relating to practice, new ways of valuing professional knowledge, personal practical knowledge as knowing-in-action, as well as the theoretical knowledge that has long been valued by the universities. There are now calls in the research literature for stories of teachers and teachers' stories, stories in which teachers and those working with teachers talk about the ways that teachers make sense of their practice, their knowing-in-practice as Schön would say.

Michael Connelly and I note that this means our work as university professors would need to be conducted jointly with teachers so that we learn to make sense of practice as we live our lives with them in their practice. This changed relationship would lead to a kind of conversation of practice in which researchers and practitioners hear each other's voices and the ways that the other's knowing is expressed in practice.

University professors in a faculty of education are embedded within the institutional narratives of universities, professional schools, and school practice. These institutional narratives have shaped the ways we live and tell our stories. For university professors used to being seen as experts in relation to practitioners, the familiar story is one of holder of the knowledge to be applied to practice. Practitioners have learned, in their relationships with university professors, to ask for solutions to their problems in practice. This mutually constructed way of knowing is bred in our bones.

As we began to construct and tell a new story of teacher education, our intent was to tell it as a collaborative story between university and schools, among university teachers and school teachers and student teachers. There was a lot of necessary restorying to reshape both our own relations with each other and the relations between the institutional stories.

## LIVING NEW STORIES IN THE ALTERNATIVE PROGRAM

I want to explore the ways in which our lived stories as university teachers became problematic both in our relationships with each other and in our relationships with cooperating teachers and student teachers. As I began to make sense of the field records and various documents from our program, I came to one way of telling the story. I began to see it as one of trying to learn to live new stories, embedded as we are within powerful institutional narratives.

I cannot begin to tell the story of each of the university teachers who worked in our program for those are theirs to tell. What I can share here are the ways I have come to story my experience in the program. I began the program with a great deal of enthusiasm, a sense that the institutional boundaries of the program were visible features of time, space, course numbers, hours of instruction, evaluation. Those were the issues I and my colleagues spent time discussing and that I sensed as problematic early in the program. At that time I was unaware of the many complex ways in which my knowing had been shaped by institutional narratives and of the ways in which the teachers and student teachers with whom I worked would shape my knowing as I worked in the program. The taken-for-granted ways of knowing I had learned to live in my stories within the institutions were like glass walls that formed the boundaries of my knowing.

## THE EARLY DAYS OF THE INQUIRY:
## LEARNING TO WORK WITH EACH OTHER

As I read the field notes and documents collected from the days before we began to work closely with cooperating teachers, I see how I thought that both I and the other participants in the program could learn to live a new story of teacher education as easily as we could tell a new story of teacher education. Even then, as we worked together and tried to construct possible new stories of teacher education, we struggled. It was not an easy task to imagine and tell new stories.

It was also difficult to live stories of collaboration with each other. I found it difficult to tell my stories of teaching to my university colleagues. Sharing personal stories of practice is not usual behavior for university teachers who live within an institution that encourages, even demands, competition between colleagues and considers individual research a key mark of success and accomplishment. Learning to live a new story was difficult but I felt we were making some progress as we met each week to talk, plan, tell our stories, and try to construct new stories of teacher education.

In those early planning sessions there were five people who were most heavily involved in the program. Four of us were university teachers with doctorates who worked at the university in tenure-stream positions. One of us, Pat Hogan, was a university associate with a master's degree, a teacher seconded from the board. The position of university associate is common to many faculties of education. University associates work with student teachers and cooperating teachers in practica and often help university teachers in their methods courses with talk about recent problems in practice. Their place in some ways is seen to keep university teachers connected to practice. Their short-term appointments, in our case 2 years, mean they are very recently taken from practice and will return to it quickly. In our institution, associates often do not become closely involved with academic faculty. In part, this is because their heaviest work load comes when the students are in practica. At that time, the faculty load is lightest. The differing instructional cycles then work against closer collaboration. Partly too, however, they remain strangers because they come and go from the institution too quickly to form connections. Full-time faculty do not have an opportunity to get to know them well as people or as unique practitioners.

When we first came together to talk, I saw our group as telling the stories of the Alternative Program in ways that would have us all be collaborators in the joint inquiry. I saw us collectively trying to imagine new possibilities for teacher education. We talked about doing work as if we would all be engaged in similar tasks. This would be a shared inquiry characterized by mutuality and equality. And early in the program before teachers and student teachers began to work with us, it did seem that we were able to live and tell such a story. As I write this chapter I see that we were already constructing a story with a radically different plot line from the regular program. Pat, as a university associate, would be a co-inquirer with tenured faculty. That was a changed place for a university associate. A second major alteration in the story was a change from the institutional narrative of competition and individual work to collaborative, shared work with each other.

## BECOMING COLLABORATORS WITH TEACHERS AND STUDENT TEACHERS

As I reconstruct the story as I write this chapter, I see dramatic changes as new characters began to work with us. While we continued to tell the same new story of teacher education as teachers began to work with us both on the steering committee and in large group meetings, the lived story started to feel different, at least to me. As I reread the notes and program documents, I feel a sense of a different story being lived out, a story that seems more like the old story of teacher education. When teachers and university teachers were together, it seemed that university teachers responded and lived out the more taken-for-granted story of university professors in relation to teachers. I saw how quickly we began to see ourselves as needing to have the answers for teachers. Rather than talking about the wonders, the nature of the discussion changed to giving answers to questions from practitioners. The powerful institutional narratives drew us back to the old story where university teachers gave answers to teachers seeking our knowledge. In one discussion on campus, the five of us talked about it. But because, as I now reconstruct the story, we had no language and little insight into the glass walls of the institutional narratives in which we were embedded and that shaped our knowing, we knew only that something was not right. It was hard work.

But something else happened. Pat, the university associate, began to be storied by the university teachers as "over there" with the practitioners. We began to respond to her in the same way we responded to the collaborating teachers, that is, not as colleagues working together in an inquiry but as people who could serve our university purposes as we began to figure out new stories of possibility for teacher education. I see now as I write this chapter that one way of telling this story is to see it as university teachers using teachers as research tools. We had begun to live out a story in which teachers were tools to help us further our ends rather than colleagues with whom we were trying to figure something out. Pat, as university associate, was caught in the middle. She was to be the one who stood between theory and practice, the one who would help us serve our purposes by solving our problems with teachers.

In June 1989, in the first meeting among student teachers, cooperating teachers, and university teachers and in subsequent small planning meetings of university teachers, the tension was evident. We had no language for talking about the tension and we all put it down to being tired and stretched at the year's end. We had, after all, to match up the student teachers with cooperating teachers; get the letters out to both student teachers and cooperating teachers; get the fall planning done for our courses; and get on with other commitments for summer work and vacations. It was a hard time of year and we were all tired. It was easy to see it as a problem of exhaustion.

## INSTITUTIONAL STORIES THAT SHAPED
## THE LIVED STORIES

When we began the Alternative Program in the fall, we were still trying to be open to ongoing possibilities for collaboration and for ways to continue to construct new stories as we went along in the inquiry. However, we increasingly became aware of the ways we were used to responding, that is, we became aware of our taken-for-granted world. For example, when problems of practice came up, the university teachers turned to Pat to have her solve them. She came to be seen as the one who had the connections to practice, the one who could solve our practical problems, the one who would buffer us from the complexities of practice and the particularities of people's lives. We find much evidence of this in our field records and notes. For example, when a school principal expressed a concern about the difficulty one of his teachers and her student teacher were having in establishing a working relationship, the university teachers looked to Pat to go out and work with the problem. As I reflect on it now, this was the story that we had most often lived as university teachers. We were not accustomed to working closely with student teachers and cooperating teachers. University associates usually did that for us. We had to remind ourselves that Pat's place in our inquiry was different. She was already committed to working with a small group of student teachers and cooperating teachers. She had similar commitments to the other university teachers. The problem was not in her group. We figured out another way to work with the teacher and student teacher. A different team member took responsibility for working with the pair. A few days later, we needed to find a new placement for one of the student teachers whose teacher had been moved to a non-teaching placement. Once again, our group's response was to turn first to Pat to solve this problem. She was, after all, the university associate, the one connected to practice who could solve this kind of problem. Once again we caught ourselves. These two examples are illustrative of how difficult we were finding it to live a new story in relation to Pat, as university associate, and in relation to our work with practitioners.

During the first 6 weeks of that fall, I think we all found it difficult to work with teachers and student teachers. As teachers experienced difficulty in working with student teachers, they wanted "the university" to come in and solve the problems. They too were accustomed to living a story in relation to the university in which the university supplied answers to difficult problems. We heard more than once the question, "What does the university want us to do with this problem?" As I reflect back now, I see how difficult it was for all of us to live out a new story of teacher education as we lived out the old story of relations between university teachers and teachers, between university and schools.

## LEARNING TO LIVE A NEW STORY IN OUR OWN TEACHING

As we tried to live a new story of teacher education, we became aware of another way in which the institutional narratives had shaped our knowing. As university teachers we were not used to living our teaching as an inquiry process, as a process of living out a joint construction of meaning with teachers and student teachers. The institutional narrative of university teaching requires teachers to have a course outline prepared early in the term that lays out the knowledge objectives and methods of course evaluation. These objectives are then fulfilled in lectures and discussion groups.

To learn to live a story in which our teaching was a kind of inquiry conducted with many participants — student teachers, cooperating teachers, and each other — was very difficult. In our weekly group meetings of university teachers, we began to shy away from questioning what was happening in our small in-school seminar groups and in the integrated methods of instruction courses. Our small group meetings began to be discussions of technical problems, things like arranging for meetings with principals or with cooperating teachers, scheduling assignments and marking assignments, and ways of letting our colleagues in the faculty know what we were doing. We began to have trouble talking about what we were figuring out through closely examining our own teaching and our relations with student teachers and cooperating teachers. Our conversations began to be marked by giving answers to each other.

## CONFRONTING THE COMPLEXITIES OF PRACTICE

When we met with all the teachers at a second large group meeting in October 1989, we struggled to maintain a sense of the collaborative inquiry during the meeting. It was difficult to maintain a sense of the mutuality. Even in small groups where we shared stories of our experiences, some cooperating teachers pushed for the university teachers to supply the answers, to tell them ways to do particular tasks. In Chapter 15, Kerry Black highlighted the plea from one cooperating teacher to turn our attention to working together in order to figure out what kind of colleagues we wanted, rather than pressing the university teachers for answers to technical problems such as the number of hours student teachers should teach and whether cooperating teachers should stay in the classroom or should leave student teachers on their own.

We saw that teachers were also struggling to learn to live new stories of teacher education, stories in which university teachers were collaborators rather than solution finders. It was a difficult process for all of us. One of the principals who attended the meeting wondered, at meeting's end, if he was still a participant in an alternative program. For him, it seemed to feel more like the old story of university–school relationships in which the university teachers gave answers to questions that should have been opened to inquiry among collaborators.

## FEELING FRUSTRATED: LACKING INSIGHTS

I remember feeling anger and not wanting to deal with what clearly were important issues in the inquiry. My reluctance was partly because we were all working very hard in the program. There were journals to respond to, seminars to attend, classes to teach, assignments to mark, and, for each of us, our commitment to this program was only a small part of our work. So even while we encouraged our collaborators to be reflective about the stories they were living and telling in their practice and while we worked with them in figuring out what was happening with student teachers and with our small seminar groups, we were not able to engage in an inquiry into what was happening with our group at the university. We all pleaded too many commitments, too little time. Partly also we didn't deal with the issues because the problem was seen as a technical problem, one of communication that could easily be solved if we all took time to hear what the others were saying. We even blocked out a longer than usual time to do this at one point. Our intent was to have time to learn to figure out what seemed problematic. This could, of course, have been part of the problem. We did not take enough time to really work together to work through what was happening. However, as I reconstruct the story of our work as university collaborators, I think a more telling account turns on the ways we were trying to live new stories with each other, with teachers, and with student teachers, while we remained embedded within the institutional narratives that shaped our personal practical knowledge.

## FINDING A WAY TO TELL THE STORY

As I noted earlier there are other possible ways in which this story of collaboration among university colleagues could be constructed. This is one account that helps me make sense of what happened. In this final section I want to highlight three interrelated points that became apparent as I made sense of the narrative data.

It is difficult to construct new stories of teacher education bounded as we are by the personal, institutional, and cultural stories in which we find ourselves. We managed to begin to tell new stories. In the pages of this book, we have told something about restructuring teacher education. However as I reflect on my work with my university colleagues, I see how much more difficult it is to live new stories of teacher education than it is to tell them as possible stories. Telling and living new stories are closely connected but, for me, learning to live new stories in my practice was particularly difficult.

A second, related point is the importance of collaboration for being reflective about the ways in which we live these new stories. I came to see the importance for me to be in collaborative relationships in which I felt safe enough to question and to hear other possible tellings of my stories. I saw the value of being in relationships where I could be open to having my stories given back. That is very difficult within university settings based on what Elbow (1986) calls the doubting game and competition. This necessitates living our stories as university teachers differently so we can work together in collaborative ways in order to have others draw attention to the complexities in the plot outlines of our stories. Immersed as we are in the expressions of our own personal practical knowledge in our practice, it is difficult to know our own stories without working with colleagues who give back our stories and whose response we hear.

A third point is connected to the first. As I told this story, I tried to

give a sense of how difficult it was to begin to work with teachers differently, to live with them as collaborators who were engaged with us in trying
to figure out their practices and ours and the ways in which we could work
with student teachers in educative ways. As I reflected on my experience in
the Alternative Program, I became aware of how inappropriate it is to
have university associates stand between university teachers and teachers, as
go-betweens between theory and practice. As we restructure teacher education, we need to find ways to work with teachers in their classrooms and
with student teachers in contexts similar to those in which they will eventually practice. The place of university associates as standing in the gap between theory and practice, between university teacher and cooperating
teacher, will work against trying to tell and live new stories of teacher
education. We need, I think, to begin to imagine new ways to work with
teachers as collaborators and new ways for them to be engaged with us in
teacher education. The stories told in this book are models of possibility.

## REFERENCES

Clandinin, D. J., & Connelly, F. M. (1992). Teachers as curriculum makers. In P.
    Jackson (Ed.), *Handbook of research on curriculum* (pp. 363–401). New York:
    Macmillan.
Eisner, E. (1988). The primacy of experience and the politics of method. *Educa-
    tional Researcher, 20*, 15–20.
Elbow, P. (1986). *Embracing contraries: Explorations in teaching and learning.*
    Oxford: Oxford University Press.
Lanier, J., & Little, J. (1986). Teacher education. In M. Wittrock (Ed.), *Handbook
    of research on teaching* (pp. 527–569). New York: Macmillan.
Schön, D. (1983). *The reflective practitioner: How professionals think in action.*
    New York: Basic Books.
Schön, D. (1987). *Educating the reflective practitioner: Toward a new design for
    teaching and learning in the professions.* San Francisco: Jossey-Bass.

CHAPTER 19

# A Moment of Improvisation: Constructing Assignments Collaboratively

*Annie Davies, Barbara Kennard, and Pat Hogan*

Our buzz of excited chatter spilled out of a classroom at the University of Calgary on a late January morning. The topic of conversation was the renegotiation of assignments in the four methods areas of language arts, mathematics, science, and social studies. In a three-way dialogue that included student teachers, their cooperating teachers, and the university teachers, we discussed new possibilities to fulfill the course requirements.

A snapshot of the room would reveal some paired conversations, heads bent together as student teachers and cooperating teachers mapped out ideas, while other collaborative pairs joined forces in order to inspire each other. The picture would also show the involvement of the university teachers as they listened to various proposals and gave suggestions. If this snapshot was mounted in an album, the caption written by one of the student teachers might read "a moment of relief," or written by a cooperating teacher, it might read "the moment of collaboration," or written by a university teacher, perhaps it might read "a moment of restorying." In any event each one of us recognized the personal significance of what we were engaged in. Collectively we explored the possibilities for new assignments based on individually situated experiences that student teachers had found important to their learning. Such assignments could replace the generic methods assignments given to student teachers in September. At this point in time the university teachers let go of their authority to frame the assignments and welcomed the collaborative input of individual student teachers with their cooperating teachers. The cooperating teachers finally had a place, and permission, to be as involved as they wanted to be and to negotiate that involvement on a personal basis with their student teachers and the university teachers.

The importance of the inclusion of the cooperating teacher's voice can be seen in student teacher Benita Dalton's description of her new sense of being "comfortable," of "gaining focus," of being "able to exchange ideas" and to "figure out what is important." As possibilities for the assignments were discussed and openly shared it became clear that certain assignments could address two or more curricular areas. Student teachers could also plan to write more extensive papers, allocating a higher percentage of their marks accordingly. Student teachers could still have the option of writing papers based on the original assignments. Student teachers in consultation with their cooperating teachers and university teachers constructed assignments that gave appropriate coverage to the four methods areas.

The university teachers were prepared to undertake the complexity inherent in marking such varied assignments. They also provided the space for joint papers to be authored by student teachers and those cooperating teachers involved in graduate programs. The mood at the end of the meeting reflected each individual's new sense of collaborative involvement. It had been a wonderful morning.

The impetus for that morning had come out of an earlier meeting and out of a moment of improvisation. Moments of improvisation in which we begin to restory are not planned. They occur as connections are made in the conversations of friends trying to make sense of their experience. Such a moment occurred one evening in early December as four of us—Pat, Jean, Annie, and Barb—met together to try to make sense of recent experiences with the practicum. The conversation focused on the student teachers' assignments. Snippets of experience were shared and as the connections between them clarified, a common theme began to emerge. Signals that had been ignored or misunderstood for several months distilled into a single notion, an understanding of the need to bring everyone together to figure out the place of the assignments in the experience of the practicum.

Annie shared a story of recent efforts to edit a paper for Benita, efforts tinged with surprise as she read pages of hypothetical possibilities that were distant from the realities of the classroom in which Benita worked. The paper was a science assignment. Busy with other things, Annie and Benita had not discussed the assignment or Benita's approach to it beforehand. As she spoke of this, Annie wondered about the nature of the assignment and about Benita's apparent difficulty in responding to an assignment that was tied to classroom practice. Annie was surprised by Benita's work, which had seemed to be an attempt to tailor her response to her perception of what it was she thought the "professor" wanted.

Pat and Jean spoke of their mounting concern that assignments were not being completed as quickly as they had expected. They wondered about the reasons why gentle nudges had not brought any response. They shared stories of a group of student teachers who had chosen to complete a social studies assignment on field trips and had found themselves again working on hypothetical possibilities. As university teachers they too wondered about the difficulties the student teachers seemed to be having writing about their own experiences in the classroom as part of the assignments.

In turn, Barb wondered why her student teacher, Lynn, had not shared her assignments with her. It had been Barb's observation that Lynn was anxious about all the assignments that were coming due and that her attention to her classroom work had been diverted. Her efforts were being spent on the assignments instead. In an effort to provide support, Barb had offered to work with her on a science paper. She spoke of her sense of surprise when she learned through Lynn's amazed response that Lynn had never asked for her involvement, thinking that Barb would not be interested.

While this was an opportunity to work with Lynn on something that seemed important, Barb felt that Lynn's involvement with this particular assignment was minimal. The telling of a child's story of science unrelated to the ongoing work in the classroom appeared, as in an old story of university assignments, to be a mere exercise. Together Annie and Barb wondered about the sense of disconnection in an assignment they had assumed would be rooted in experience.

Through the twists and turns of the conversation Annie and Barb explored their feelings that as cooperating teachers they remained outside of the assignments. They recognized that, while helping their student teachers, both had assumed the role of editor, reading papers in which they had no part. Neither of them had seen any of the assignment sheets and were unclear as to their intent. They felt frustrated in their desire to help their student teachers complete meaningful work.

As they spoke of their experience, Jean and Pat began to hear their stories and the stories from other student teachers and cooperating teachers in a new way. The signals they had been hearing throughout the weeks and months of the practicum highlighted the noncollaborative nature of the way in which the assignments had been addressed. They recognized more clearly their own surprise that the student teachers and cooperating teachers had not, in all cases, shared the assignments.

Pat and Jean heard in the stories shared that evening an echoing story of the cooperating teachers who had not felt a part of the assignments and thus were experiencing a sense of disconnection. They began to recognize that without the involvement of the cooperating teachers, the assignments could never be rooted in an experience that was situated in the real classrooms in which the student teachers were working. It was a recognition through which Pat was able to distill all of the stories of the assignments into a single moment of improvisation, wondering aloud about what would happen if all the participants were brought together at the same time to talk about the assignments and to figure out what to do. In response, Jean remembered that money was available that could be used for such an undertaking. In an instant, the conversation turned to the possibilities suddenly revealed.

When Jean and Pat look back and try to remember what led us to the moment of improvisation that resulted in the meetings in the university classroom and the renegotiation of assignments, it is a bit like trying to unravel a wad of string. There are bits that can be teased out of the knots but they don't seem to lead anywhere. There are strands that make better sense but they break off from the jumble and exist as only pieces of the story. It is only now that we can begin to take a closer look at some of those pieces and begin to understand how they contributed to our felt need to act in a way that was responsive to the signals.

Some of the signals we experienced as moments of surprise. One of those moments came early in the practicum year when we called together all the cooperating teachers to a meeting in one of the schools. We had been with the student teachers for about a month, meeting them in university classes, in small group seminars, and in their schools. But our contact with cooperating teachers had been on an individual basis, and we wanted to bring them together so they could talk to each other and with us about how they were figuring out their experiences with this kind of practicum. The meeting took place in a room where teachers were gathered around three or four large tables. We suggested that people might like to talk informally with the others at their table, and we made some attempt to have each of the university teachers sit with a group or circulate among the tables. After a lengthy period for talk in the small groups, we asked that someone from each group report on the discussion that had taken place at the table. One of the comments that we remember particularly was a request made by Barb.

During the large group discussion Barb asked if the cooperating teachers could be provided with a copy of the assignment sheets. It surprised us a little that student teachers had not shared their assignment sheets with their cooperating teachers, but at the time we were unable to read this as a signal that there was something amiss in the way we had structured assignments. We remembered how the steering committee had given us responsibility for constructing the assignments and how we had lived out the institutional story of university teachers in this regard. We probably assumed that student teachers would show the various course outlines and assignments to their cooperating teachers. It was not until now that we could see how this bit of the story contributed to a new way of thinking about assignments.

Another piece of the story came about a month later as Annie talked to us about a conversation she had with Benita regarding one of the assignments. In some ways it echoed the concerns raised by Barb. Benita had tried to talk with Annie about a particular approach to learning that was seldom used in Annie's classroom. Annie puzzled over Benita trying to attempt an assignment that seemed so disconnected from the classroom situation. From the conversation Annie tried to piece together what the assignment might look like. Annie spoke of hearing the student teacher's version of the assignment as if it were "coming to her through a wooly scarf." Like Barb, Annie suggested it would be a good idea if cooperating teachers were given a copy of the assignment sheets. As we look back, we remember conversations with other cooperating teachers that indicated their lack of feeling connected to the assignments or that showed that they had difficulty seeing how the assignments were connected to their particular classroom situations. We attempted to listen to their concerns but we did not yet see how we could try to live out a new story of collaboration.

Student teachers were also giving us signs that they were having difficulty feeling confident about attempting the assignments, but again we had difficulty reading the signs. In large numbers student teachers asked for extensions on the assignments that were due before Christmas. They came to us in small delegations and spoke of the large number of assignments they faced in six courses and of the additional assignments they were being asked to undertake in their classroom situations. They spoke of not being ready or of not knowing enough. We granted the extensions they requested and tried to understand the demands that were being placed on their energy. Yet we continued to think that our assignments were tied to practice. We continued to think that the assignments could easily be accomplished with the student teachers' everyday contact with children.

We continued to think this way until finally there were so many signs that we had to start listening and looking at the whole question of assignments in the Alternative Program in a different way. We knew we had to respond and our response was an improvisation. We arranged to bring all the participants together to try to figure out new ways of completing the assignments, new ways of connecting theory and practice, new ways of collaborating.

We are just beginning to understand how much of our early thinking was set in the institutional stories of teacher education. Learning how to ask questions about the ways we come to know and about the requirements of the institutions in which we work has been an important aspect of our inquiry. Initially we did not question who had the authority to set the assignments. Each of us, cooperating teachers and university teachers alike, had lived our own stories of teacher education in various institutions where university classrooms were very separate from school classrooms. Our personal experiences with assignments were unrelated to situated experience and most often fulfilled through discussion of readings, presentations, or plans related to hypothetical situations. As students we had attempted to give our professors what they wanted to hear in order to obtain good grades. Our own experiences with practicum had involved being parachuted into classrooms for a brief period of time where we faced another evaluative situation with unknown cooperating teachers and practicum advisors who may have been complete strangers. In those instances our cooperating teachers attempted to help us fulfill the requirements as set out by the university. At the time, few of us had questioned the gap that existed between the classrooms of the university and the classrooms of the schools. And few of us had questioned the role of the institution in setting assignments and creating rigid guidelines for the practicum experience.

When we envisioned an alternative practicum we agreed that the assignments should be connected to classroom situations but we continued to feel bounded by the institutional requirement to have university teachers set out the assignments prior to the beginning of the school term, prior to knowing the individual students and their classroom situations. It wasn't until we started to listen differently to stories of how participants were experiencing the assignments that we began to understand possibilities for collaboratively constructing assignments that were situated in individual teachers' practices.

CHAPTER 20

# Living the Story of Received Knowing: Constructing a Story of Connected Knowing

## Pat Hogan and D. Jean Clandinin

Our schools and colleges, institutions of the patriarchy, generally teach us to listen to people in power, men or women speaking the father tongue; and so they teach us not to listen to the mother tongue, to what the powerless say, poor men, women, children: not to hear that as valid discourse.

I am trying to unlearn these lessons, along with other lessons I was taught by my society, particularly lessons concerning the minds, work, works, and being of women. I am a slow unlearner. (LeGuin, 1989, p. 151)

LeGuin's words remind us of our own struggles to unlearn the stories we learned to live as received knowers. It was not easy to unlearn the lessons we had learned so well in our own school experiences, in undergraduate and graduate experiences, and in the places where we worked as teachers. We learned to take notes in lectures and libraries and to give back the contents of those notes in examinations and in papers. We learned to take our selves out of our writing and our speaking when we wanted to be heard by our teachers and those in power. We learned how to quote authorities and reference them properly. We learned to complete long-range plans for our administrators that had no place for our voices and the children's voices.

Gradually we began to unlearn these lessons. When we found ourselves in relationships where we felt we could risk to begin to tell another kind of story, speak in another kind of language, and where we felt we were heard, we began to gain confidence in our own knowing. We began to hear our own voices, to listen to how we told stories of our lives, and to recognize that knowledge didn't reside outside us but was constructed by us. We came to understand the meaning of personal knowledge in the ways that Polanyi (1962) spoke about it.

The unlearning, to borrow LeGuin's phrase, was set within a process of constructing and reconstructing our knowing as we storied and restoried our lives. Each time we found ourselves in new situations with theory; in new relationships with children, colleagues, and friends, in new schools and positions, we learned to make new sense of the stories that we were living and the knowledge that we were constructing. Each experience cast new shades of meaning onto the ways in which we made sense of the world. We came to new ways of knowing and we also came to new insights into what it meant to know.

Coming to these understandings of our knowing and of knowledge was particularly difficult, situated as we were within institutions where the teaching–learning relationship, the theory–practice relationship, had a long narrative history. We struggled to learn to speak a new language and to question the taken-for-granted ways of knowing that pervaded our practices when we worked within these institutions. The dominant voice and way of knowing was both patriarchal, as Belenky and her colleagues (1986) have illustrated, and theoretical, as Schön (1983) suggests. The voices of women and practice were excluded. We began to think about ways to include these voices within the educational institutions.

We began to value our own knowing and to speak of constructed knowing within the institutions of university and school. We set up a program where constructed knowing was central to being a participant. We expected cooperating teachers and student teachers to be able to quickly unlearn the lessons of received knowing. Furthermore, we expected them to do that unlearning within the constraints of the university and schools that too often valued received knowing rather than constructed knowing.

Helen Mahabir (1990), one of our student teachers, wrote the following account of how she experienced moving into new ways of talking about her knowing. (See Chapter 2 for more of Mahabir's story.)

My first four years in university presented me with a degree, but it also conditioned me to believe in the expert. The professor, the textbook, and the theories defined the knowledge that I needed to comprehend to enable me to pass. I, as the student, was a mere sponge, there to soak up their wisdom. My personal experience did not matter.

I entered the Faculty of Education at the University of Calgary believing in the idea of the expert, the all-knowing person. I pictured the faculty as a factory. The students were the input, the raw materials. The courses and the practicum were the throughput. And the output or final product was the certified teacher. A real teacher who possessed the skills, the knowledge, the key to teacherhood and TADA! I would be all done. What a surprise I had when I discovered the reality of the situation. The reality for me lies within the story I share with Pam, the story of our collaborative relationship.

What we see in Helen's words is an expression of her image of the university and the process of learning to teach as one that is disconnected from who she is as a person and from her lived story. Her image is one in which someone does something to her, fills her up with knowledge, and then she is a teacher. She talks about her sense of surprise in discovering that what was valued was her story and her way of making sense. She alludes to the way in which she learned to construct her knowing within a relationship with Pam, her cooperating teacher.

Benita Dalton, another of the student teachers, was beginning to develop some insights into her relationship with the institutional story as she reflected on an article written by Donald Murray (1978). She wrote in her journal:

This was a wonderful article and I agree with him totally. He talks about writing as "traditional, imitative, standard, noncritical, non-threatening . . . students not using language." This is how I see a lot of university writing. Everyone at university strives for excellence by giving the teacher exactly what he wants to hear and SEE! I have struggled for many many years on writing because I am so concerned about how it works or if it says the right things. (Journal entry, October 23, 1989)

Benita is just beginning to make sense of a new way of constructing her own knowledge, a way that allows her to use theory to reflect on her knowing. The new insight that Murray offers to her about the ways in which writing could be used allows her to look at her own experience and the experience of others in university. She acknowledges her struggle in the space that Murray's article makes for her.

As we reflect on the restorying or unlearning that we asked of the student teachers and cooperating teachers, we see clearly how much we had asked of them. We had taken years to come to make sense of this and we asked them to make sense of it within a short period of time and within the context of teacher education with its narrative history.

We needed to be reminded many times of the new ways of thinking about knowledge and experience that we expected of the participants in our program. On many occasions over the course of the inquiry, we were surprised. The surprises caused us to question again how participants were learning to restory themselves.

## JOY: TRYING TO READ THE TEXT OF
## PRACTICE FOR THE ANSWERS

Joy was a student teacher in our program long accustomed to writing down the words found in the texts of the university and the schools. She wrote down professors' words and words from books in order to be able to find answers to the problems that were given on assignments and on tests. As Joy saw it, the answers were always out there, always belonging to someone else and she could learn them if she wrote them down or heard them given in a class. Joy had learned to live a story of received knowing. She reminded us of the difficulty of learning a new story of constructed knowing when we read her journal, in which she recorded fragments of classroom practice. Her way of reading the classroom text was to record such details as where her cooperating teachers stood, the words they spoke, and the way they moved their hands. She wanted to record such details as a way of finding the answer for how she should teach. She knew that she needed to record a lot of details for she saw the complexity of classrooms. For Joy writing down such fragments of information was similar to writing down words from lectures and books in order to find the answers for tests and papers. Joy came to understand what she was doing as she looked back in a reflective interview at the end of her year's experience (Dyck, 1990). Joy's struggle reminded us of how different a story we were asking participants to live.

## HEDY: PLAYING THE GAME OF KEEPING THE PERSONAL
## OUT OF THE UNIVERSITY

The first assignments for student teachers were ones that asked them to follow individuals or small groups of children as they worked on classroom tasks within particular subject areas such as mathematics and language arts. We wanted the papers to be ones in which student teachers told their stories, their ways of knowing practice as they tried to figure out what children were doing. Hedy's paper was an account of children working on a math project. She interspersed transcript fragments of the children's talk with fragments of quotations from motivation and learning theory. She tried to leave out her own narrative history and her own knowing and to look to the experts to give the only word on what sense the children were making of the project. Hedy's paper reminded us again of how we were asking for a very different kind of writing. Instead of asking for theory to explain practice and for papers to be written in distant and objective language, we were asking for connections to the personal and practical. Hedy

came to new understandings as she reworked the assignment with her cooperating teacher in ways that let her tell her own story of making sense of
her knowing within that particular situation.

## BARBARA: NAMING "THE UNIVERSITY" AS KNOWING

We were excited to have Barbara participate in the program because
we knew her well. We had worked with her in the classroom, in a research
project, and in graduate studies. She had come to understand what it meant
to construct her own knowledge during her masters program. She too was
excited about taking that new way of knowing into the classroom and into
her work with a student teacher. She participated with us on the steering
committee, attended meetings with us, and worked closely with us on all
aspects of the Alternative Program. We were surprised when, during a
discussion of evaluation at a steering committee meeting, Barbara turned
to us and said, "What does the university want us to do?" At the time we
laughed and joked about how she was turning us, her friends and colleagues, into an institution. We teased Barbara about it for the remainder
of the year. However, when we consider the narrative meaning behind her
question, we understand how easy it is to go back into the old story of
received knowing. The story of received knowing is a comfortable one in
the face of the uncertainty that was the context of our inquiry. Barbara's
experience reminded us of how difficult it must have been on many occasions for other cooperating teachers to have confidence in the construction
of their own knowledge within the context of this work. Many times in
their conversations with us we heard echoes of Barbara's question as they
too sought their answers in knowledge that came from outside themselves.
For all of us the inquiry was being lived out in a series of new situations.
We had to remember that new situations could put us back into silence or
into being received knowers. Barbara's question became a reminder of the
difficulty of learning to live a new story, of unlearning the old lesson.

## SONIA: GETTING DOWN THE TEACHER'S WORDS

Sonia tended to be quiet during our Wednesday afternoon seminars.
She said she liked to listen and take in what everyone was saying. However,
as it became time for the first assignment to be written, Sonia initiated a
discussion about what it was that the university wanted. Other members of
the group offered their perceptions on how the assignment might look. Pat
also spoke for a few moments about how papers might look. It was a

surprise to her at this point to see Sonia pull out a pencil and attempt to write down everything she said. When Pat finished Sonia looked a little frustrated and asked Pat to repeat her words. Sonia had not managed to record everything. Pat explained that she had been just imagining a possibility rather than giving a model for the paper. She couldn't repeat her words exactly, much to Sonia's disappointment. Others in the group laughed and made a joke of the fact that Pat had actually said something worth writing down. Pat laughed too but later thought about the narrative meaning of Sonia's actions. As is the case with many university students, Sonia was accustomed to recording a professor's words at the moment of utterance in order to take them away and use them as a prescription for completing assignments and papers. The professor's words are used to frame the task and to give shape to the paper. It is the story of received knowing in our universities. Sonia's actions were particularly surprising to us because she had impressed us with her stunning practices in the classroom and her insights in her journal. As we reflected on how difficult it was for Sonia to move to a new story of writing papers as a constructed knower, we wondered about the difficulties being experienced by other students as they struggled with the new ways of knowing we were asking of them. As she came to trust her own voice, Sonia wrote unique papers that told us a great deal about how she had learned to construct her knowledge from theory, from her own story, from the children's stories, and from her work with Jude McCullough, her cooperating teacher.

## LEARNING TO CONSTRUCT KNOWING

Carol, a student teacher, gave us insight into the ways in which we all learned to figure out new stories of being constructed knowers. She wrote:

> Part of finding a voice is living with uncertainty. Knowing that we don't have to be one hundred percent sure of ourselves or our situation. This isn't easy! I like deadlines, schedules, answers. I don't like books with non-ending endings. I like to know there is a way to do something and a way it should turn out — whether it be a paper or my life. There is security in answers. But perhaps there is a security in not having the answers — a different type of security. You don't have to live someone else's answer. When there are no answers, you can make up your own and change them if you wish. There is more room to grow when you don't have an ending to meet. When there is uncertainty there is more opportunity for growth and discovery. You find your own way — rather than follow only one. (Flather, 1990)

Carol's words, beautifully written, help us to see that there will always be a tension as we tell and live our stories between received knowing and constructed knowing. There will always be times when we want the answer to come from outside ourselves, when we want certainty. As we live out our lives as teachers, however, our stories are always lived in uncertain contexts and we are always trying to figure out what is the best action to take at any time. The tension remains in our stories, a constant presence.

Carol is beginning to tell her story as constructed knower, beginning to talk of knowing as "something she can make up and change" as she finds herself in new situations. She is beginning to tell of her knowing in a language of practice that tells of her experience, a language that is personal, emotional, moral, tentative, and changing. Carol reminds us that in order to construct our own knowing, we have to speak in a language of practice. It took Carol time to unlearn the lessons of the institutions. It takes time for all of us to learn a new language, to live a new story, to become constructed knowers. We are all slow unlearners.

## REFERENCES

Belenky, M. F., Clinchy, B., Goldberger, N., & Tarule, J. (1986). *Women's ways of knowing: The development of self, voice and mind*. New York: Basic Books.

Dyck, R. (1990). Becoming a teacher. Unpublished manuscript, University of Calgary.

Flather, C. (1990). Unpublished manuscript, University of Calgary.

LeGuin, N. (1989). *Dancing at the edge of the world: Thoughts on words, women and places*. New York: Harper & Row.

Mahabir, H. (1990). Unpublished manuscript, University of Calgary.

Murray, D. (1978). Internal revision. A process of discovery. In C. R. Cooper & L. Odell (Eds.), *Research on composing — Points of departure*. National Council of Teachers of English.

Polanyi, M. (1962). *Personal knowledge: Towards a post-critical philosophy*. Chicago: University of Chicago Press.

Schön, D. (1983). *The reflective practitioner: How professionals think in action*. New York: Basic Books.

# PART FIVE

# LEARNING FROM OUR STORIES: NEW POSSIBILITIES FOR TRANSFORMING TEACHER EDUCATION

In the final part of the book, we editors have collectively turned our attention to reflecting on our experience of the program. In Chapter 21, we use the metaphor of improvisation as a way of giving an account of our experience in this inquiry. We develop a metaphor of teacher education as an improvisatory art guided by an ethic of caring. In the final chapter we discuss how we have seen our work as creating new spaces for teacher education. We discuss the implications for institutional restorying in order to permit the creation of these new spaces.

# CHAPTER 21

# Teacher Education as an Improvisatory Art

## Pat Hogan, D. Jean Clandinin, Annie Davies, and Barbara Kennard

As we thought about the inquiry and as we lived and told stories of it, the metaphor of improvisation was often one that we used to express how we were making sense. When we found Bateson's (1989) book *Composing a Life*, her ideas of the art of improvisation and especially her notion of desperate improvisation resonated with our way of knowing. For us, her idea became a metaphor for the inquiry in which we were engaged. As we continued to make sense of what we were doing, it became important to write about our inquiry into teacher education as improvisation. Our writing is a kind of conversation with her text, our response from our experience of the inquiry.

In her book, Bateson (1989) draws our attention to the ways in which we worked by improvising, "discovering the shape of our creation along the way, rather than pursuing a vision already defined" (p. 1). As we think about our inquiry, this captures the idea of a program that, as far as we know, had not been done before. We were trying to construct a new program that would evolve as we worked together collaboratively. We had no vision for how the story would unfold for each participant or for how the story of the program would be lived out. We often spoke about how we hadn't done anything like this before and how we didn't know what we were doing. We knew that improvisation would be important and we trusted that as we worked together we could shape our stories into meaningful ones that would allow us to make new sense.

Bateson reminds us that in improvisation, we begin with our past experiences, with our taken-for-granted ways of being in the world, and that we are involved in "recombining partly familiar materials in new ways, often in ways especially sensitive to context, interaction, and response" (p. 2). We had been reading and thinking about our ways of knowing and what worked for our own growth as teachers and as women. Ideas such as fidelity and caring from Nel Noddings, ideas of personal practical knowledge from Jean Clandinin and Michael Connelly, ideas of the myths of teaching and ideas of voice from Deborah Britzman, the idea of the believing game and the doubting game from Peter Elbow, and the idea of improvisation from Bob Yinger were the partly familiar materials that we brought to the inquiry. We also brought our own stories of teaching and teacher education. For example, we had engaged in writing dialogue journals with student teachers in regular teacher education programs and with practicing teachers in graduate classes and in other settings, but we had not attempted a written three-way conversation. A dialogue journal where all three kinds of teachers were trying to engage in conversation was unfamiliar. As we brought these partly familiar materials to the new context of the Alternative Program, we recognized the need to be especially sensitive to the new situation, to all participants and to the ways in which we responded to each other. We wanted to be open to new possibilities.

Bateson talks about each person learning "to combine and vary familiar components to say something new to fit a particular context and evoke a particular response, sometimes something of very great beauty or significance" (p. 3). As we thought about our inquiry, we knew that individual participants came to the project with their own particular stories and learned to make sense of the situation in which they found themselves in ways that were connected to their ongoing stories. We read student teachers' papers in which they constructed metaphors of mirrors, of dance, and of journeys that eloquently described their ways of knowing themselves and their teaching. Participants' experiences were different as they responded to different aspects of their situation. Because each participant's experience was unique, each learned to construct new ways of knowing. In telling the stories in the pages of this book, we want to convey the significance of personal practical knowledge and the beauty in those moments when participants learned new ways of thinking about their practices and their stories.

Bateson draws her examples of improvisation from the common everyday experiences of women. She compares improvised meals with planned meals and talks about the improvised meal as being "certainly riskier, but rich with the possibility of delicious surprise. Improvisation can be either a last resort or an established way of evoking creativity. Sometimes a pattern chosen by default can become a path of preference" (p. 4). As we lived out the inquiry and now tell stories about it, we see the risks that we undertook but we also are reminded of the joy of "delicious surprise." With so many participants, each making her own sense, we were always being surprised by new insights and being reminded of new risks in what we were doing. We were well into the inquiry when we realized that assignments needed to be constructed collaboratively with space for all participants' voices. Now we cannot imagine setting up assignments without allowing for the possibility of collaboration. For us, inquiry or improvisation is an established way that continues to challenge us all to create new possibilities in our stories. It is now our path of preference.

Bateson looks to women's lives and sees them as expressions of the art of improvisation. She sees "the ways we combine familiar and unfamiliar components in response to new situations, following an underlying grammar and an evolving aesthetic" (p. 3). She reminds us that we undergo each new situation in ways that allow us to make connections to what has gone before in our lives. As we make the connections between past and present, we can begin to see narrative patterns and themes. For us, narrative themes have come to mean the rhythms, unities, tensions, continuities, and discontinuities that occur as we continue to story and restory our lives. These themes are the underlying grammar and evolving aesthetics in our narratives of experience.

For us, the themes have an emotional and moral dimension that brings out the underlying ethic of caring that guides our responses. It is in this sense that we renegotiated assignments with student teachers and cooperating teachers. Our improvisation in this instance was guided by an ethic of caring. Our understanding of an ethic of caring is informed by Noddings's (1984) work. For us, this implies responsibility to ourselves as teacher educators, to the student teachers and cooperating teachers and especially to the children in the classrooms where we work. As we understand this improvisation in our narrative inquiry into teacher education, we see how we attempted to open up the question of assignments to allow all participants to make moral choices. We see this as transforming a situation that did not ask anyone for a moral response into a situation that asked every participant for a moral response. We see more clearly the ways in which teacher education — and education itself — is an improvisatory art. We see ways in which teacher education is part of our ongoing story with its narrative themes in our past, expressed in our present, and leading into the future. These narrative themes help us to construct meaning as we fashion new understandings, the past gives meaning to present action, and we begin to see the evolving aesthetics in how teachers' moral lives are written.

Bateson uses the theme of aesthetics and writes about the ways "our aesthetic sense, whether in works of art or in lives, has overfocussed on the stubborn struggle toward a single goal rather than on the fluid, the protean, the improvisatory" (p. 4). She examines our culture's notion of "achievement as purposeful and monolithic . . . rather than something crafted from odds and ends, like a patchwork quilt, and lovingly used to warm different nights and bodies" (p. 4). Bateson's notion about achievement reminds us of the ways that we came to see achievement in the Alternative Program.

Traditional programs in teacher education have overfocused on a linear progression of skills to be acquired, conditions to be met, standards to be achieved. Like Bateson, we questioned this monolithic view. We saw instead that each particular situation drew out different aspects of each individual's narrative of experience. For example, once assignments were crafted by the participants, each student teacher was allowed to gain a sense of achievement through the pursuit of personally meaningful goals.

## CONSTANCY AND CHANGE

Bateson draws our attention to the world in which we live when she reminds us that "constancy is an illusion. After all, our ancestors were immigrants, many of them moving on every few years: Today we are migrants in time. Unless teachers can hold up a model of lifelong learning and adaptation, graduates are likely to find themselves trapped into obsolescence as the world changes around them" (p. 14). In our own classrooms, we hold a similar view of the world. As teachers we need to work with children as lifelong learners, adapting to the changing cultures and societies in which we work. Living is an inquiry, as Dewey reminded us many years ago, and we need always to be seeking new ways of making sense of the situations in which we find ourselves. Our student teachers will be teaching children from many cultures, children who will live in a changing social and technological world. We want the student teachers to be able to make sense of their lives and, in turn, to help the children in their classrooms to write more moral lives.

Bateson's concern that "society's casualties are men and women who assumed they had chosen a path in life and found that it disappeared in the underbush" (p. 7) was also our concern. As society changes, our schools and classrooms need to change. Teacher education also needs to change. For ourselves as teachers and for student teachers, we wanted to figure out how to be responsive to changing situations so that, as Bateson tells us, "far more could be lived" (p. 8). We need to be open to new possibilities. It seemed to us that teacher education had not changed very much to respond to what was changing in our lives and classrooms and in the lives of children. Bateson wrote that "the central survival skill is surely the capacity to pay attention and respond to changing circumstances, to learn and adapt, to fit into new environments beyond the safety of the temple precincts" (p. 231). As teacher educators we need to question the taken-for-grantedness of our day-to-day lives in order to be responsive to the ever-changing lives of the children in our classrooms. In the Alternative Program we came out of the temple precincts, out of the university, to situate our lives and our student teachers' lives in classrooms. We wanted to work with all participants in the program and with each other in ways that were both responsive to current changing circumstances and meaningfully connected to our past experiences.

As we look at the classrooms in which we teach, we see children who come and go quickly. We see how teachers are also migrants in time. We, like Bateson, are concerned with teaching "the skills for coming into a new place and quickly making it a home" (p. 17). Bateson speaks of the ways in which we "reshape our pasts to give them an illusory look of purpose" (p. 17). She goes on to say that "our children are unlikely to be able to define their goals and then live happily ever after. Instead, they will need to reinvent themselves again and again in response to a changing environment" (p. 17). We knew that the participants in our program would continue to story and restory themselves in response to the ways they were working as educators. We too wanted to use strategies that were "not strategies for victory but for survival and adaptation" (p. 239). We wanted to speak with our student teachers and with children in our classrooms in ways that allowed us to express the moral dilemmas we experienced as we wrote our own lives. Part of what we were trying to do in the dialogue journals, in our small group seminars, and in our conversations was to create a space where all participants could speak in a language of uncertainty, in a language of story that left them open to restorying their lives.

## WRITING OUR LIVES IN UNCERTAIN SITUATIONS

As we thought about the uncertainty in our own lives and about the discontinuities and tensions that we experienced as we worked, we thought about the inquiry as a way of helping each of us learn to make new sense of our own stories and of teaching. We saw our own lives as stories that were continually restoried as we tried to make sense of interruptions and changing circumstances. We had seen as we looked back over our lives, our own ways of coping with discontinuities. We saw these ways of knowing as strengths that allowed us to adapt in ever-changing ways. As we thought about our program we wanted to work with each participant in ways that helped us each learn to build on these strengths. Bateson gave us a new language and a way for thinking about this when she wrote: "Fluidity and discontinuity are central to the reality in which we live. Women have always lived discontinuous and contingent lives . . . which turns women's traditional adaptations into a resource" (p. 13). In the program, we recognized that whenever we work in a truly collaborative manner there can never be "one right way" to experience learning to teach. We tried to support one another in the notion that we could and would develop strategies to cope with collaborative inquiry in the uncertain contexts of classroom life. Our experiences of practice and our experiences at home and with children required "the ability to shift from one preoccupation to another, to divide one's attention, to improvise in new circumstances" (pp. 13–14). Bateson also suggested to us that "by examining the way women have coped with discontinuities in their lives, we may discover important clues that will help us all, men and women, cope with our unfolding lives" (pp. 13–14). When we thought about our inquiry with the participants in the program, we knew we would find important clues to how we might learn new ways to think about knowing practice and becoming teachers, from the ways we had learned to live our lives. As we told stories in journals and in papers, in seminars and discussions, we each looked back on our life and on the ways we had learned to cope with discontinuities.

We thought about our program as a narrative inquiry and we considered the ways in which we brought forward the past to make meaningful sense of our actions in the present. Bateson helped us "look at discontinuity differently. The lesson each of us has drawn from multiple fresh starts is that there is always something in the past to work with" (p. 236). We learned to look back to see the patterns and themes in our own lives. We encouraged participants to learn to write reflectively in order to find their own narrative themes. For us and for Bateson, "writing has been the constancy through which I have reinvented myself after every uprooting. Often continuity is visible only in retrospect" (p. 223). Journal writing and story writing were central features of the program. As we shared stories, opportunities to restory connected events presented themselves. As we looked back over our writing and asked questions of each other, "each of us has repeatedly had to pose the question of who we are" (p. 213).

We all wrote and told stories, creating a multiplicity of stories to think about and talk about. As we listened to each other's stories, we learned new ways of seeing our own stories. It was important to us to have a diversity of possible stories in order that each of us could "look at multiple lives to test and shape our own. . . . I believe in the need for multiple models, so that it is possible to weave something new from many different threads" (p. 16). In our program we frequently tried to create opportunities for students to make sense within the community that was created in the university classroom. In other words, we tried to give the student teachers each other so they could learn from their stories, from the stories of the university teachers, and from the stories of their cooperating teachers. Each sharing of stories "provokes a dialogue of comparison and recognition, a process of memory and articulation that makes one's own experience available as a lens of empathy. We gain even more from comparing notes and trying to understand the choices of our friends" (p. 5). In the sharing of stories, we were trying to help students within the community address the notion of what constitutes a caring response. A caring response allows us to explore the moral dimensions of our actions in the lives of children. It was this perspective that we tried to foster in bringing students together in a community.

As we heard each other's stories and tried to find new meaning in our own stories, we came to understand the importance of response, of feeling heard and of connecting with others. Bateson helped us think about response when she wrote about "a life whose theme is response rather than purpose, response that makes us more broadly attentive rather than purpose that might narrow our view" (p. 237). We saw our mode of action as responsive "based on looking and listening and touching rather than the pursuit of abstractions" (p. 234).

## MODELS OF POSSIBILITY

In our inquiry, our language is a language of possibility for teacher education. As we worked together we talked about ways of seeing new possibility in our practices as teachers, as teacher educators, and with children in our classrooms. As we saw possibilities in our professional lives we also came to see new possibilities in our personal lives. Bateson's words resonated with our own thoughts when she wrote:

> Women today, trying to compose lives that will honor all their commitments and still express all their potentials with a certain unitary grace, do not have an easy task. It is important, however, to see that, in finding a personal path among the discontinuities and moral ambiguities they face, they are performing a creative synthesis with a value that goes beyond the merely personal. We feel lonely sometimes because each composition is unique but gradually we are becoming aware of the balances and harmonies that must inform all such compositions. Individual improvisations can sometimes be shared as models of possibility for men and women in the future. (p. 232).

We see our inquiry as just such a model.

## REFERENCES

Bateson, M. C. (1989). *Composing a life*. New York: Atlantic Monthly Press.
Noddings, N. (1984). *Caring: A feminine approach to ethics and moral education*. Berkeley: University of California Press.

# CHAPTER 22

# Finding New Ways to Work Together: Living in the Middle Ground

*D. Jean Clandinin, Annie Davies, Pat Hogan,
and Barbara Kennard*

This book tells many of the stories that emerged from our experiences of trying to restory the ways in which the institutional narrative of teacher education has been lived. When we tried to think about the features that marked the program and what we learned in the inquiry, a metaphor of creating a middle ground, a new space for teacher education, emerged. When we began the inquiry we saw teacher education as situated in the gap between the universities and the schools. For student teachers, their practicum experience was supposed to bridge that gap. Many of them, however, felt lost within it. The gap silenced those of us who worked at the university as well as those of us who worked in the schools. As we tell the story now, we see that we wanted to figure out how to live in that middle ground of connection.

When we began the inquiry, we had no metaphor of middle ground as a guide. We began our work with each of our stories. We wanted to acknowledge our own stories, stories of who we were and how we were making sense of our lives and our practices. As the year progressed, we all shared stories of how we were making sense. Theory in the shape of research papers, philosophical books, other teachers' and students' stories were all used to help us reflect on our own stories. We had seen our purpose then as making connections between who we were and how we were writing our lives, and between our lives and how others had envisioned writing their lives in teaching. We approached each of the pieces, the written stories of teachers, children, researchers, and philosophers with a sense of conversation. In these conversations we responded within an ethic of caring in which we were able to question the moral dimensions of our actions. It is only now that we can see how the sharing and responding to each other's stories was a beginning step in creating that middle ground, a new space for teacher education. As we write this chapter, we see the ways other practices that developed in this program shaped the middle ground.

In other chapters we have talked about the program as an inquiry, a desperate improvisation in uncertain contexts. Too often we think we engage in alternative programs with a sense of distance, with a sense of not really engaging in the inquiry. As teacher educators, we have not often been reflective about our own practices. Our inquiries are situated outside of ourselves. In this program, however, it was important that all participants saw themselves as engaged in the inquiry. Student teachers, cooperating teachers, and university teachers wrote, talked, wondered, and improvised as we both restoried our own lives and imagined new possibilities for teacher education.

One of the most important points in the program was seeing teacher education and teaching as an ongoing inquiry for all the participants. We became aware that if one of the participants, university teacher or cooperating teacher, stood outside and saw the inquiry as ongoing only for the student teachers, a sense of possibility was lost. When only some participants see the need to look at their stories and to see the possibility for restorying, then connections cannot be made. As we learned to make connections and to engage in that process of storying and restorying, we came to know, in important ways, that we were doing so in uncertain contexts. We also began to recognize that the contexts and our practices were both moral and emotional ones.

This year has been a year of restorying for each of us. For university teachers, we have come to see ourselves as needing to work more collaboratively with teachers and student teachers in the schools. For cooperating teachers, we have come to see the need to tell our stories and to feel heard even as we listen to the university teachers' stories in more attentive ways. For student teachers, they have begun to live their lives as practitioners in school situations and to see themselves as engaged in a continual process of teacher education. As we saw in their stories, they came to see teacher education as an ongoing process of inquiry in which there was a continuous dialogue between theory and practice, between themselves and children, between their pasts, their presents, and their futures.

So, we start to see the middle ground as peopled with teacher educators who are university teachers, cooperating teachers, and student teachers. We have to acknowledge we are all learning from each other, from our experiences, and from our conversations with theory and practice. This acknowledgment of each of us as a teacher educator blurs the distinctions we have traditionally made between teaching and learning in teacher education.

We found that what we read about the expert–novice relationship did not resonate with our view of personal practical knowledge. When we stayed within the expert–novice view we were not open to constructing and reconstructing all participants' knowing. The expert–novice view silenced everyone. In our program, we came to recognize the personal knowledge that all participants brought to the inquiry. While student teachers' personal knowledge had not been made practical in school situations, we valued their knowing. We also valued the knowledge that university teachers and cooperating teachers brought to the inquiry and we worked hard to find words to make explicit our knowing. Valuing these many ways of knowing shaped the middle ground.

The small group seminars held each week were places to make connections between a particular university teacher, a small group of student teachers, and their cooperating teachers. It was in these small groups held in schools that we came together and asked our wonders, shared our journals, and laughed and cried about the complexities of teaching and living our stories. The journals were a three-way written dialogue in which all participants shared stories and responded to each other. They were a place for figuring out experience through writing. We became aware of the importance of having all participants see journals as places to make sense. As university teachers and cooperating teachers wrote responses, they came to see their practices in changed ways. Because the journals brought stories of practice to university classrooms and because the journals reflected university discussions to the cooperating teachers, they became an important feature of the middle ground. The journals became a way for the teachers to be represented at the university and for the university teachers to be represented in the classrooms. This allowed the teacher's voice to be heard in the university and the university teacher's voice to be heard in classrooms. All participants came to feel comfortable with the sounds of others' voices in what had been their own place. This sharing of journals and stories, this feeling of being comfortable, of being at home, was an important part of the middle ground of connection.

While we all had a sense of each individual story as unique, we saw in the program that there was not one story being lived and told but many stories. These stories, lived and told in relationships throughout the year, changed and were restoried. We came to see as we worked with each individual, each paired relationship, each seminar group, each methods class, each classroom, that stories are multiple and always changing.

In the large classes and in the small group seminars one of our tasks was to figure out ways of giving students each other. We had, for too long, seen the dialogue as existing only between teacher and student. In this program we wanted the students to come to value each other and their ways of knowing. We wanted them to figure out how to be invited into each other's stories so they could make a collaborative connection and live a story different from the one usually lived and told within the university. We encouraged them to see each other as colleagues learning with and from one another, rather than as competitors for grades.

As we worked in the program we came to new insights into evaluation. While we all started with the notion of self-evaluation and wanted to encourage our students to engage in that process, we came to see that evaluation was both in the person and in the situation. We needed to figure out ways to help students and ourselves understand evaluation as contextualized. It is, for us, important to acknowledge that our knowing is an expression of ourselves that is drawn out in the particular situations in which we work. Because we are always changing, storying, and restorying ourselves, and because the situations in which we work are always changing, we came to see that evaluation must give a sense of the changing, growing, developing sense of knowing each of us has in our practice. This view of evaluation in the middle ground requires that we give up the privileged stance of expert in order to be attentive to all voices. In collaborative evaluation, one voice does not carry more authority than another.

We now see this view of multiple voices in evaluation as reflected in our renegotiation of the assignments. Initially we had attempted to write assignments prior to making connections with student teachers and cooperating teachers in their classrooms. In this initial construction of assignments we could not allow spaces for their voices. When we became aware of the ways in which the assignments were being lost in the gaps between the university requirements and the requirements of practice, we came together to talk about ways to make connections in that gap. We wanted the assignments to bring together the work of the student teachers at the university and in their schools. We also wanted to bring together cooperating teacher, student teacher, and university teacher in collaboratively constructing the assignments. And we wanted to make a space for student teachers to complete assignments that would help them figure out the lives children in their classrooms were writing and the ways they were writing their own lives as teachers. The renegotiated assignments formed another connection among the student teacher, cooperating teacher, and university teacher. In the middle ground we came to see the assignments that the student teachers completed as an expression of their conversation between theory and practice.

## THE MIDDLE GROUND OF TEACHER EDUCATION

Let us think about this middle ground, about what is necessary for its creation. What do we ask of the two institutions, university and schools, by way of change? As we wrote this chapter and looked back, we were reminded of Bateson's notion of having "the skills for coming into a new place and quickly making it a home" (Bateson, 1989, p. 17).

When we look at the smooth faces of the two institutions and their taken-for-granted relationships, it seemed initially there was little possibility for change. It was when we became aware of the discontinuities in the institutional narratives that we sensed the possibility for creating a new space, a new place where cooperating teachers, university teachers, and student teachers could feel at home. When we began the program, we had little sense of the many changes we were asking of ourselves and of the institutions in which we worked. It is only now, retrospectively, that we can see those changes and understand the metaphor that had tacitly guided our practice.

In order to create what we now see as a middle ground, we recognize how each institutional narrative needed to be restoried. At the university, extensive changes were required in the temporal organization. In trying to create a middle ground between the university and schools' cyclic organization, we extended the practicum over an 8-month period and we placed students in one classroom for the entire period. Rather than having the practicum follow the methods coursework, the students began their university year in both classrooms and the university. Weekly timetables were organized to provide blocks of time in both the classroom and the university. In addition, we scheduled full weeks when students could experience the full cycle of classroom life and one week each university term for reflective writing on their assignments. We also found it necessary to integrate methods courses to reflect more realistically how teachers viewed their classroom practice. This required changing the usual university course organization and temporal cycles from individual course times to large blocks of times where the four methods courses could be taught in an integrated way.

Temporal change was reflected also in the evaluation cycle. While we worked within the broad framework of the university year, we had to bring the university evaluation cycle in line with the longer, 8-month practicum cycle. A departure from the usual university process of cooperating teacher evaluation of student teacher was the collaborative nature of evaluation in the Alternative Program. The collaborative nature of the assignments was also a radical change in the university narrative. This valuing of the student teachers' and cooperating teachers' voices in the evaluation process and in the assignment construction was also reflected in the possibility of their participation in the selection of their partners. Instead of a university-school relationship wherein institutional requirements dictate who becomes a cooperating teacher, individuals came to work in this program based on their personal connections with university teachers and other cooperating teachers.

Another change in the university–school relationship was reflected in the willingness of the university teachers to move beyond what Bateson has called "the temple precincts" into the schools, both to visit classrooms and to work with the small group seminars. Every Wednesday afternoon each university teacher met with six to eight student teachers in one of the schools. These sessions were places where we told our stories and, through conversation, tried to make sense of our practice. The connections that were formed in the seminar groups and the classrooms were strengthened in the dialogue journals where all participants reflected on their practices. This was also a marked change from the usual university–classroom relationship.

While the university narrative underwent changes in order to allow the creation of the middle ground for teacher education, changes were also required in the school narrative. As in the university narrative, many of the changes were temporal in nature. Cooperating teachers began their school year working with a student teacher, making a commitment to the longer, 8-month practicum cycle. They also had to deal with the interrupted weekly cycle of student teachers, who worked in the classroom every other day. The cooperating teacher–student teacher relationship was altered as the two groups took on more collaborative ways of working together as partners. The partnerships in journal writing also changed for many cooperating teachers, who now wrote with, and responded to, their student teachers rather than with their colleagues. For other cooperating teachers, dialogue journal writing was a new undertaking. While cooperating teachers were accustomed to evaluating student teachers and providing feedback on their classroom work in logbooks, most of them had not attempted a conversation of practice with a student teacher. The changes that were required in the schools were not only of the cooperating teacher. The entire staff, including the administrators and support staff, were required to make a place for the student teachers as colleagues in the school. But perhaps the most radical changes in the school narrative involved asking cooperating teachers to trust university teachers and student teachers with their stories of classroom practice. The stories were discussed in university classes and in the seminar groups, and the cooperating teachers trusted that the responses to the stories would be guided by an ethic of caring. Their stories as well as the stories of university teachers and student teachers became part of the ongoing inquiry. This stance of being participants in an inquiry required that they see themselves as equal participants in teacher education.

Changes in the institutional narratives of schools and universities altered the lived experience of children in our classrooms. We asked them to accept the student teacher as another teacher in their classroom. We asked them to accept the interrupted weekly cycle of the student teachers. Our concern for the children caused us to ask ourselves continually how what we were doing would become part of their stories of school. The moral responsibility was always in how the children were making sense of what we were asking as we attempted to create this middle ground for teacher education.

We began with our stories but, as we look back, we see we have created a new space, a middle ground for teacher education. It is a space that we initially saw as a way of being more attentive to our own stories as university teachers, student teachers, and cooperating teachers, a space where we could make personal connections that would help us all be more thoughtful about the lives we were writing. As we lived out the stories in this program, we saw the need for changes in the institutional narratives of schools and university and their relationships in teacher education. We understand it also as a matter of changes in the relationships between all participants, between university teachers and cooperating teachers, cooperating teachers and student teachers, classroom teachers and children. As we look to our future lives as teachers, we see possibility for changed practices in our work and in the work of the student teachers who have begun to write what we hope are more thoughtful lives as educators of our young children.

## FINAL WORDS

This chapter and this book are closed best, we think, by a journal dialogue between Annie Davies and Benita Dalton. It is the end of the practicum, the final days. Annie has written a letter and a poem to Benita. We share both of them with you here.

Dear Benita,

We'll not be doing goodbye because you don't do beginnings and I don't do endings . . . so let's live the middle ground of connection. It's where the energy is.

Each of us has our own stories of this year. We may never know the text of the other's chapter. Mine is full of snapshots . . . special moments in time where the images are my own . . . they are images that blend into a feeling of what collaboration can be.

From a distance, this may look like any practicum but we know it differently, "as friends."

Thank you for all that you are.

Love,

Annie

### THE BELIEVING GAME

two days ago
you walked beside me . . .
I listened . . .
you voiced
chains of thoughts and feelings
you wondered
you questioned . . .
still . . . I listened . . .
you paused . . .
I
looked at you . . .
you
said . . .
"You're not going to give me answers . . . "
    RIGHT!

"Right!" I said as you laughed
I treasure that memory
I "SEE" the teacher in you
I "FEEL" the teacher in me.

A. D. (April 16, 1990)


## REFERENCE

Bateson, M. C. (1989). *Composing a life*. New York: Atlantic Monthly Press.

# Epilogue

What matters is that lives do not serve as models; only stories do that. And it is a hard thing to make up stories to live by. We can only retell and live by the stories we have read or heard. (Heilbrun, 1988, p. 37)

As we read back over the lived and told stories in the chapters of this book, we want to make explicit the views we hold about teacher knowledge, teaching, teacher education, and the relationships between the schools and universities in teacher education programs. Our purpose is to outline the policy implications of our work for preservice and in-service teacher education.

We view teacher knowledge narratively. Teacher knowledge is experiential, embodied knowledge that is constructed and reconstructed as we live out our lives, both in and out of schools. It is emotional, moral, and aesthetic knowledge developed in historical, social, and cultural contexts. This knowing is called forth by the particular situations in which we live and work. This view of knowledge acknowledges that teachers' lives are composed over time and their stories are lived and told and relived and retold as teachers encounter new situations in their lives. Our teacher knowledge, then, is produced by each of us in the ongoing experience of composing our lives.

We view teaching as an ongoing inquiry. From this perspective, teaching is seen as a narrative inquiry into our lives, the lives of the children in our classrooms, and the ways in which we are all engaged in making sense of the subject matter and of the contexts in which we work. This view recognizes the complexity of practice. This acknowledgment of the complexity of practice provides a space for recognizing, naming, and voicing our uncertainty. Teaching is the process of making sense of practice through the construction and reconstruction of experience. Teaching is a moral act, a process of staying open to questions that arise in practice and engaging in conversations in response to these questions.

We also view teacher education from this narrative perspective. A metaphor of teacher education as reconstruction is central to this perspective. We think of teachers' and student teachers' lives as central to the

218

curriculum of teacher education. We understand that student teachers, co-operating teachers, and university teachers bring with them their life stories, stories they have lived but rarely told in the sense of creating narrative texts that become ways of giving accounts of their lives. This narrative perspective insists that we acknowledge the need to give voice to all participants' experiences. As participants in the ongoing inquiry of teacher education we need to listen to the multiplicity of voices. Teacher education is a process of learning to tell and retell educational stories of teachers and students. Teacher education is a sustained conversation in which we need many responses to our stories in order to be able to tell and retell them with added possibility. Conversations with theory, research, social conditions, different cultural groups, other teachers, and children allow for a response-filled environment and encourage more mindful retellings. These tellings and retellings are education.

Our view of teacher knowledge, teaching, and teacher education lead us to a different view of the relationship between schools and universities. When we are listening to a multiplicity of voices, one voice is not privileged over others. Relationships between the participants become collaborative as we begin to look at ourselves as members of a community and participants in the conversations. Each of us brings our own narratively constructed knowledge to the conversation and a new quality emerges in the dialogue. In the new conversation there is space for every voice to be heard and spaces for voices to respond to each other in ways that allow growth and change.

Teacher education programs cannot be conceived at the university and implemented in the schools. Rather, teacher education programs must be situated in a middle ground created by the conversations among university teachers, cooperating teachers, and student teachers. In this view we move away from hierarchical negotiation toward collaborative conversation in which each participant contributes to the telling and living out of teacher education programs.

It is through living and telling the stories in this book that we have been able to articulate our views. When we listen to the current conversations about teacher education, we do not often hear these views expressed. In this final section, we want to address the implications our views have for several specific areas of teacher education. We do not see these implications as prescriptive but rather as possibilities for restructuring. We imagine there are many teachers who will share these views with us. We expect they work in many different contexts. We hope through reading our stories, they will begin to figure out how to come together and engage in their own inquiries into teacher education.

In the current conversations on teacher education, concern is often expressed about what constitutes an appropriate professional knowledge base. For us, the question needs to be rephrased. Instead of asking about particular skills and strategies that must be learned, we want to ask what kind of situations can support the narrative inquiries of student teachers, classroom teachers, and university teachers. We imagine that certain conditions such as trust and an openness to questioning are two of these conditions. It is within the grounded nature of each inquiry that it becomes clear what the relevant knowing is. No longer can we think of teaching as something that can be demonstrated and transferred, modeled and imitated. The notion of experts and novices dissolves as we look at learning to teach as an ongoing inquiry throughout each teacher's life.

Teacher assessment is also part of the talk of reforming teacher education. There is much concern over what constitutes an appropriate standard for judging teacher competence. For us, the question of assessment needs to be redefined from a narrative perspective. Instead of determining external standards, we need to think of assessment that is connected to each individual's narrative of experience. When we understand classroom practice as situated in teachers' and students' narratives, assessment becomes a sustained conversation, a way of making sense of classroom experiences. Within these sustained conversations there is an ongoing negotiation of meaning in which stories of experience are told, responded to, and retold with new insights. We recognize that many stories can be told about any particular classroom event and that each telling and each response allows us to see the experience in more mindful ways. It is through this dynamic process that each individual continues her own inquiry.

Talk of working relationships permeates every conversation of teacher education. The talk is often of collaborative working relationships. For us, collaboration is about caring relationships between people. Caring is an ethical activity. Our notion is informed by the work of Noddings (1984). Just as we cannot mandate caring relationships, we cannot mandate collaborative relationships. In collaborative relationships, teachers come together to engage in conversation and inquiry. The work undertaken in collaborative relationships is uncertain and improvisational. We cannot predetermine our inquiries. Certainty is not found in the situations of our work or in the lives that we compose for ourselves. For us, the only certainty in collaboration is the caring that guides our responses.

In the conversation of teacher education the issues of autonomy and accountability are often raised. Frequently in such conversations, it is implied that teachers are free agents, accountable to no one, free to tell their stories without response. Our view calls for a redefinition of the issues, a redefinition that involves recognizing that our moral responsibility is ultimately to the lives of the children in our classrooms. Our task becomes one of figuring out how to set up collaborative relationships, interpretive communities that keep us responsive to children, parents, colleagues, and changes in society. Through participation in interpretive communities all of us can continue to raise questions and to respond from within an ethic of caring. The notion of interpretive communities leaves behind power and control inherent in hierarchical relationships.

We are often asked to provide people with information about how to set up our program in different contexts. These requests remind us of Don Schön's 1987 AERA address where he told what we have come to call the grandfather clock story. It goes something like this. Once upon a time there was a kindergarten teacher whose children, in their imaginative play, used an old orange crate, a clock face, and a pendulum to construct a grandfather clock. This construction emerged out of their experiences in the classroom with stories, songs, and science. One day, a school superintendent visited and observed the clock play. He was so excited he mandated similar constructions and play for all kindergarten classrooms in his jurisdiction.

Our stories are not a mandate or a prescription for programs in collaborative teacher education. We know our program took the shape it did because of the particular people, their relationships, their stories, and the contexts in which we came together.

When the stories in this book become part of the conversations of reforming teacher education, we hope they will suggest fundamental changes. We see possibilities for changed relationships among teachers, student teachers, and university teachers, and between schools and universities. As we worked together, each trying to figure out his or her own practice, the distinctions among university teacher, student teacher, and cooperating teacher blurred. Our experience in this program has illustrated for us that we are all always engaged in learning how to teach and in understanding what it means to be a teacher. When we acknowledge that both teaching and learning to teach are ongoing processes of inquiry, we can no longer talk about knowing and not knowing, about who knows and who does not know. What had seemed certain to each of us in our own practices became less certain as we asked questions and tried to stay open to the possibilities in the responses. We began to see that our knowing in practice is an expression of who we are and the kind of lives we are writing for ourselves. It is an expression of how we tell the stories of the children in our classrooms and the kind of lives they are writing for themselves. These views are the ones that find expression in our practices. They are, at this moment, the horizons of our knowing.

The Alternative Program in its original form no longer goes on at the University of Calgary. The participants in the program have gone on to compose their lives in new settings. The student teachers have gone on to teaching and continue to write and talk to their cooperating teachers and university teachers. For example, Sherri Pearce journals regularly with Deb Nettesheim and talks often to Pat Hogan and Jean Clandinin. Angela Barritt and Kerry Black continue to journal together. Benita Dalton and Annie Davies share journals and conversation. Sonia Menzies visits Pat Hogan's classroom to prepare to teach in her own classroom. There are many connections among us.

The cooperating teachers continue to write about their practice in journals and papers. They have found new and imaginative ways to work with student teachers within the confines of the traditional practicum. The Alternative Program has provided a model for the university teachers as they try to move to more collaborative forms of teacher education.

For each participant, the experience of the Alternative Program continues to shape our lives.

## REFERENCES

Heilbrun, C. (1988). *Writing a woman's life*. New York: W. W. Norton.

Noddings, N. (1984). *Caring: A feminine approach to ethics and moral education*. Berkeley: University of California Press.

Schön, D. (1987). Instructional supervision and teacher education in the 21st century: Educating teachers as reflective practitioners. Invited address to the annual meeting of the American Educational Research Association, April 20–24, 1987. Washington, D.C.

# Index

# About the Contributors

**Angela N. Barritt** is employed by the Calgary Board of Education. She currently works with 5- to 8-year-old children at Colonel MacLeod Elementary. She was a student in the Alternative Program and now holds a B. Ed. degree from the University of Calgary.

**Kerry E. Black** is employed by the Calgary Board of Education. She is currently a member of a team working with 8- to 11-year-old children at University Elementary School, a demonstration facility for preservice and in-service teachers. She holds a B. Ed. degree from the University of Alberta and an M. Ed. degree from the University of Calgary.

**D. Jean Clandinin** is currently an associate professor and Director of the Centre for Research for Teacher Education and Development at the University of Alberta. She misses being in the same city as her friends who worked in the Alternative Program. She counts herself fortunate to have a community of such amazing people who continue to engage with her in her inquiry into what it means to be a woman composing her life.

**Kathryn Cope** was a student in the Alternative Program. She graduated from the University of Calgary in 1991 with a major in special education. Now in her first year of teaching, she has worked with special needs children and in a grade-3 classroom.

**Benita Dalton** is a native Albertan residing in Calgary. Her goal has always been to work with children, and it was for this reason that she attended the University of Calgary. She majored in elementary education, participated in the "Alternative Practicum" program in 1989–90, and graduated in 1991. She is currently working for the Calgary Board of Education. She finds teaching to be a fulfilling and rewarding profession, and continues to learn from each experience what it is to be a teacher.

**Annie Davies** is a grade 3 teacher at Ranchlands Community School in Calgary. Her desire to figure out how to become a better classroom teacher led her into a masters program at the University of Calgary in 1985. Her M. Ed. degree in 1990 was her first collaborative degree. Jean Clandinin has one-third of the certificate, and Pat Hogan has the other. Annie continues to think hard about what it means to collaborate.

**Jean Fix** is a recent graduate from the University of Calgary and is currently teaching language arts and math in Airdrie to youngsters who have stories similar to hers. While completing her degree, Jean was involved with the Alternative Program, which provided her with the experience and opportunity to reflect and write on these reflections. Jean and her two children reside in Calgary.

**Carol A. Flather** grew up in Airdrie. She moved to Calgary to attend university. She entered the Faculty of Education in her second year and then the Alternative Program in her third year. The practicum convinced her that she belonged in teaching. She graduated from the University of Calgary in 1991 with a B. Ed. degree.

**Gary Godfrey** graduated with his B. Ed. degree in 1991 when he was 38 years old. He is presently teaching dyslexic children. He wishes to pursue graduate work in the area of dyslexia, reading/writing process, and curriculum. He enjoyed being a student teacher in the Alternative Program.

**Pat Hogan** is currently teaching grade 1 at Connaught Community School where her team partner and her English as a Second Language children are helping her to continue figuring out what it means to collaborate and to teach. She enjoys her continuing relationships with Alternative Program participants and the opportunities for further projects that these relationships provide. She hates it that Jean is in Edmonton but counts herself fortunate that Annie and Barb remain in Calgary. She looks forward to the day when they can all work together again in the same city.

**Lynn Johnston-Kosik** began her studies at the University of Calgary in September 1986 after graduating from Sundre High School. She chose to study elementary education, majoring in language arts. She was a student teacher in the Alternative Program and graduated with her B. Ed. degree in 1991. She is now living in Olds, Alberta, where she is a teacher for the County of Mountain View. She hopes to eventually further her studies in teacher education.

**Garry Jones** was born and raised in Calgary. He attended the University of Calgary and has taught school in that city since 1977. He has taught kindergarten and grades 1 to 6. He has written a children's musical, *Writing and Primary Science*, and *Crocus Hill Notebook*. He is currently completing an M. Ed. degree at the University of Calgary.

**Barbara Kennard** is currently at Dr. J. K. Mulloy School in Calgary. As an administrator, a teacher, and a person she continues to restory her life as she is presented with new possibilities in the stories of those with whom she lives and works. She thanks her friends Annie, Pat, and Jean for helping her to know what it is she could possibly have to say.

**Helen Mahabir** remained in London after graduating from the University of Western Ontario. She worked part time in a day care center and found herself intrigued with the little individuals she met there. In September 1988, she began working toward a B. Ed. degree at the University of Calgary. There she met Pat Hogan, Jean Clandinin, Pam Rinehart, and Annie Davies, four women whom she admires, respects, and has grown to love. These women empowered her through acceptance, encouragement, and support to be the best teacher that she could be. She returned to her hometown and began teaching at Bryan Southwood Public School. The "purple glow" (her teaching career) is the reality of the challenges, expectations, and rewards that she anticipated . . . and more.

**Deb Lloyd Nettesheim** is a graduate from the University of Guelph where she majored in psychology. She received her B. Ed. After Degree from Hamilton Teachers College and is currently completing her diploma in teaching and learning at the University of Calgary. Deb has taught elementary school in Ontario, British Columbia, and Alberta. Presently, she is team-teaching a multi-aged year 1- and 2-class at University Elementary School, an observation school affiliated with the University of Calgary. She is married with two beautiful daughters. They enjoy spending their summers swimming and windsurfing on Georgian Bay and being near old friends and family.

**Lori Pamplin** is employed by the Calgary Board of Education. She holds a B. Ed. degree from the University of Calgary and has studied at the University of Ottawa, the University of Montreal, and the Sorbonne in Paris, France. Lori and Joan Payne, a student teacher in the Alternative Program, worked together at University Elementary School, a demonstration facility for preservice and in-service teachers. Currently on professional improvement leave, Lori is completing an M. Ed. degree at the University of Calgary.

**Sherri L. Pearce**, a student teacher in the Alternative Program, recently graduated from the University of Calgary with a degree in education. She is a native Calgarian raised in a family of teachers. Sherri's energy and enthusiasm for teaching are matched only by her love for hiking with her friends and her dog Jasper, in Kananaskis Park and the foothills of Alberta.